PRAISE FOR

APPROACHING THE HEART OF PROPHECY

Truly awesome! This book is prophetic voice that has embraced the loving nature of God and the season of grace that Jesus ushered in on the cross. The reader will clearly understand why prophetic judgment is not an option today and why God will not speak in a way that belittles or devalues a believer's life. Every word spoken in the name of God should be spoken in the hot pursuit of love and for lifting our head so we might gaze into the beauty of Father's tender loving eyes.

Jack Frost
Shiloh Place Ministries

Graham Cooke's new book, *Approaching the Heart of Prophecy*, is destined to be one of the most practical tools the Holy Spirit will use to enrich and deepen the lives of many who desire to move more powerfully in the gift of prophecy. I love the way the book is structured and the very practical applications and readings at the end of the chapters. The sidebars telling the stories of great people in the kingdom of God who moved in prophecy after the apostolic age are a great encouragement to us who do believe God still speaks to His church. I am excited about this first of six books in this series that Graham will write. I will encourage its reading by the students at our Global School of Missions, Church Planting and Supernatural Ministry. I consider Graham Cooke one of the most respected persons I know who not only has a prophetic gift, but who is in the office of a prophet. It will be hard to find a more practical book to help you grow in prophecy. Graham has walked through many rough seasons in his life, and I am proud to watch him live out his life with great integrity and faithfulness to the author of all prophecy. Graham has been faithful to continue to bear the testimony of Jesus which is the spirit of prophecy.

Randy Clark
Global Awakening

Once again, Graham Cooke delivers an extraordinary book on prophecy. His unique ability to communicate spiritual truth is refreshingly authentic and theologically sound. As one who ministers in the prophetic, I am indebted to the wisdom of years that Graham has put into this writing. *Approaching the Heart of Prophecy* is truly a one-of-a-kind manuscript that reveals the heart and mind of one of the foremost prophets and thinkers in the church today. It is a must read that will help you navigate through the deep waters of prophetic ministry.

Larry Randolph
Larry Randolph Ministries

I highly recommend Graham's new book. He has profound insights into the nature of the prophetic ministry and never loses sight of the practical application.

Jack Deere
Evangelical Foundation Ministries

Graham Cooke's writings and teachings always leave me hungering and thirsting for more — more of God, more divine revelation, more understand of God's heart, ways and values. His writings whet my appetite for the deep things of the Spirit because the truths Graham presents come alive within my heart. *Approaching the Heart of Prophecy* is full of divinely inspired revelatory treasures — treasures that took years of searching, refining and preparing to bring them as gifts to you, the reader. The richness of its contents reveals that the writer has truly paid a great price to pen its pages. I love this book!

Patricia King
Extreme Prophetic

In *Approaching the Heart of Prophecy*, Graham Cooke has clearly articulated truth that is attainable and achievable. He demonstrates what is possible for those who are concerned to grow churches that announce and demonstrate the kingdom of God. Graham provides practical and incisive insight that releases a congregation to move forward together into who they are called to be. There is absolutely no doubt that this book will both initiate the way forward and build the future for churches that are intent on cultivating an appetite for God.

Peter McHugh
Senior Minister, C3Centre

I had hardly advanced into the first chapter when I ran smack into a classic Graham Cooke revelation. He wrote, "God is more interested in creating collaborative prophetic communities than He is in birthing a new generation of prophetic superstars." If this is so (and I think it is), then God will surely use the new book as a tool to shape the skills and disposition of a new generation of prophetic voices. This new generation will have the ability to collaborate with one another and the throne room in a manner that will build a canopy of agreement between heaven and earth. Asaph taught his musician sons how to flow in the prophetic anointing of David's tabernacle, and I believe Graham's counsel will tune the instruments of the sons and daughters that God is raising to flow in the prophetic tabernacle that covers us in these last days.

Lance Wallnau
Lancelearning Group

I received a new level of faith in the prophetic reading this book. Graham reveals the intentionality of God's love and encouragement towards us, and makes it clear how we are to hear His voice, know His heart and prophesy confidently.

Julie Anderson
Prayer for the Nations

There is a curious tendency in "Spirit-filled" church life to promote the giftings of the New Covenant Spirit in the context of what is really Old Covenant practice. No wonder that we struggle with certain anomalies. However, there is brilliant news! Graham Cooke's new book, *Approaching the Heart of Prophecy*, is a significant and mature contribution to the prophetic teaching arena, and his approach is best summarized by his comment, "Any time someone receives a prophetic word, grace should explode in his heart." Well said! The rest of the book is consistent with that statement in both its well-developed content and easily implemented practical exercises. This book is worthy of wide endorsement and exposure. We need a healthy, life-giving approach to the understanding and practice of prophecy, and Graham manages to accomplish this extremely well.

David Crabtree
Senior Pastor, DaySpring Church, Sydney, Australia

I've always enjoyed Graham's writings and public ministry. His recent bite-size, interactive format is just in time for a faster thinking, activational and demanding generation. He makes me think and take time to pause with insights that act as keys, unlocking my own creativity. Keep those keys coming… let's see what treasures lie ahead!

Steve Witt
Edify Ministries International, Author of *Experiencing Father's Embrace*

It's rare to find a prophet who can prophesy *and* train other to do the same! Graham's new book puts a rich treasure into the hands of the church, not just to understand the nature of the prophetic, but to develop a sensitive heart to the voice of God. When Graham first came to CFC 16 years ago, he prophesied many things which we are now walking in. But he also empowered us to develop the prophetic when he left. If you can't get Graham to come and visit you personally, then this book is a very close second! It imparts God's heart, has wonderful insights, is easily understood, and at the same time gives very practical instructions on how to develop the prophetic. I doubt iff there is a better book on the prophetic in print.

Paul Reid
Leader, Life Link Team, Christian Fellowship Church, Belfast

In Graham Cooke's new book, *Approaching the Heart of Prophecy,* he outdoes himself, as I've come to expect. He continually amazes me with each line in this book. How can one man come up with so many quotable quotes? Wow! Based solely on Scripture yet lived out in his own life, the content of Graham's new book will walk you through the real purpose for prophecy today. This book is about transition in the prophetic gift currently operating and accepted within the church. So, use this as a primer for yourself, your friends, or even your own church group. You will never think of prophecy in the same way again!

Steve Shultz
The Elijah List

My personal acquaintance with this author makes my endorsement to be both a privilege and a responsibility. There are few voices in the realm of the prophetic dimension in which there would be the freedom to recommend a manuscript without reserve. Graham Cooke is one that has excelled in this needed realm. He has been given an unusual ability to remain biblically accurate and spiritually insightful while wrapping every instruction and expectation in the love of the Father. If your heart hungers to know and become involved in the prophetic dimension, don't hesitate to make this volume your very own.

Bob Mumford
Lifechangers

APPROACHING THE HEART OF PROPHECY

BY GRAHAM COOKE

THE EXERCISE OF PROPHECY

THE PROCESS OF PROPHECY

THE PURPOSE OF PROPHECY

www.BrilliantBookHouse.com

Approaching the Heart of Prophecy is the first of six books in the *Prophetic Equipping* Series.

Brilliant Book House LLC
865 Cotting Ln, Ste C
Vacaville, California 95688 USA
www.brilliantbookhouse.com

Brilliant
BOOK HOUSE

DEDICATION

I dedicate this book to two groups of people. Firstly, to the leadership team and the people of The Mission, Vacaville, California. The journey we are on is one of love, laughter and celebration. It is a dream come true to worship and live with a bunch of people who are passionately enjoying the journey into the heart of God. We can't all get it together, but together we can get it all.

Secondly, I dedicate this book to all people everywhere who are going through the process of transition. Transition is a journey into the bigness of God for you. In that series of steps you get to experience a transformation that opens up the heavens and makes a way for you on earth. Never forget it is the process that makes you rich, not the outcome.

ACKNOWLEDGMENTS

My love and thanks to David and Deborah Crone for providing friendship, leadership and a place for a prophet to be himself in life and in calling. Blessed are you.

To all my friends around the world, too numerous to mention. What a great company of warriors, worshippers and comedians we are together. I love the way we perceive, think about and love the Lord with all our hearts. You have all been so very intentional in your love for me and I am profoundly grateful to the Father for all that you are and do in my life.

To John (now with the Lord) and Mellie McKenzie. Thank you, thank you, thank you. Your generous financial support has enabled me to get started in the USA.

Jeanne Thompson, my personal assistant. I love the unfailing energy, capability, professionalism and generosity that you bring to all the many and varied initiatives that I plague you with each week. Thanks for all your hard work on the manuscripts in particular.

Thanks to Mark and Sophie for running the store so amazingly and creatively.

Kudos to Jordan Bateman, good friend, great editor and all round good guy. My love to the queen and the princess.

My love and appreciation to Joan Johnson and Karen Jacklin at Punch Press. Thanks for putting relationship before business. Thanks for the laughter and passion that turns all our business meetings into labors of love.

Finally my thanks to the Holy Spirit, whose comfort and genius I have never needed more than in these past few years. I love the picture of the Father and the Lord Jesus that you have painted in my heart and mind over many years. This book bears your image.

CONTENTS

INTRODUCTION

And it shall come to pass afterward that I will pour out My Spirit on all flesh; your sons and your daughters shall prophesy, your old men shall dream dreams, your young men shall see visions. And also on My menservants and My maidservants I will pour out My Spirit in those days. (Joel 2:28–29)

THE WORLD CHANGED THE DAY the Holy Spirit fell on Jesus' remaining disciples in that famed upper room in Jerusalem. The Spirit of God, reserved in the Old Testament for a select few, had now been placed on anyone who sought and loved Christ. With that outpouring came the gifts of the Spirit. While once only a few could prophesy, suddenly everyone could.

I have been in the prophetic ministry since 1974. I began prophesying the year before. That's more than thirty years of sharing the love God has placed in my heart. Amazingly, I'm still learning — and I never want to stop. Every year, I understand something new about God and His ways. He never ceases to intrigue me.

More than a decade ago, my book, Developing Your Prophetic Gifting, was first published. It has been a greater success than I could have ever imagined. It has gone through many re-printings, several publishers have taken it up; it has been written in many, many languages; and it still is on the best seller list; and yet the material I teach now is light years beyond that original manuscript. I have come a long way in the years since I wrote that first book. For one thing, I have taught countless prophetic schools during that time. As I work with students and emerging prophetic voices, I have had my own gift shaped and honed. "As iron sharpens iron, so a man sharpens the countenance of his friend," as it says in Proverbs 27:17. The people I have met have pushed me further into the things of the prophetic. They have challenged me to find fresh ways of equipping, explaining, and encouraging.

For several months, I have felt the Lord prompt me to rewrite Developing Your Prophetic Gifting, adding the material I have taught in my schools over the past ten years since it was published. This book is the first in a series of six that will more fully equip people longing to speak the words of God to those around them.

Following the unqualified success of the spirituality journals in the Being With God Series[1], I have decided to develop this material into the same format.

Each book has assignments, exercises and meditations which, if followed, will bring each individual into an experience of God within the context of the material.

Together, we will study the practical elements of hearing God, of moving in the Spirit, of knowing God's nature, and of representing His heart to someone else. We will learn how to be grounded in the love, grace, and rhythm of God. It is my prayer that these books will give you something fresh about who God wants to be for you. As you read the principles and illustrations within, I pray that you will be excited and inspired to venture further into what God has for you.

> *A small mind is incompatible with a big heart*

Prophecy comes when we have a burden to encourage and bless the people around us. There is no magic formula to prophesying; it all depends on our love for God. When we love Him fully, that love should spill over onto the people around us. Prophecy is simply encouraging, exhorting, and comforting people by tuning them into what God has for them. In every church in the world, there are people who need that life-giving word from God. These aren't just the individuals who are obviously struggling; some appear to have everything together. But God knows what's really going on.

Everyone could benefit from a prophetic word, even those for whom everything is soaring. I love to prophesy over people who are doing really well. If we can target those people and increase their faith at a critical time, they can fly even higher in the things of the Spirit.

New Testament prophecy will be spoken through the context of the Gospel of Grace. Jesus has received the judgment of God for sin for all those who are living, to enable them to find repentance through the goodness and kindness of God.

Prophecy is now in the context of a family; a company of called out people who are learning together to become the beloved of God; the Bride of Christ. There is a new language in the Spirit to learn and the unity of the Spirit to maintain and enjoy, as a people together.

Of course there are necessary tensions in all good relationships and prophecy is not the way to resolve conflicts. Clearly we need wisdom for those situations.

---

1   See www.brilliantbookhouse.com for more information

I believe strongly that the more encouraging, exhorting, and comforting prophecy we have the better our churches will be. Blessing and encouragement stir up anointing. The more of this kind of prophecy we can have in church, the less we will need intensive, time-consuming pastoral care. People will actually be touched by God and come into the things of the Spirit themselves. Individuals will realize that, yes, they are loved personally by God. That kind of revelation will stoke up their faith in ways a counseling session never could.

> *When the church runs out of encouragement, the world runs into wickedness*

I know I need that kind of encouragement every day from the Holy Spirit. I can't remember the last time I asked Him to encourage me and He didn't. He may not speak it out immediately, but He always meets me at the point of my greatest need. That's just who the Holy Spirit is, and what He loves to do.

This book can help you go further in the prophetic than you have ever hoped. After all, *"Eye has not seen, nor ear heard, nor have entered into the heart of man the things which God has prepared for those who love Him,"* (1 Corinthians 2:9).

Approaching the Heart of Prophecy is divided into three chapters: The Exercise of Prophecy, The Process of Prophecy and The Purpose of Prophecy. These chapters are not meant to be read in a day or a week; instead, I encourage you to take your time going through each, reading them until you understand the themes and thoughts they contain. Furthermore, don't neglect the exercises, case studies, and Bible readings included at the end of each chapter — they are valuable practice tools which will take the lessons taught and put them into practice in your life.

Throughout this book, I have included several sidebar articles about some of my prophetic heroes. These are people who lived after the Bible was finished being written, heard the voice of God for themselves, and did marvelous exploits for the Kingdom. I hope this will open your eyes to a few of the people who have gone before us.

I have also included some suggestions of resources that may help you further explore the themes contained in this book. I hope they prompt you to dig deeper into the things of the Spirit.

Blessings on your journey into the prophetic!

Graham Cooke.

February 2006

MODULE ONE

THE EXERCISE OF PROPHECY

The Exercise of Prophecy

WHAT YOU WILL LEARN IN THIS SEGMENT:

- To develop confidence in God for your own journey.
- Prophesying for the common good?
- Developing self-control in your language.
- The pursuit of love as a prime response to life.
- To represent the New Covenant in prophecy.
- Judgment is replaced by admonition and exhortation.
- To be in tune with the heart of God.
- Moving in the opposite spirit to what comes against us.
- Become a model of grace and truth.
- To be an ambassador for reconciliation.
- Freedom as a core doctrine of the prophetic.
- Develop your life message concerning the nature of God.
- Cultivate a great perception of God.
- Speaking what could be!
- Central themes of prophetic speech.
- Only humility restores people. Judgment comes back on you.
- How to perceive and use grace growers.

The Exercise of Prophecy

WHAT YOU WILL LEARN IN THIS SEGMENT:

- The objective affects the Delivery. Purposefully prophetic.
- Hypocrisy is always disciplined.
- The Diagnosis and Prognosis of Prophecy.
- Prophesying the solution not the problem.
- Treasure seeking in the Kingdom.
- Discernment aids Direction in proclaiming breakthrough.
- The difference between a grace issue and a discipline issue.
- Moving in the peace of God rather than the pressure of man.
- Dealing with frustration.
- Seeing in the Spirit.
- The difference between personal and private prophecy.
- Working with building and blessing prophets.
- Case studies in the prophetic.
- Recording prophecy is vital.
- Exercises and Assignments to help you grow.
- What contributes maturity and immaturity in the practice of prophecy.
- How to develop a partnership with leaders in this context.

The Exercise Of Prophecy

G OD IS IN THE BUSINESS of developing prophetic companies around the world. I believe He is more interested in creating these collaborative communities than He is in breeding a new generation of prophetic superstars. His heart is to bring the whole body of Christ under a prophetic umbrella. To live in Christ is to live in the prophetic nature of God. The revelatory gifting is part of God's DNA, implanted in us at creation.

We are made in the image of God (Genesis 1:26, 27). Jesus came to restore that broken image through His death and resurrection. Image counts for something in the Kingdom. All good prophets are concerned with restoring the Christ-like image to the church. All prophecy is connected to rebuilding God's image in the Body of Christ. This is why we build into the Spirit and not against the flesh. What we build up (edify of Christ) in the image of God will automatically remove the flesh from the life of the believer.

Man has an inbuilt capacity to be drawn towards revelatory insight whether they are in Christ or not. It is part of the DNA in all people that they are drawn to the supernatural. It is the image of God. The Father did not remove His DNA because man had sinned. All people are made in His image. Until Christ reforms it, that image is fractured but it still contains the propensity for spiritual experiences beyond the natural realm. If not Christ, then another power will seek to usurp that God shaped vacuum in all people.

A church that denies the Holy Spirit and His presence and power is simply not able to compete in a post modern culture where the organ for receptivity of truth is the eye and no longer the ear. People are not open to hearing about God. They want to see God at work because they live in a show and tell world.

Every one of us in the church has the capacity to prophesy. We can be a prophetic statement of what the Kingdom of Heaven is — showing people

> *Prophecy is in our DNA because...*

what Christ is really like — by our lifestyle, our actions, our thoughts, and our identity. We're a prophetic voice of who God is, how He speaks, and what He's doing on the earth. We cannot help but be prophetic; it is in our very bones. It is who God made us to be.

It seems to me that the whole earth is waiting for something to be revealed. I sense that very clearly in my spirit; God wants to reveal something in these days that the earth has never seen. He is acutely interested in creating prophetic companies of people willing to hear His voice. He wants to finish better than we started — Pentecost was a wonderful beginning for the gifts of the Spirit, but God has even more in store.

Of all the billions of people walking the earth today, I believe that Christians should be the most confident. And out of that confidence should flow courage and boldness. We all need confidence for ourselves, to enable us to walk with God effectively and to overcome the world, the flesh and the devil. Prophecy is centered on restoring confidence, trust and faith to everyone who has an ear to hear. God wants a bold people, a prophetic company of declaration and proclamation. For far too long, the Church has been a people of explanation. God has not put us here to explain Him; He doesn't need our help, and we're not very good at rationalizing Him anyway. We can't explain Him, and we're certainly not supposed to apologize for Him. No, we are here to declare who He is. We are here to proclaim His majesty, and the best way to do that is by living it. Confidence is the lowest form of faith, but every Christian should stand at least at that level.

> *...we are made in the image of God*

Prophecy can help build people's faith by revealing more of God's nature to them. In 1 Corinthians 12:4–7, we read more of the Holy Spirit's role in this:

> *Now there are varieties of gifts, but the same Spirit. And there are varieties of ministries, and the same Lord. There are varieties of effects, but the same God who works all things in all persons. But to each one is given the manifestation of the Spirit for the common good.* (NASB)

That final phrase, "for the common good," is at the very heart of the revelatory gifts. The gifts of the Holy Spirit, including prophecy, are not just for our own personal benefit; they enable us to benefit the Church for the common good of everyone who is present. The gifts of the Spirit should never be abused — they are used only to bless the common good. The gifts of the Spirit are for the purpose of releasing and expanding the Kingdom not just empowering the church. The "common good" therefore is about the benefit for all humanity and not just believers in Christ. Prophecy as much as all aspects of Christ's spirituality has relevance for all people everywhere at all times.

When God is vague about something it is always for a purpose. Clearly here He does not want us to know specifically what the "varieties" are of gift, ministry and effects. If He had specified exactly what these different varieties were then humanity would have locked up the experience to only those elements. This is an invitation to be open in our thinking and practice. It is an ongoing call to intentionally explore the heart of the Father for all people and all circumstances. It is a summons to live a life of sensitivity to the Holy Spirit so that He may always give us not only the best gift but the most suitable expression of it to that individual or people group.

Jesus only mentioned the word "church" two or three times in Scripture, but mentioned the "Kingdom" almost eighty times. He clearly wanted to keep our understanding of the Church as fluid as possible. *Ekklesia*, the Greek word for *Church*, means more than just a simple gathering; it can also mean a company of called out people. We are a committed band of people, meeting together for a common purpose. Church is not a place we go to. It is who we are together.

God didn't list the full variety of gifts because there are endless ways He can do things. He knew that if He had laid everything out for us, we would stop exploring the Spirit and quit experimenting with His gifts. In the past thirty years, I have worked with eighteen different kinds of prophets. I am sure there are more — I just haven't met them yet. I love discovering what kind of prophet a person is, and what the nature of their particular calling includes. God is not one-dimensional. He is multidimensional and far bigger than anything we could dream of.

Old Turns New

In 1 Corinthians 12–14, the Apostle Paul took great care to teach us how to use the vocal gifts. Three passages are particularly important to this study:

For to one is given the word of wisdom through the Spirit, and to another the word of knowledge according to the same Spirit; to another faith by the same Spirit, and to another gifts of healing by the one Spirit, and to another the effecting of miracles, and to another prophecy, and to another the distinguishing of spirits, to another various kinds of tongues, and to another the interpretation of tongues. But one and the same Spirit works all these things, distributing to each one individually just as He wills. (1 Corinthians 12:8–11)

If I speak with the tongues of men and of angels, but do not have love, I have become a noisy gong or a clanging cymbal. If I have the gift of prophecy, and know all mysteries and all knowledge; and if I have all faith, so as to remove mountains, but do not have love, I am nothing. (1 Corinthians 13:1–2)

Pursue love, yet desire earnestly spiritual gifts, but especially that you may prophesy. For one who speaks in a tongue does not speak to men but to God; for no one understands, but in his spirit he speaks mysteries. But one who prophesies speaks to men for edification and exhortation and consolation. One who speaks in a tongue edifies himself; but one who prophesies edifies the church. Now I wish that you all spoke in tongues, but even more that you would prophesy; and greater is one who prophesies than one who speaks in tongues, unless he interprets, so that the church may receive edifying. (1 Corinthians 14:1–5)

The vocal gifts of the Holy Spirit must lead us to do two things: pursue love and do everything for the purpose of edifying the body of Christ. We are to build each other up in every way possible. New Testament prophetic people are called, just like every Christian is, to be an ambassador for Christ: *"Now then, we are ambassadors for Christ, as though God were pleading through us: we implore you on Christ's behalf, be reconciled to God"* (2 Corinthians 5:20). As part of that call, we must represent the heart of God to people around us. We must give evidence of the essential nature of who God is within the New Testament covenantal relationship He has with us.

We cannot escape the new covenant; it is who we are. We have to represent that new covenant in every single thing we do. John the Baptist was the last of the Old Testament type of prophets, sent to prepare the way for Jesus. Christ was the first of the New Testament series of prophetic figures.

John's mission was to bear witness to the arrival of a Messiah who came as prophet, priest, and king. Jesus Christ was that individual.

In Himself, Jesus taught how the prophetic was to be refashioned and remodeled in the new covenant. In His revolutionary Sermon on the Mount in Matthew 5–7, He repeatedly used the phrase, *"You have heard that it was said to those of old… but I say to you."* He knew the things He taught were causing controversy and consternation, because they were pushing a culture out of its Old Testament thinking and into a new day with God. Where once only a few could interact with God, now all would be able to.

> *The Father sees you in the future and...*

In the Old Testament we see a prophetic concentration of the gift in only a few people who represented the Lord. In the New Testament we discover a prophetic distribution of the gift because now the Holy Spirit lives in all God's people who have surrendered to Him. Jesus said *"My sheep know my voice,"* (John 10:3,4,16,27!)

This does not make everyone a prophet, that is a specific calling. However we have all been given a lifestyle that involves communion verbally. It is impossible to build a successful, dynamic relationship with God if we cannot hear His voice. In chapter 10 John puts forth the truth that we can know by hearing and therefore not just by knowing scripture or the witness of friends.

Paul's statement that "I wish even more that you would prophesy" (1 Corinthians 12:5) resounds as strongly today as in the early church. God's intentionality is part of His divine nature, unchanging and eternal.

Jesus wanted to prophesy because He loved to edify, exalt, and comfort. He shared the same passion for encouragement and tenderness that God the Father has. God is constantly looking at each of us, planning ways in which He can build us up. He loves us deeply, and has called us to pursue that same love.

> *... loves to speak to that in your present*

To properly release the prophetic gift in our lives, we must remain in the love of God. We have to learn how to see people the way God sees them. Then we need to learn how to speak to them the way God would speak to them. Our interaction with people should cause them to understand and appreciate who God is and who He wants to be for them.

When God speaks, it is an event. Something is created and birthed. Something is supposed to happen in people's hearts when they receive a prophetic word or action. *"Let your speech always be with grace, seasoned with salt, that you may know how you ought to answer each one,"* Paul taught in

Old Turns New

Colossians 4:6. *"Let no corrupt word proceed out of your mouth, but what is good for necessary edification, that it may impart grace to the hearers,"* he added in Ephesians 4:29. We are taught to put away malice, anger, wrath, slander and abusive speech from our mouth {Colossians 3:8]. We are enjoined to pursue the things that make for peace and the building up of one another (Romans 14:9). We are commanded to speak whatever is true, noble, just, pure, lovely and of good report (Philippians 4:8). Our conversation — whether "everyday" or what we would term "prophetic" — must operate from the same grace base. This was the shift Jesus brought to the realm of the prophetic.

Prophecy And Grace

God punished Jesus for the sins of the world because Christ made Himself available for judgement as we read in Romans 8:31–34:

> *What then shall we say to these things? If God is for us, who is against us? He who did not spare His own Son, but delivered Him over for us all, how will He not also with Him freely give us all things? Who will bring a charge against God's elect? God is the one who justifies; who is the one who condemns? Christ Jesus is He who died, yes, rather who was raised, who is at the right hand of God, who also intercedes for us.*

God delivered Jesus up for all of us, and now no one can bring a charge against us. As prophetic people, we must carry that same positive outlook. We represent the essential nature of God, including the Galatians 5 fruit of the Spirit. Being prophetic does not exempt us from being Christ-like. It doesn't mean we live one way and talk another. We don't get to live lovely in Christ but talk nasty in the spirit. Instead, we must display the character of God — loving, kind, gentle, patient, peaceful, joyful, good, and meek. Perhaps the hardest fruit for a prophetic person to show is self-control. Yet self-control is the only form of control that is acceptable in Church life. This is the basis for all true maturity, purity and integrity. People must take responsibility for how they speak in every circumstance. If the fruit of self-control is not visible in a person's life then it is hard to trust the character of the one speaking.

We live in a prophetic season of grace.

In the New Testament Church, there is no place for judgment. When someone sins, they have an advocate in Jesus. We cannot bring charges against each other or we fly in the face of grace. *"My little children, these things*

SAINT FRANCIS OF ASSISI

Lived: 1182 to 1226

Prophetic Synopsis: Born the son of a wealthy merchant, Francis turned his back on his former life when he heard God tell him to "Go, Francis, and repair My house, which as you see is falling into ruin." Francis followed this revelation and worked to fix a rundown local church. Despite being mocked and beaten, Francis kept building the little church by lugging huge stones and putting them in place. He did indeed fix that chapel — even at the cost of his relationship with his greedy father.

In 1208, Francis was touched by a sermon on Jesus sending out the disciples without money or extra clothing. He took that command to heart and gave away his remaining goods. Others joined him as he rebuilt several churches. Eventually, the Franciscans became their own Catholic order.

He traveled and preached, following his famous creed — he spoke the Gospel always, but only used words when necessary. His love for nature became legendary, and he wrote the magnificent Canticle of the Sun: "Most high, all powerful, all good Lord! All praise is Yours, all glory, all honor, and all blessing. To You, alone, Most High, do they belong. No mortal lips are worthy to pronounce Your name."

Key Comment: "0 Divine Master, grant that I may not so much seek to be consoled as to console; to be understood as to understand; to be loved as to love."

More: Read *The Little Flowers of Saint Francis of Assisi* by Saint Francis of Assisi

Source: St. Francis of Assisi. *The Little Flowers of Saint Francis of Assisi*, trans. Thomas Okey (New York: Dover Publications, 2003).

I write to you, so that you may not sin. And if anyone sins, we have an Advocate with the Father, Jesus Christ the righteous," says 1 John 2:1–2. *"And He Himself is the propitiation for our sins, and not for ours only but also for the whole world."* The prophetic ministry points to that advocacy. While there is a place for correction, discipline, and chastisement, judgment must be thrown out of the equation. We read more about this in 1 John 4:7–11:

> *Beloved, let us love one another, for love is from God; and everyone who loves is born of God and knows God. The one who does not love does not know God, for God is love. By this the love of God was manifested in us, that God has sent His only begotten Son into the world so that we might live through Him. In this is love, not that we loved God, but that He loved us and sent His Son to be the propitiation for our sins. Beloved, if God so loved us, we also ought to love one another.*

A truly prophetic voice is very in tune with the heart of God. Our role in the earth is to proclaim His love, seeing people as God sees them — not how we see them in the natural. Prophets speak to the all-sufficiency of Christ for people. We represent who God is in word and deed.

We are not subject to judgment because God has already judged Jesus. We are in a prophetic season of grace. God judged Jesus on the cross and He will judge us when the books are opened in eternity. Between then and now, however, we live in a season of grace. There is no judgment now, only the chastisement and discipline that comes because we are maturing into full sons and daughters of God.

Was Jesus punished enough? If the answer is yes, then...

Every day, the Holy Spirit is trying to bring us into cooperation with the Father. He has a series of adjustments He wants to make in our lives because He loves us. Unfortunately, there are times when those adjustments go unnoticed; we ignore them, but they don't go away. Many times, we just wait the will of God out rather than change.

Discipline that is not adhered to doesn't go away; it accumulates. It grows to a point where God has to chastise us. We can ignore discipline, but it will not ignore us. Eventually, it reaches the level where God has to practically beat the living daylights out of us because He loves us so much.

When a handyman lays a floor, he knows the first row of tiles is the most important. If those are off even slightly, the floor will look worse and worse as he continues to build it. Eventually, it has to be completely

... there is no judgment in life only...

redone. By ignoring God's call to realign that first row of tiles, we end up having to have our entire life pulled up and re-laid. Sensible Christians know this and keep a short account with God. They constantly repent for their sin and open themselves to His subtle touch. Hundreds of small adjustments are better than six really big changes. Being taken behind the woodshed by God is never fun. Discipline and chastisement are a part of our spiritual journey because they show that God loves us, that He wants us to change, and that there is no judgment for us now. So called prophecies that are centered on sin, judgment and death tell us nothing about the nature of God but may reveal everything about the person prophesying! It is a significant witness to their lack of relationship with God. It witnesses to their inability to live, move and speak out of the fruit of the Holy Spirit (Galatians 5:22–26). It demonstrates the poor quality of their love and attitudes towards people.

In the New Testament judgment becomes a sober assessment of what is right and wrong. Judgment does not always imply condemnation in the Bible. When used in relation to scriptures it consistently refers to the evaluation of a believers work in the context of them gaining reward from the Father (1 Corinthians 3:10–15).

God is not looking for opportunities to destroy people but to reveal His own nature to the earth. He is merciful. He is kind. He is good. It is the goodness and the kindness of God that leads us to repentance (Romans 2:4). Jesus ever lives to make intercession (Hebrews 7:25). The whole world now belongs to the Father because the spirit of redemption has been released through Calvary. We are now God's prime ambassador's reconciliation.

We are His visual aid to the earth to demonstrate the Kingdom of Heaven and to reveal the Name and Nature of God to a sin sick and hurting world.

There is a rising tide of evil in the earth and there is no rising tide of goodness to combat it. "We overcome evil with good" (Romans 12:21). What if the problems in the world are not lawlessness and crime; not poverty and sickness; not greed and selfishness; not drugs or terrorism; not abortion or immorality? What if the biggest problem in the earth is simply the lack of goodness?

The ambassadors of Christ are spewing out judgment in the name of righteous indignation and the world is going to hell because we have mis-understood the glory of God.

... the law of sowing and reaping and ...

When Moses asked to see the glory of God, the Father showed him His goodness whilst proclaiming His compassion. The world is wanting to know what

God is like. Jesus came to put a face on God, the church is present to put a face on Christ. "He who has seen Me, has seen the Father".

Millions of people are caught up in bondage. Many, many millions more are victims of evil and are living with no perception of the majesty of God's goodness. The sex slave trade is greater now than at any other time in history. Child abuse is at an all time high. Poverty has never been bigger in the history of man. More wars have been fought in the past century than ever before. Where is the goodness of God? Where is the church? Why are the people of God consumed by judgment and negativity when they should be leading lives overwhelmed by the goodness and the kindness of God. The Good News must become the Good News in our lives. The church is an agent of freedom. It is for freedom that Christ has set us free. Not just our own freedom, but that of every living soul. We are caught up in a war between darkness and light. We are not fighting people but dark forces arrayed against us that persist in their intention to enslave all God's creation. Let us preach the gospel of reconciliation and the goodness of God to all men everywhere, whilst at the same time taking authority in the name of Jesus over principalities and powers, and interceding for the victims living in hear and bondage.

Christians must live and operate within the nature of God. We must demonstrate the fruit of the Spirit. We cannot function outside of His lovingkindness and mercy. Indeed when James and John asked for the fire of judgment, Jesus rebuked them gently: "You do not know what kind of Spirit you are!" (Luke 9:54–55).

There is a difference between a judgmental spirit and the Spirit of God, as seen in the face of Christ the Redeemer. We live in an age of redemption and we must live in that Spirit. The Old and New Testament anointings particularly with regard to the prophetic are manifestly different.

> ... judge and you will be judged

How do we maximize grace and mercy without reducing all forms of sin to a misdemeanor? There are some heinous sins being committed across the earth that clearly cannot be ignored. The church must understand her role in the earth. Firstly, to act as ambassadors of grace and mercy through reconciliation (2 Corinthians 5:18–19). Secondly, to expose sin and to release people in bondage. "Mercy triumphs over judgment" (James 2:13). Unless it triumphs in the heart of each individual believer they will never know the fullness of God's presence.

God comes to our perception of Him or not. When Jesus asked the question: "Whom do people say that I am" (Matthew 16:13) He was wanting to know about peoples perception. From peoples perception of us we can gauge how we are going to be received. The Father builds the church on the right perception of Him. We apprehend what we perceive, whether that is good or bad.

If we perceive God to be harsh, demanding and prone to judgmentalism, then our experience of Him is not going to grow into any great place of relationship. How do you make friends with a tyrant? It is impossible, because fear governs the relationship. Fearful of making mistakes; of saying the wrong thing; of doing a wrong act? Paranoia rules and peace is impossible.

However, if we perceive that the Father has huge wells of compassion and mercy, which never run dry. If we know Him as being One who is full of grace, rich in love and abounding in love and truth. If He is slow to anger and incredibly patient toward us. If He is joyfully happy, with a sunny disposition. If His very cheeriness can over the world. If He is scandalously forgiving and generous. If He is the very epitome of goodness; so much so that we can only be transformed when we link our repentance with His goodness and kindness. If these things are true and form a large part of our practical and spiritual theology of life, then our whole personality is formed by such values.

Jesus was always accused of lavishing too much time on sinners (Matthew 9:11–13) and always had an answer for the religious people. God desires love and compassion in His people.

We are called to pray not condemn. We are called as Jesus is to intercede for a depraved world to the God who cares. God takes care of His own wrath, He does not need our help. We have favor to request mercy (1 Timothy 2:1–2). The Father wills that all people should be saved. In that case we must declare the goodness and kindness of God so that repentance may come (Romans 2:4).

Jeremiah knew the goodness of God and he also understood the prophetic role in a country where the One, True, God was not worshipped. It is to seek the good of the place where God has sent you and to pray on behalf on its inhabitants. Blessing comes to blessing (Jeremiah 29:7).

Judgment comes to judgment (Matthew 7:1). We are told numerous times to pray for people not against them. We have the honor of praying in line with the Holy Spirit's revelation of the Father. Therefore we can appeal favorably to His compassion and mercy which never fails (Lamentation 3:21–23) for they are daily renewable. The God who has always identified with sinners is unchanging in that respect. Read Isaiah 53 in order to understand the Christ-like nature. Jesus always opposed the spirit of the Pharisee by moving in the opposite spirit Himself. We must choose between being Christ-like and becoming a Pharisee. Jesus numbered Himself with sinners.

In our thinking we must focus on mercy and grace or we will be mentally judging others. Jesus is "with us" and He is "for people". Pharisees define themselves by what they are against, thus putting themselves on the wrong side of God.

Jesus' appeal to the church is to "be merciful, just as your Father is merciful" (Luke 6:36).

We are in a prophetic season of grace so, prophetically, let's be gracious. It is God's kindness and goodness that lead people to repentance, not our hammer of revelation. God's love is impossible to resist. To communicate it properly, our hearts have to be soaked in that love. We need to be completely overwhelmed by the grace of God.

Like any other secular group/organization the church today contains people who are skilled at running off at the mouth. We criticize one another, saying nasty, sarcastic, and disrespectful things. We ignore God's command that our ordinary speech be full of grace. We talk trash all week and then sing praises on Sunday. Such a lifestyle smacks of immaturity and a lack of self-control.

We all have choices to demonstrate our allegiance either to Christ or ourselves. There will always be difficult, hard-nosed people seeking to put their mental, emotional and spiritual imprint upon our lives. How we move in the Spirit in those situations will tell an awful lot about us. What comes out of our mouth either glorifies the Father or defiles our heart and ministry. When we are trapped in a situation where people are being nasty and negative, we can choose to be Christ-like. If we don't choose the path Jesus would have taken, I guarantee that such sin will show up and influence our ministry. That negativity will be reflected in the way we prophesy. Our everyday conversations must have the flavor of God in them.

> *Every situation is about who you choose to be in that circumstance*

"For out of the abundance of the heart the mouth speaks," Jesus said in Matthew 12:34. It is great to worship and have our hearts filled with presence of God. But what fills our hearts when we're in a negative situation: is it bitterness, sarcasm or something cynical? It is in those moments that we can win only by exercising self-control. We have to better than we have been. We have to become Christ-like, for it is in those situations that our prophetic voice is established. It is so important that we develop a lifestyle of moving in the opposite spirit to what comes against us.

The Exercise Of Prophecy

In tough situations, we must ask God what the need of that moment is. Do we need something? Does the other person need something? Instead of speaking out the first nasty comment that jumps to our minds, we must settle into the Spirit of God and speak a word of edification. If we can get into a lifestyle of gracious speaking in our everyday conversations, our prophetic ability will grow in leaps and bounds. The heartbeat of God will become clearer and clearer to us.

"But now you yourselves are to put off all these: anger, wrath, malice, blasphemy, filthy language out of your mouth," Paul wrote in Colossians 3:8. How could God be any more obvious than this verse? We must put those evil behaviors away and live a life of grace in word and deed. A prophetic voice cannot speak love and kindness one breath and hate and bitterness the next; a fountain cannot give out both sweet and salt water. Being prophetic takes a tough choice about our lifestyle of communication. What will we speak out? No one can say ungodly things in conversation and expect to prophesy at a meaningful level. God will not honor such hypocrisy.

Our ordinary conversations show the Holy Spirit if we can be trusted with something remarkable. *"Therefore let us pursue the things which make for peace and the things by which one may edify another,"* says Romans 14:19. Perhaps the most famous passage in Scripture on this theme is found in James 3:8–12:

> But no one can tame the tongue; it is a restless evil and full of deadly poison. With it we bless our Lord and Father, and with it we curse men, who have been made in the likeness of God; from the same mouth come both blessing and cursing. My brethren, these things ought not to be this way. Does a fountain send out from the same opening both fresh and bitter water? Can a fig tree, my brethren, produce olives, or a vine produce figs? Nor can salt water produce fresh.

If we do not tame our tongue, our gift will hit a glass ceiling and level off. Operating in the prophetic takes two things: we must trust God with everything, and He must bring us to the place where He can trust us. We can aspire to higher and deeper levels of the prophetic but the cost of that is controlling our everyday conversations.

Jesus: The Model Of Grace

Jesus was full of grace and truth, and the perfect example for Christians to follow. Prophecy and grace must come together in our lives as they did in Christ's. *"Finally, brethren, whatever things are true, whatever things are noble, whatever things are just, whatever things are pure, whatever things are lovely, whatever things are of good report, if there is any virtue and if there is anything praiseworthy — meditate on these things,"* wrote Paul in Philippians 4:8. Jesus did just that: concentrated on truth, justice, nobility, purity, love, and virtue. He was unbelievably kind.

God understands our struggle in this because Jesus was wonderfully human, as we read in Hebrews 4:14–16:

> *Therefore, since we have a great high priest who has passed through the heavens, Jesus the Son of God, let us hold fast our confession. For we do not have a high priest who cannot sympathize with our weaknesses, but One who has been tempted in all things as we are, yet without sin. Therefore let us draw near with confidence to the throne of grace, so that we may receive mercy and find grace to help in time of need.*

> **Prophecy promotes confidence**

No one reading this book has the burning desire to be the worst Christian who ever lived. But do many of us have a plan to be the best one? In all of our hearts, we have a hunger to be Christ-like. We want to be significant in the spiritual realm. The prophetic anointing allows us to see this desire in other people. It doesn't just tap into God's heart, but it lets us see others as God sees them. We can see the hunger, purity, and loveliness of another person. We can see their earnest desire for God.

Prophetic ministry is about drawing out of people what God has already put in them. Christ understands our weaknesses for He too was human. Because of that fact, we can approach His throne of grace boldly. The prophetic word presents people with grace and truth. The truth about grace and the grace to be truthful with a real impartation of love!

Confidence in Christ is the only antidote for inadequacy and insecurity. When we learn who He is, our doubts about ourselves fade. We know that His grace is sufficient for us, and that we can enter His presence because we belong there. We can come before His throne with boldness because it is the very place where we receive mercy. By coming to Him, we gain the grace we need to face any situation in life.

New Testament prophets release individuals to that same place of confidence. When a true prophet ministers, no one is afraid. Instead, confidence in God builds within the listeners. Those who hear start to see God as He really is and begin to fall in love with Him all over again. The grace of God is intoxicating and irresistible. Prophets help inspire people to obtain mercy and grace.

When the Holy Spirit convicts of sin He always brings us the gifts of mercy, grace, righteousness and forgiveness. He uses these gifts to restore our fellowship in line with our relationship with God in Christ. The Father has put us into Christ (relationship); it is the work of the Holy Spirit to teach us to abide there (fellowship). Literally to establish the Christ life and likeness in us. All prophetic input is towards the same purpose. Edifying (1 Corinthians 14:3–4) leads to the establishing of our identity in Christ Jesus.

It is important that we all understand this basic, but vital, truth about Christ and life in the Spirit. We cannot prophesy outside of that revelation — we prophesy within that power.

New Prophecy For New Times

The New Testament form of prophecy started by Jesus was startling in light of what had come before it. In Acts 10, Peter was given a new paradigm of how God worked. When he saw that sheet come down from Heaven, filled with every manner of "unclean" animal, he was sickened. He refused to go anywhere with Gentiles like Cornelius because they were "unclean."

> *In prophecy God invites us to see what He is seeing... in Christ*

Three times, God had to shake Peter's upbringing off him: *"What God has cleansed you must not call common,"* (Acts 10:15).

God wanted Peter to see the Gentiles differently. All of his life, the burly fisherman had been taught to not go into a Gentile home, not mix with any of them, and certainly not eat with one of them. And suddenly, after decades of living like this, God told Peter that He wanted him to do all of those things. You can almost hear Peter's protests: "I don't do that sort of stuff, Lord. It's not kosher. You wrote the book on that, remember?"

"What God has cleansed you must not call common."

This was a major shift for not just Peter, but the entire Jewish culture. Acts 11 shows the hot water such a revolutionary act landed him in. The other disciples, Peter's dear friends and colleagues, couldn't believe their ears. Peter's comment to them is astounding! *"Who was I, that I could stand in God's way?"* (Acts 11:17). What Peter experienced in his connection with the household of Cornelius was revolutionary and mindset changing!

Every single one of us is going to go through a similar kind of mental shift. God will change our paradigm about something. It will be as difficult for us to accept as it was for Peter. As prophetic people, we share the Lord's burden for releasing people from whatever imprisons them.

It is for freedom that Christ has set us free. All people who prophesy and those called to the prophetic ministry and the higher office of a prophet are jealous for people to have life and freedom in Christ. They want to see a people of promise and power emerge who know their God and who are living in His fullness.

Prophetic input leads us into an experience of the faith, hope and love of the Lord. Prophesy should turn our heart towards the love of God. Even if the word convicts of sin there must be a clear call to repentance in God that brings renewal (Revelation chapters 2 and 3).

In Luke 4, Jesus came out of the desert full of the power of the Holy Spirit. He walked into a synagogue, picked up a scroll, and opened it to Isaiah 61. Just the fact that Jesus took the Scripture out of sequence must have shocked all who were present. After all, the Jews would pick up God's Word from where they ended the previous reading. Jesus wasn't terribly interested in sticking to such a tradition. He just turned to His life message and read:

> *"The Spirit of the* LORD *is upon Me, Because He has anointed Me To preach the gospel to the poor; He has sent Me to heal the brokenhearted, To proclaim liberty to the captives And recovery of sight to the blind, To set at liberty those who are oppressed; To proclaim the acceptable year of the* LORD.*" Then He closed the book, and gave it back to the attendant and sat down. And the eyes of all who were in the synagogue were fixed on Him. And He began to say to them, "Today this Scripture is fulfilled in your hearing." (Luke 4:18–21)*

As prophetic people, we all need a life message about who God is and what He is like. Jesus' understanding of God the Father was that He loved the poor, brokenhearted, enslaved, oppressed, and sick. This call on His life focused His prophetic gift. He was constantly kind and generous to those whom He was called to help.

Jesus was full of grace and truth as a prophet. It's important that we are too; but truth by itself will only change people. Truth causes transformation when it is powered by grace. When those two spirits work together, they have an incredible

> *Prophecy can open any prison door*

SAINT MARTIN OF TOURS

Lived: 316 to 397

Prophetic Synopsis: Martin was a young soldier when he came across a beggar at the gate to the city of Amiens, France. Gripped by compassion for the poor, freezing man, Martin tore his own cloak in two and handed it to the man.

That night, Martin had a vision of Jesus Christ dressed in the piece of cloak he had given to the beggar. Jesus smiled, looked at the angels around Him, and said proudly: "Martin … clothed me with this robe." Smiling, He quoted Matthew 25:40 — "Inasmuch as ye have done it unto one of the least of these my brethren, ye have done it unto me."

That revelatory vision changed his life. Martin left the army and became a monk: "I have served you as a soldier; let me now serve Christ. Give the bounty to these others who are going to fight, but I am a soldier of Christ and it is not lawful for me to fight," he said. Once, a group of thieves robbed him — and he led one of them to Christ on the spot.

Throughout his life, Martin followed the insight given to him in his dreams. He used that gift to plan pilgrimages, trips, and moves. His contemporaries record that he operated strongly in the prophetic. Even in his final days — having known through a prophetic word that he was about to die, he traveled a long distance to reconcile two warring factions within a church.

Key Comment: "Place me alone in the front of the battle, with no weapon but the cross alone, and I shall not fear to meet the enemy single-handed and unarmed."

Source: Bateman, Jordan. "The Mindfulness of St. Martin." AWE *Magazine*, Winter 2003, pp. 8–9

effect upon humanity. It doesn't matter if the individual is Christian or pre-Christian, truth and grace affects them.

There is a difference between change and transformation. Change can seem a temporary alteration of behavior during a particular season. It could be that people drive their carnal behavior underground when confronted and then return to it when the heat is off.

Transformation occurs by the action of God's grace on truth when we allow the Father to touch our innermost place and we surrender life at that point. It is possible to have great truth but ruin it with poor grace. People then feel brow-beaten by the truth rather than seeing the beauty of what the Father is offering in Christ. Pharisees are inveterate bullies.

I am fascinated by the idea that Christ proclaimed His life message — *"The Spirit of the* LORD *is upon Me… to set at liberty those who are oppressed"* — to the Church of His day. He did not read from the scroll, or paraphrase it, during His Sermon on the Mount, or when He fed the five thousand. He didn't tell the masses that He would save them, but He told the religious community. "I'm going to release you from prison," He prophesied to them.

The Church of Jesus' day was locked in its religious, pharisaical prison. Its system had bred thousands of brokenhearted, oppressed captives. These people had to be freed, and Christ knew it.

Our Perception Of God

What we think about God is the single most important thing in our lives. Whatever we perceive God's nature to be will color how we live spiritually, physically, emotionally, and relationally. It is unavoidable. *"For the testimony of Jesus is the spirit of prophecy,"* says Revelation 19:10. Our testimony of who Jesus is for us will drive our prophetic gift for the rest of our lives. For better or for worse, how we connect with God's nature will determine how we prophesy.

> When your personal revelation of God is increased, your…

In Exodus 33–34, Moses had a unique encounter with God. The Lord lovingly maneuvered Moses into asking for the very thing He wanted to give him. Because everything originates in God, we know that Moses' desire was placed there by Him. *"Please, show me Your glory,"* Moses asked in Exodus 33:18. In Heaven, God smiled. Moses had caught the very thing God wanted to give him.

God placed Moses in a small cleft in a rock. *"So it shall be, while My glory passes by, that I will put you in the cleft of the rock, and will cover you with My hand while I pass by,"* He said in Exodus 33:22–23. *"Then I will take away My hand, and you shall see My back; but My face shall not be seen."*

That experience changed Moses. As God walked past him in Exodus 34:6–7, He prophesied to Moses about Himself:

> *Then the Lord passed by in front of him and proclaimed, The* LORD, *the* LORD *God, compassionate and gracious, slow to anger, and abounding in lovingkindness and truth; who keeps lovingkindness for thousands, who forgives iniquity, transgression and sin; yet He will by no means leave the guilty unpunished, visiting the iniquity of fathers on the children and on the grandchildren to the third and the fourth generations.*

Suddenly, Moses had a whole new revelation of who God wanted to be for him.

God never changes. He is still merciful and gracious, and all of the other things He told Moses. But our ability to understand His character traits grows and deepens as we spiritually mature. The nature of God is constant, but we are not. That's why we need to spend time with Him, learning as much about His character as we can. Moses' burning bush experience paled in comparison to seeing the back of the Almighty. He had proven himself worthy and grown to the next level. He was changed by what he saw from the cleft in the rock; even his face glowed afterward.

I believe the world is ready for a revelation of who God truly is and what Christianity is really about. We're ready to come to a place of deep truth where the prophetic nature of God bubbles within us. God wants to give each of us a unique vision of Himself — sharing what He is like, what He loves, what He sees, and what He dreams. This revelation is so profound that it will change the way we think forever. When we walk through dry places, it will sustain us. It is water for our spirits.

> *... prophesying goes to a whole new level of intimate proclamation.*

Speaking What Could Be

God always speaks to our potential. In Luke 19, we read that Zacchaeus, a much-loathed tax collector, was up in a tree trying to see Christ. He was an obnoxious person who had defrauded most of the community. Some say he may have been up the tree because he couldn't see over the crowd, but I think he was up there for security purposes as well. A crowd that big, full of people who hated him — it was just a matter of time before he took a knife between his third and fourth ribs.

Hiding in trees wasn't the life Zacchaeus had dreamed of. He yearned for more. He wanted to be loved and accepted. As Jesus walked through Jericho, He had the option to eat with anyone there. Everyone would have loved to have had Him over for a meal — they would get to meet Him, and then brag to their friends afterwards. So who did Jesus choose? The one man everyone hated.

"Zacchaeus," Jesus said in Luke 19:5, *"make haste and come down, for today I must stay at your house."*

That acceptance changed Zacchaeus's life. Jesus never prophesied his sin to him, but instead loved him. The fruit of the encounter was immediate, according to Luke 19:7 — *"Look, Lord, I give half of my goods to the poor,"* Zacchaeus said. *"And if I have taken anything from anyone by false accusation, I restore fourfold."* Jesus merely filled Zacchaeus's need to be loved, and the rest flowed from that.

From the one simple positive act towards a loathsome individual the whole village experienced a blessing. Money flowed into families that had been defrauded. It was like the whole village won the lottery!

It's amazing what can occur in a community when we suspend judgment in favor of blessing.

When prophetic people confront someone with their sin, they inevitably hold onto it. Without grace, the truth is useless. Our call is to speak to their potential.

It is important that our hearts are exercised in giving grace and mercy. *"Mercy and truth have met together; righteousness and peace have kissed,"* says Psalm 85:10. We need to live within that embrace, so that we can bear fruit according to Isaiah 32:17 — *"The work of righteousness will be peace, and the effect of righteousness, quietness and assurance forever."* This is the very foundation of the Kingdom of Heaven: *"The kingdom of God is not eating and drinking, but righteousness and peace and joy in the Holy Spirit"* (Romans 14:17).

Righteousness and peace are two themes central to the prophetic gifting. Anyone who wishes to speak God's words must remember passages like James 3:17–18:

> But the wisdom from above is first pure, then peaceable, gentle, reasonable, full of mercy and good fruits, unwavering, without hypocrisy. And the seed whose fruit is righteousness is sown in peace by those who make peace.

There is a beauty in the Lord that is amazing!

Hypocrisy is a major pitfall for many prophetically-gifted people. The Bible assures us that hypocrisy will be disciplined. One needs only look at Romans 2:1–7 for evidence of that:

Therefore you have no excuse, everyone of you who passes judgment, for in that which you judge another, you condemn yourself; for you who judge practice the same things. And we know that the judgment of God rightly falls upon those who practice such things.

But do you suppose this, o man, when you pass judgment on those who practice such things and do the same yourself, that you will escape the judgment of God? Or do you think lightly of the riches of His kindness and tolerance and patience, not knowing that the kindness of God leads you to repentance? But because of your stubbornness and unrepentant heart you are storing up wrath for yourself in the day of wrath and revelation of the righteous judgment of God, who WILL RENDER TO EACH PERSON ACCORDING TO HIS DEEDS: to those who by perseverance in doing good seek for glory and honor and immortality, eternal life…

When we despise the richness of God's goodness, forbearance and longsuffering, then we open ourselves up to becoming Pharisaical and judgmental.

Judgment has become part of the spirit of the age. The world acts out its condemnation on the news channel with approval ratings. On reality TV people are voted out summarily by others with a vested interest in taking their place. We have poll ratings for everything so that everywhere people can execute their perceived right to judge another.

The justice of God does fall on people. When it does, it is not a pretty sight. My advice to anyone playing with such a possibility is to stop everything and immediately repent. You don't want God's justice to smash down on you. Like a rock falling from the sky, it will crush you. Severe chastisement is not fun, enjoyable, or easy to recover from. Let go of your stubbornness and ask God to soften you to His Spirit. In Matthew 7:1–5, Jesus Himself is every bit as clear as Paul was on the sin of hypocrisy:

"Do not judge so that you will not be judged. "For in the way you judge, you will be judged; and by your standard of measure, it will be measured to you. "Why do you look at the speck that is in your brother's

eye, but do not notice the log that is in your own eye? "Or how can you say to your brother, 'Let me take the speck out of your eye,' and behold, the log is in your own eye? "You hypocrite, first take the log out of your own eye, and then you will see clearly to take the speck out of your brother's eye.

With the same standard we use to measure people, we ourselves will be measured.

A friend of mine was once stuck in a bad church situation. It was a place where cynicism and criticism were in control. One day, a particular individual came to him and began tearing down other people in the church. Every time he started talking about someone, my friend would literally duck beneath him. When he would start attacking someone new, my friend would again duck. Finally, the man demanded to know what was going on.

"Why are you doing that?" he asked.

"That plank in your eye — every time you swing it around, I'm afraid it's going to knock my head off," my friend replied. What can I say? He has a strange sense of humor, but he did get his point across.

Brethren, even if anyone is caught in any trespass, you who are spiritual, restore such a one in a spirit of gentleness; each one looking to yourself, so that you too will not be tempted. Bear one another's burdens, and thereby fulfill the law of Christ. (Galatians 6:1-2)

People become inconsiderate when they fail to renew their own humility. We can only restore people when we are living our lives in a state of meekness before God. Meekness is not weakness it is strength under control.

Beware lest your truth have wrong companions, such as anger and not grace! If you enjoy putting people straight, you may need to examine your own heart.

Correcting people is an awkward process requiring great love, humility and fruit of the Spirit. Truth when preceded by grace, will transform.

Grace Growers

It's not easy to love everyone, but it is the call on every prophet's life. To test us in this, God deliberately puts people around us who are meant to be loved by us. Oftentimes, we will have to be very creative to love them; some of them, by design, are not easy to love. But those unlovable ones, ironically, teach us the most about God's heart.

I call people like these grace growers. They cultivate the grace in my life by forcing me to be intentional about loving them. In Luke 6:27–36, Jesus taught us about grace growers:

> *But I say to you who hear, love your enemies, do good to those who hate you, bless those who curse you, pray for those who mistreat you. Whoever hits you on the cheek, offer him the other also; and whoever takes away your coat, do not withhold your shirt from him either. Give to everyone who asks of you, and whoever takes away what is yours, do not demand it back. Treat others the same way you want them to treat you.*
>
> *"If you love those who love you, what credit is that to you? For even sinners love those who love them. "If you do good to those who do good to you, what credit is that to you? For even sinners do the same. "If you lend to those from whom you expect to receive, what credit is that to you? Even sinners lend to sinners in order to receive back the same amount. "But love your enemies, and do good, and lend, expecting nothing in return; and your reward will be great, and you will be sons of the Most High; for He Himself is kind to ungrateful and evil men. Be merciful, just as your Father is merciful.*

The Lord chooses some strange people to convey His heart…

I first learned about grace growers in the 1980's when I began doing schools of prophecy in the U.K. They were among the first of their kind and so attracted a lot of attention both positive and negative. There were several "ministries" who felt threatened by what I was doing and there were various people who were totally convinced that training people to hear God's voice was demonic!

Three such men began to follow me around convinced it was their calling from God to expose me and protect the body of Christ from my ministry. They genuinely thought that they had a mandate from God to oppose me and pull me down (John 16:2). They would visit cities where schools were booked and try to persuade pastors to warn their people not to attend. They would be outside the venues on the day holding placards and handing out leaflets warning people. Then they would come into the school, put their placards at the back of the hall and sit in the front row directly in front of the lectern. They would take copious notes and afterwards write a newsletter explaining the teaching and why I was a heretic. We called them the three stooges.

…you are probably one of them!

This went on for two years. They booked in to every school! I cried out to the Lord, "Please, kill 'em". Well that prayer didn't work so I modified it to maiming, "Lord cut off their writing hand... do something!"

Several weeks later He answered my prayer, though not in the manner I had envisioned. One night I had a dream. I am used to dreaming. Most of my revelatory dreams begin in the same way, so that I am able to retain what I see, hear and experience in the dream.

God is on His throne. I am sat on one arm of it with my legs over His lap and our heads are together talking. In this particular dream the Father had something to show me. When I readily agreed, He gave a command off to one side of His throne. An angel walked in with a huge block of the most beautiful marble I had ever seen. It was six foot high, four feet wide and three feet deep. It was glorious and breathtaking.

Jesus came into view, smiling that lovely slow, small smile of His. He dug a finger into the marble and made an outline of a figure in the stone. I watched entranced. The Father asked "Would you like to see it made?" I nodded enthusiastically and He gave a command. Three pairs of hands and arms (up to the elbow) appeared. Each pair held a hammer and chisel and at the command of the Father began sculpting this figure out of the marble.

"If you encourage them, they will work faster and it will be completed more quickly". He said, smiling at me. I began tentatively to bless and encourage them but it didn't seem to make any difference. "My son, you must always be wholehearted in your encouragements." He said laughing. I began to exhort, bless and encourage loudly encouraged by the Father. At one point I was standing on the arm of His throne with my hand on the Lord's head (for balance!) shouting encouragement at the very top of my voice! Everywhere was pandemonium! There was huge laughter and cheering all around me. One angel was lying on the floor beating it with his fists and screaming with laughter. The draft of his wings almost knocking me off my perch.

Eventually the work was finished and the noise became peace. I was exhausted and sank down to my original position. I starred in awe at the figure that had been created. "Do you know what it is?" the Father breathed into my ear. When I shook my head, mute in awe and wonder, He turned my face to look in His eyes.

"It's how I see you, my son. It's the man I am making you into." I looked again at the figure and began to cry. "But it's so beautiful my Lord." I whispered. He smiled gently, looking full into my face. "Would you like to thank the sculptors He asked with a smile. "Sure!" I said, turning back to the statue. My smile of thanks turned to one of total shock and horror when the three stooges suddenly appeared next to the sculpture. "Aargh!!" I screamed at the top of my voice; so loudly in fact that I woke myself up!

Suddenly a flood of revelation filled my waking heart and mind. I began to realize the purpose of the Lord over the last two years. God allows in His wisdom what He could prevent by His power. All their opposition had driven me to strive to be an excellent teacher. Their criticism had pushed me into a place of continuously upgrading my material and the quality of presentation. School of Prophecy was gaining an excellent reputation because I had consistently upgraded it in the face of their antagonism. What had not been upgraded, I realized, was my own nature and character. Their hostility had not produced in me an opposite spirit that craved Christ-likeness. I had been offended, angry and affronted. I had affected a grieved spirit believing it was justice.

I had not at all seen that the purpose of the Father was also to change my character and personality. He was seeking to beautify me by making me like Jesus. I saw His plan and I wept. I cried because of my stupidity. Why could I not have foreseen His purpose early on in the circumstance? I began to understand that I valued my material and my ministry more than being made in the image of Jesus. I wept for that.

I saw the value that the Father placed on my becoming like Him. I resolved to change my ways with the help and support of the Holy Spirit. To put character transformation at the top of my list of responses to the workings of God.

I got it. I understood the purpose of grace growers. They were present in my life to teach me the grace that is currently mine to be made in the image of Jesus. Grace growers provide an unconscious opportunity (on their part) for us to experience a breakthrough in the image of God. I had only approached the situation from a functional and not a relational paradigm. Pride, vanity had made me change my product but not my heart.

> Grace growers provide us with a shortcut to enter the Presence of God at a deeper level of response

My attitude changed. I thought through the effect that these men had been on my outlook and my personality. Suddenly, all the clues were there to be seen; so obvious now. I was supposed to learn patience with joy; blessing and not cursing; how to love those who were in enmity; how to be kind and gracious in the face of unkind opposition.

The next months were vastly different. Now I prayed positively for these guys. I had compassion, kindness and love for them. I lost my victim mindset. I ceased to be offended by their actions and became profoundly grateful to the Lord instead. I learned my lesson and it has been the foundation of all ongoing transformation since.

Grace growers are people you love to hate and who hate to love you. They are a gift of God to bring a pressing transformation to bear quickly on our lives. Better the grace grower you know, than the new one who will have to take their place!

God puts these people in our lives to teach us about being Christ-like. How do we love our enemy? By refusing to see him as such. We all have difficult people around us, but they are going to experientially teach us how to discover and explore the love of God. It will kill us to love some of them; such struggle cracks open our heart to the Holy Spirit. God wants us to look at His children with the same love He feels. The harder they are to love, the more God will pour Himself out on us to accomplish that action.

What a mystery this is! The very people we find the hardest to get along with can bring us the closest to Christ. To connect with someone, we must see them as Jesus sees them. We have to look beyond the rubbish, "looking for the baby Jesus under the trash," as U2 sings. We must look beyond the brave fronts we all put up and see each other for who we truly are. When we see someone the way God sees them, we can speak to that treasure.

How Prophecy Starts

In prophecy, the first thing we need to receive is a sense of burden. When we give ourselves fully to God's love and grace, our hearts are tuned to the same wavelength as God's. We inherit a sense of ownership for the church community He has placed us in, and, out of the burden, God will express His heart.

We need to be intentional and look around where we live, asking God, "Who, Lord, do You want to speak to in my church, on my street, or in my daily life? Lord, give me a burden." Once we receive that burden — or compulsion to pray for someone — we can explore it further by asking God several questions:

- What are You really saying through this burden?
- What are Your hopes and dreams for this individual?
- What is it You want me to do?
- At the end of this prophecy, what do You want to achieve in this person's life?
- What is Your objective?

We can never assume that we will immediately know all of the right answers. A strong sense of burden can take time to work through and explore with the Holy Spirit. But God will give us a sense of objective. To develop an understanding of how God's heart works towards people is very important. Why is He picking this person out to receive prophecy? What does He want to achieve through this word?

Having a sense of God's objective helps us to be clear, specific, and significant in what we are prophesying. It is similar to what schoolchildren experience when they are taught how to write an essay: we must support and develop God's thesis, His key theme, for that person's life. Without a sense of objective, we sometimes fudge the words or pad the prophecy with too many human insights. We see a blurrier picture because we do not have a sharp focus on what God wants to do.

God's objective also affects our delivery; we must present the word in a manner that connects with whatever God wants to do. *"Most assuredly, I say to you, the Son can do nothing of Himself, but what He sees the Father do; for whatever He does, the Son also does in like manner,"* Jesus said in John 5:19. If God wanted to impart His peace to a person, you usually wouldn't grab the individual by the scruff of the neck and yell into his face: "Thus says the Lord, 'BE AT PEACE!'" If it was the Father's love that was to be shared, you probably wouldn't be harsh to a person. The objective and delivery cannot be at odds with each other, or there will be no impartation.

> The objective affects the delivery of prophecy

If the objective is to strengthen people, to add resolve and determination to their lives, our prophesying will reflect that aim. We will prophesy in a bold, forthright manner, dwelling on the supremacy of God and taking care to release a confidence into the people concerned. If we have received a word from the Lord about His love for an individual, we should communicate that in a way that causes God's love to be spread into that heart.

Diagnosis Versus Prognosis

When we receive a sense of objective, we then begin to focus in on what God wants to say to the individual. Often, the first thing we receive is diagnostic. A significant difference exists between a prophetic diagnosis and a prophetic prognosis. A diagnosis is the process of determining the nature and cause of a person's need. A prognosis is how God weaves Himself into that diagnosis. In medical terms, we can be diagnosed with the flu, and given a prognosis of full health after a few days of rest, orange juice, and chicken noodle soup.

Sometimes, we can see a vision or have an intimation that is quite negative. We may see a fault, a wrong, or a sin. Often, this first impression is simply diagnostic. Prophecy is made up of three elements: word of knowledge, gift of prophecy, and word of wisdom. A word of knowledge opens up the issue, a prophetic word speaks God's heart into it, and a word of wisdom tells us how to respond to God.

> Do to others what you would have them do for you

That first shred of negativity we sometimes get may actually be a word of knowledge, not a word of prophecy. God can give us information about a person's life in order to contextualize, for us, the prophetic word to come. "This is what is happening," God says. "I need you to understand it before it can be spoken into." God is telling us what He wants to overthrow next in that person's life (Jeremiah 1:10) so that He can build or plant something better.

Most people prophesy the first thing they receive. We can actually prophesy a word of knowledge that God gave us as information. It is called prophesying the problem and has probably damaged more people's lives than any other activity in the prophetic realm. Never give the first thing you receive; don't be in a hurry to prophesy. It's not a race. You are dealing with sensitive issues in a person and can hurt them greatly. We must not feel that we have to get a word out of our mouth as soon as we get it.

We must perfect the art of stepping back into our spirits when we receive revelation. We can dialogue with God when we receive that first impression. "Thank You, Father," I often say. "I understand that about his life. Now, in light of that, what is it You want to say to him?" What He gives us next could be the complete opposite of what we first saw because the grace of God may need to come into operation.

The word of knowledge, in many cases, is for diagnostic purposes. The Lord reveals the situation to us as it is at the moment. However, the prophetic word we give may relate to what the Lord is going to do both now and in the future. We can give the individual their prognosis. Diagnosis identifies what is, while prognosis indicates what is to come.

Context is incredibly important to God. When we receive a word of knowledge, we need to ask ourselves two questions:

- Is this word diagnostic?
- If so, is it for me personally, so that I can become familiar with the situation?

If the answer to both questions is "yes," then we have a context, or set of circumstances, into which God wants to speak. We need to use that privileged information wisely — being sensitive to the Holy Spirit and respecting the people concerned.

One of the hardest things for prophetic people to learn is that not everything that we receive is to be given. Many prophetic ministries speak out everything they see and hear from God, broadcasting a person's innermost fears and flaws to a packed auditorium. We must become constrained by love, and remember Jesus' golden rule: *"And just as you want men to do to you, you also do to them likewise"* (Luke 6:31). Prophesy the second thing you get.

Speak The Second Thing

I learned this principle for the first time in a Welsh church in 1986. God set out a precedent for me, and I have held fast to that ever since. My first evening there, I had dinner with a number of leaders. One thing led to another, and I ended up praying for some of the elders there. I prophesied over the pastor of the church — for the sake of this anecdote, I'll call him David. I was working my way around the room when I came to an elder named John. Touching his shoulder, I told him that I just wanted to wait on the Lord and see if God had anything He wanted to say. In my spirit, I asked God what He saw over John.

Immediately, the Lord showed me a picture of John holding an eighteen-inch-long knife in his hand. It was a wicked-looking blade, tapering from four-inches-wide at the hilt to a sharp point, and serrated on both sides. John took his knife and began stabbing the main leader, David, in the back over and over. He didn't do it just once or twice, he stabbed him twelve, fifteen, twenty times. He plunged the knife into David, trying to get it in as deep as it could go. From every conceivable angle, John stabbed David in the back. I was stunned, to be honest. I couldn't believe how vicious it was.

I asked the Lord for an interpretation. "What's this all about?" I said to Him in my spirit. God showed me that John thought he should be the leader of the church. He thought he was more anointed, had a better ministry, and felt he was a better-equipped leader. In private, he took every opportunity to run David's ministry down. He sullied his reputation, his gifting, his style, everything. John desperately wanted to build a platform for himself; he wanted status and was profoundly jealous of David's popularity.

> The Spirit always gives life

At that moment, to be perfectly honest, I felt a sense of dread. I was suddenly aware that what I did next was going to be incredibly important — not just for John, but for me. I stepped even further back into my spirit and asked God what I was supposed to do with this information.

Imagine if I had prophesied the first thing I saw! "John, thus saith the Lord: stop it, you backstabbing little rat!" I held John's life in my hands in those few seconds. I could either release him from what he was doing, or bring him to a place where he would be finished in that church. If I exposed him, no one in that room would ever trust him again. Those other leaders, and especially David, would have been wary of him. A stigma would be placed over his life because I exposed something that God wanted me to use only for diagnosis. He would have been humiliated. Of course, I would have come out looking great and wonderfully "revelatory." I could have rationalized away what I did to that poor man by saying, "truth is truth."

Yes, truth is truth. But there is also grace, compassion, and mercy that come with it. We can express God's desires in a way that does not water down the truth, but is also in line with His love for the individual involved.

In my spirit, I asked the Lord what he wanted to do. "How do I handle this? What am I supposed to say?" I asked. Instantly, the peace of God came over me.

"Grae," I felt the Lord say, "I want you to know what is going on in his life. But I want you to say something that is going to release him from that." If I had prophesied the problem, I would have locked him up for years. He would have been known as that backstabber for the rest of his life. I wouldn't have freed him; I would have turned him into a prisoner of other people's fears and perceptions. He would have had to move to a new city to be free.

Fortunately, God showed me exactly what to do. I asked John and David to stand up, back to back. I looked around and found an old broom handle, and placed it in John's hands.

"John, I want you to pretend this broom handle is a sword," I said. "The Lord has brought you two men together. He has stood you back-to-back, which is a fighting position. He is giving you a charge into your life, John, to guard David's back, to look after him because the enemy wants to have and destroy his life and pull him down by any means possible. He is giving you a charge to guard him and keep him prayerfully. Defend him against the enemy. Be aware that the enemy strategy is to ruin him through the hands of men who lust for power. He has given him to you as a friend to watch over his life, pray for him, bless him, and stand with him. He wants you to be his friend and brother. You have been brought here for such a time as this. The Lord has brought you here to guard this man's back because the enemy is seeking to destroy him. He wants to kill him because he knows that if he cuts off the head, the body will die. But your friendship is going to be significant throughout the whole region. There are spirits of accusation going out against this man all the time; there is a weakening in the spiritual realm around this man's life. The enemy wants to kill him, to destroy his reputation, because there is a father's heart emerging in him. There is an apostolic calling on his life. The Lord has brought you here to guard his back. Not to be his yes man, but to be his strong right arm."

As I spoke, John began to cry. The others in the room thought it was because of the incredible privilege God had given him. That may be partly true, but he was also crying because I was speaking to him on one level, and God was speaking to him at a deeper one.

> *The Blessing of the Lord makes rich…*

It is not a prophet's job to convict someone of their sin. That's the work of the Holy Spirit and, quite frankly, He doesn't need our help doing it. As I prophesied blessing on John, he was being convicted of his sin at that same moment. He realized that he was on the wrong side of God, and he had been doing the very things the enemy wanted him to do. He was being convicted even as blessing was being poured out on him.

John felt very guilty in that moment, but that's okay. After all, guilt is a friend because it convinces us that we are wrong and need to repent. Guilt is different than condemnation, which makes us feel so bad that we cannot approach God for forgiveness. Guilt, however, leads us back to Christ.

At a time when any human being would have slapped John around for his sin, God gave mercy and grace. "Isn't it time we changed this?" God whispered to him. Even as I prophesied the blessing, God was showing him the root of sin. He was prompting John to change from vicious backstabbing to his true call. Where sin abounds, grace abounds so much more.

In the spirit, I could feel John's resolve strengthen. He determined that he would answer the call of God on his life. "I want to be that man," he prayed, and he has been since that day. His heart broke when God honored him — and he responded.

Almost twenty years later, John and David are best friends. They have held on to each other through good times and bad. Their friendship has been significant regionally, drawing churches together around their ministry. Both guys teach on how to live together and deal with confrontation. Their ministry is superb.

Later that weekend, I took John aside and asked if everything was okay with him.

"You have no idea how God has blessed me this weekend!" he said. At that point, I felt the Lord nudge me to tell him what I had been shown.

"Actually, I think I might," I said. "On Friday night, I saw you with a knife in your hand, stabbing David in the back."

He broke down in tears; a contrite spirit knows the kindness of God. The fact that the Lord knew his sin, but redeemed and blessed him publicly without exposing it, softened his heart.

"You didn't say anything," he said.

"God had something better to say than that," I said.

... and adds no sorrow with it

"Why did He bless me?" he asked.

I looked him in the eyes. "John," I said, "that's what God is like. He's the kindest person I've ever met in my life. God was only being true to his essential nature. It's impossible for Him to be anything but kind. God is good, and His goodness leads us to repentance."

That is the beauty of the prophetic. Anyone can speak to what is there, but only God can go beyond that and speak to what could come. Why speak to the flesh when you can speak to the treasure? If we do not understand the diagnostic principle, we may prophesy a problem and cause major damage. The Gospel is redemptive; a prophet must be good news, even if that news is repentance.

"We have this treasure in earthen vessels", Paul said (2 Corinthians 4:7). It is better to speak to the treasure rather than just the clay pot. Whatever you speak to in people will rise up. If you speak to nobility it emerges. If you speak to the Christ-like nature, He is revealed. If we connect with someone's carnality, it will rise up too.

Sometimes because of our intransigence, the Lord will have to chastise rather than mildly rebuke. This may be more formal and public than we would like. It is our non responsiveness that has brought this about and we only have ourselves to blame. But usually that only comes when we are so far down the road of no return that He considers it the only way to bring redemption. We don't have to speak the negative, even if God reveals it to us. If we fix in our minds that the Gospel is redemptive, we will be more likely to speak to the treasure God has for people.

God does not do shame

If possible draw attention to the leaders in the church before you give any corrective word (NB. Please see book 2 in the series entitled "Prophetic Protocol"). At least try to make it as private as possible so as not to cause shame or condemnation.

SAINT JOAN OF ARC

Lived: 1412 to 1431

Prophetic Synopsis: With her country under siege, God visited Joan, a young farm girl in rural France, with a series of prophetic messages. Shortly after her thirteenth birthday, Joan spent a day fasting and praying. During that fast, God spoke to her: "When I was about thirteen, I received revelation from our Lord by a voice which told me to be good and attend church often and that God would help me." From that time on, she heard various voices speak to her, including Michael the Archangel, St. Catherine, and St. Margaret of Antioch. Two or three times a week, Joan would receive a message from one of those famed servants of God.

The voices told her she had to go to end the siege of a town called Orleans, take a young ruler named Charles to a city called Rheims and crown him King of France. It was a call that would change Joan's life.

Five years later, God's voice told her to go to the neighbouring town of Vaucouleurs and speak to the captain of the fortress there, a man named Robert de Baudricourt. She immediately recognized Robert, even before he was introduced to her. Joan kept telling Robert that she had to meet Charles the Dauphin; he refused her twice. Finally, she prophesied to Robert that the French would win a battle at Herrings. They did, and Robert, impressed, gave Joan six attendants and ordered them to take her to Chinon, where Charles was.

Just as her revelation showed, Joan led the French army to victory and crowned Charles king. Burned at the stake at age nineteen for being a heretic, she died staring at a makeshift cross made by an enemy soldier.

Key Comment: "I fear nothing for God is with me!"

More: Read *Joan of Arc* by Mark Twain or *Joan of Arc: In Her Own Words* by Willard Trask.

Sources: Mark Twain. *Joan of Arc: Personal Recollections*, trans. Jean François Alden. (Ignatius Press, 1990). Willard Trask. *Joan of Arc: In Her Own Words*. (New York: Turtle Point Press, 1996).

If you are in a public event such as a conference and you receive such a word for someone and there is no possibility of a more private meeting with a few people, then care must be taken to extend grace. Give the prophecy as a general "word to someone here" and request that they see you privately. Then it is up to the Holy Spirit to lovingly confront, convict and redeem!

Grace Breaks Our Hearts

The grace of God will keep flowing into our lives most of the time. There isn't a person in any church, anywhere, to whom God doesn't want to reveal His incredible kindness. Many Christians have given up on the kindness of God; our experiences with others have been so bad that we can't help but equate God with natural relationships. But God is completely different: He is not human. He is divine, an altogether different character.

God wants to build us up any way He can. Prophecy is for the edification, comfort, and encouragement of those who receive it. God isn't just encouraging and stirring us — He is in touch with our pain as well. He wants to bring us comfort when we need it.

Ninety percent of prophecy is stating the obvious: God loves you, He cares for you, He wants the best for you, His kindness and faithfulness is with you. His love is eternal. He knows everything about your life. These are things every Christian knows and recites, but sometimes we get so locked into our circumstances that we lose sight of even those basic attributes of the character of God. We need to be reminded from time to time. We can read these same truths in Scripture, but sometimes we just need that "now" element of prophecy, allied to the Bible, to actually bring the word home to our circumstances in a dynamic way.

We must not apologize if the prophecy we have is not new or fresh. If we have received a word that God loves someone, then we have say that word in the best way possible. Prophecy communicates spirit-to-spirit as well as speaking to our minds.

The whole essence of prophecy is that we need to let the Holy Spirit fire our spirits. Personally, the fact that God loves me is the single most important truth in my life. I know that He loves me.

I wake up everyday convinced of the love of God, convinced that something wonderful is going to happen that day between me and the Lord, convinced that God is going to help me find a way through the problems I have in my life at the moment. God is going to do something terrific and dynamic, and He is going to help me fight off the enemy and fight through the difficulties. Why? Because He loves me. It doesn't matter what is facing me in life at the moment, for I know that God is going to walk with me. The worst that can happen is that my situation doesn't change at all, but I know the presence of God. God will walk me through it. I'll have to go through everything and endure everything, but even in that, God will not leave me. His presence will be with me. He will be with me even until the end of the age. The absolute best that can happen is that He changes everything and my concerns disappear. The worst that can happen is that I get to walk by faith for a little while longer. His presence is with me as I endure, and even the struggle is wonderful.

Discernment And Direction

My confidence in the love of God colors the way I prophesy. Thank the Lord it does! Sometimes when we pray for a person, we can be given the gift of discerning spirits, along with our prophetic intuition. Primarily, discernment enables us to detect and witness God at work. However, it can also enable us to understand the spiritual state of an individual. There are

> In Christ, everything is within our reach

no secrets from the Holy Spirit: He knows everything about everyone. Discernment can be helpful as it can tell us if an evil spirit is present, if the person is oppressed or possessed, and if they are under some form of spiritual attack.

In prayer times, the Lord has often shown me the spiritual state of the person I am prophesying over. For example, I have detected a profoundly low self-esteem. Of course, the last thing you want to do when praying for someone with low self-esteem is broadcast to a room of five hundred people that they have a poor self-image. We must not prophesy the problem; instead, we must speak out what God wants to be for them.

"A new confidence is going to come into your life from the Lord," one might pray over a person with low self-esteem. "Through events in your life, God is going to meet you and take you to a whole new level of peace, rest, and confidence. He'll take you to a place you've never been before and you'll love it. As He does that, the Lord says He will break some long-standing things in you. Your life is at the point of breakthrough. A spirit of breakthrough hovers over your life right now and it will enable you to get revenge over the enemy for all the areas where you have felt pushed down over the years." In Isaiah 61 we have the favor of God and the possibility of vengeance on the enemy for all of our situations.

When we exit the prison of our circumstances we are able to receive the Lord's blessing and turn our life into an opportunity to strike back at the enemy.

Whatever we have suffered and been a victim of in life, now, when freedom comes, it enables us to use our favor to set people free from the very thing we ourselves were a victim of in life. It is a critical part of the prophetic gift to declare God's heart, intention and favor to another and to proclaim that their own breakthrough will lead them to assist others in overcoming!

By speaking to what God wants to do, and not what the individual, the world, or the enemy has already done, we speak freedom into a person's life. If we see a particular sin over someone's life, it has not been revealed to us so we can pronounce judgment. We need to wait and listen for further insight and instruction from above. He shows us sin because there is a release in the Spirit over the person's life. Our question must be: "What is the nature of that release?" God is not heartless. He will not show us sin without showing us the critical point of release that's about to come into that person's life.

> Our maturity may well depend on the type of questions we ask

Seeing someone's sin prophetically boils down into one question: "Is this a grace issue or a discipline issue?" When we sense something is amiss, we have to dig into our spirit and listen very closely to what God has to say. Does He want grace or discipline? If it is a grace issue, we have to prophesy grace, mercy, and hope.

A few years ago, I remember seeing a spirit of lust sitting on a man I was praying for. It was almost oppressing him, but I felt God telling me that it was a grace issue. God showed me what was going to happen, and I prophesied it: "A new anointing of holiness is coming upon you. I see a fresh anointing for holiness that will bring you to a whole new place of purity, power, and righteousness. You've been crying out for those things and God is delighted to say yes, with all of His heart." Men break open when you prophesy holiness over them; many have been crying out for that new path, and God loves to open it to people.

There are also times when we see a sin and God declares it a discipline issue. This occurs when a person has been ignoring the grace of God for a long time. Pride and arrogance accompany that sin. In Scripture, we see this dealt with a few times — Paul, for example, told the Corinthian church to throw out a man who was having sex with his own mother. It was a deplorable, abhorrent sin and the individual had to be disciplined. We can also be disciplined in a Hebrews 12 context, where God is developing us into mature sons and daughters. *"If you endure chastening, God deals with you as with sons; for what son is there whom a father does not chasten?"* says Hebrews 12:7–8. *"But if you are without chastening, of which all have become partakers, then you are illegitimate and not sons."* Loving confrontation is sometimes required in discipline.

One rule holds true whether it is a grace issue or a discipline issue — you always deal with sin privately, not publicly. In 1986, the elders of a church I was visiting asked me to pray for a man who was going through a very hard time. His wife wouldn't go to church, wouldn't pray with him, and didn't want to talk about Jesus. They asked me to go and encourage him.

> *Discipline when stored up by our lack of response… becomes chastisement*

As I prayed for him, with the elders present, I saw a vivid picture of the man in a navy pinstripe suit, with a white shirt and red-striped tie. He was walking into the foyer of the Connaught Hotel with a redheaded woman. The woman was wearing a two-piece, dark green business suit and carried an overnight bag. They went to the reception desk and signed in under the name "Coleman." The attendant, a bald, 5'2" man in a black suit, white shirt, and green tie, gave him a key for room 213.

After seeing that, I asked the Lord what it meant. God told me that his wife was all over the place because the man had been having an affair with his secretary for three years. She knew something was wrong but didn't have any proof. She could not stand his hypocrisy and became depressed.

I had been asked to pray for a man who seemingly had a shrew for a wife; that perception turned out to be all wrong! I asked the Lord one final question: "Is this a grace issue or a discipline issue?"

"I have been speaking to this man for three-and-a-half years, Grae," the Lord said to me. "It's a discipline issue. Tell him what I've shown you."

I shared the vision and watched as the man sunk to his knees, crying. The elders were perplexed: "Who is this woman?" they asked him. "Your wife is a blond! Your name is not Coleman!"

The man confessed everything: on business trips, the two would stay at the Connaught Hotel, and the last time they were there, they had room 213.

This man was at the point of losing everything because he had resisted God's grace for three-and-a-half years. We had reached a point of critical mass and God had to deal with the issue. The man could not be trusted to respond to a grace word any longer; he had to be lovingly confronted and led to a place of confession and repentance.

Discernment And Direction

When we encounter a discipline issue, we must remember that the whole point God has brought it up is to lead the individual into confession and repentance. Paul's exhortation in Galatians 6:1 must be of paramount concern to us: *"Brethren, if a man is overtaken in any trespass, you who are spiritual restore such a one in a spirit of gentleness, considering yourself lest you also be tempted."* Judging someone will not cause them to change. Restoring them in gentleness will.

Any time someone receives a prophetic word, grace should explode in their hearts. If someone is walking in sin, they usually don't need to be told about it because they already know. We don't need to be prophesying what a person's problem is, we need to be prophesying what God wants to do at that moment in time.

I once did a conference with a team of prophetic people in the northeastern United States. We were praying during a ministry time when I came to a natural break in what I was doing. I stood back for a moment to gather myself in the spirit and found myself listening to what another speaker was prophesying over a young man.

"The Lord sees you as a very hard nut with a very hard exterior," he told the man. "In the next twelve months, God is going to crack open your life." In graphic detail, this man prophesied the pain and pressure God was going to pour out on this poor person's life, all to crack him wide open. I was getting depressed just listening to it — I can't imagine what the poor man was feeling!

"I don't like this," I said to the Lord. My heart was jarred by the words this man had given. This person had nothing to look forward to for the next twelve months; it was like his life was going to be flushed down a toilet for a whole year. The man finished prophesying and walked away, leaving a devastated young Christian in his wake. He didn't know what to do or where to look. He was totally lost.

> Always ask: what is the freedom and the release?

I walked over to him and put my hand on his shoulder. He flinched.

"It's okay, mate," I said.

"Please, I don't want another prophecy," he replied. I'm not surprised, I thought to myself.

"Okay," I said. "Why don't you and I just be two guys, two brothers, on a journey together? We're both on a quest with God, so let's just see what else He might have to say."

I asked the Lord to show me the first thing He had shown the other man. God showed me a very hard nut, one that could be pounded on a table but make no sound. It was rock hard. "Okay, Lord," I prayed. "Was there anything else you wanted to show him, something he didn't get?" Suddenly, right next to the nut in my picture was a bottle of oil.

The first prophetic person had gone with the first thing he had seen. He didn't wait or dig deeper into what God wanted to do. He didn't ask any questions. God had given him the nut picture as information to contextualize the actual word.

"What's with this nut?" I asked God. The Lord showed me that the man had lived a hard life. He wasn't rebellious or hard-hearted; life had just been difficult. He had to build a shell around him to protect himself from all the damaging things he had grown up with. He was an orphan. He lived in institutions but was never chosen for a home. He never got adopted. He never received anything. He had known all kinds of abuse. That hard shell was the only way he could have kept himself together. God showed me he was a nice kid. He had come to the front because he desperately wanted God.

God doesn't break nuts by shattering them. When I asked Him how He wanted to break this hard shell, I saw a picture of the oil bottle being opened and poured on to the nut. It didn't happen just once; it happened again and again and again and again. The mysterious ways of God softened that nut to the point that one could dig their fingernails into it and pry it apart. It wasn't hard anymore.

I told the young man that I saw a nut. His face was priceless: "Oh no, it's going to happen again!"

"Next to the nut, I see a big bottle, full of oil," I continued. "I see it being poured on to that nut, again and again and again. It is a continuous stream of activity, oil being poured out so lavishly that the nut suddenly became soft. I believe that all of your experiences of life to date have made you tough and hard on the outside. God knows everything you have gone through just to preserve your own life. And now He is saying, 'My son, My son, the days of hardness are over. These are the days of a softening, a day when the oil of My presence and beauty will soften you.' The Lord says that the next season will be a profound season of change — a transformation. You will dance your way through this time, you're going to laugh your way through this time, you're going to grin your way through this time, you're going to smile your way through this time, for the days of hardness are at an end. These are days of a continuous grace and an oil of the Holy Spirit being poured out on you. Enjoy this time."

Something in his heart began to connect with God when I prayed for him. A few minutes later, I saw him on his knees, worshiping. He was changed by that word.

Peace, Not Pressure

One of my good friends often jokes that prophecy is eighty percent preparation, twenty percent inspiration, a hundred percent perspiration, and a thousand percent trepidation. Often, the main cause of failure in the prophetic is that we have moved under pressure rather than in peace and relaxation in the knowledge of God. I am under enormous pressure, everywhere I go, to move in prophecy. I have visited churches where leaders have slept in sleeping bags outside of my bedroom, wanting a prophetic word in the middle of the night. I've gone to the washroom at 3 a.m. and been followed in by a person wanting prophecy. I have been at conferences where I have been expected to prophesy from 6 a.m. at a men's breakfast straight through to when I wrap up the main session at 11 p.m.

I accept some pressure as part of my ministry, but there is no way I can live under the weight of false, or unfair, expectations. Many churches and leaders see prophetic ministry as a glorious shortcut. Instead of laboring to create vision in the church from the roots up, leaders bring in a prophet to prophesy a vision that can be imposed on to the people from the top down.

> Prophecy involves a labor of love and a work of grace

Prophecy will confirm and broaden a vision, it can be a catalyst in the Spirit to reveal the unseen and unknown. Vision is further developed through prayer, seeking God, and sharing our hearts and dreams with people in the work.

Every day, I have to push away the burdens of other people's expectations. To be still, to live in the grace of God, to be aware of His presence, and to be at rest are the goals of prophetic ministry. Into that environment, God can drop His word, create faith, and release the prophetic flow. Worship is important to a prophet. Being at rest and peace in our relationship with God is absolutely vital.

When we do not dwell in rest and peace, we find ourselves reacting to situations. Reaction rather than rest is poison for a prophet. People moving under pressure can often indulge in mental gymnastics rather than hearing a word in their spirits. Prophecy becomes tainted.

Most people think prophecy comes from "somewhere out there" into our minds. This isn't the case. In fact, we cannot receive prophecy in our minds. The mind only receives information. Our spirit, however, receives revelation. Prophecy comes from within, through our spirit's communion with the Holy Spirit. It then moves from our spirit into our mind, through the link of faith. Faith is the vehicle that takes a prophetic word from our spirit into our conscious mind.

Our minds are very good at putting things in order. They can organize billions of gigabytes of information, sorting it and making it understandable. Revelation comes in bits and pieces sometimes. We may receive part four, then part two, followed by parts one and three. The mind is brilliant at putting those pieces into order so that they come out correctly. We must always let our faith loose on a prophetic word first, so that it can move from our spirits into our minds. This faith is simply the confidence that the word we have is truly from the Lord.

Sometimes we can get a word coming into our spirits that makes no sense whatsoever to our minds. That is because our minds cannot understand revelation; they can only process it and put it in order. Revelation, sometimes, is totally illogical. It does not always make reasonable sense. If we seek to understand revelation with our minds, we can slip into uncertainty and fear, and become paralyzed by the thought of being wrong. Our courage can evaporate as we ponder the very real possibility of looking stupid in front of other people. That fear can cause someone to cut their losses and say nothing. To make up for it, we often say something general (but dressed up in spiritual language) that our mind can cope with rather than the significant, supernatural word we've been given.

In a meeting in London several years ago, I gave an appeal for people who were experiencing relational difficulties to come forward for prayer. As I worked through the line, I came to man in his late forties. I had no idea about the relationship in his life that was causing him pain; the man said nothing to me. All I could do was reach out in my spirit and ask God's perspective.

At that instant, I had a fifty-fifty chance at being right about speaking out whether it was a male or female this individual was having trouble with. If I guessed correctly there, the odds lengthened, as I had to decide if it was a mother, wife, girlfriend, sister, daughter, employer, co-worker, church member, pastor's wife, or a hundred other relational possibilities.

As I reached out to God, I said, "The Lord wants to speak to you about your wife." At that point, I received a picture of a tall young woman in her mid- to late-twenties with long blond hair. My mind was screaming at me that this was his daughter. However, in my spirit, I heard the word "wife."

I took a second to rest in my spirit and let my faith loose on the original word. I ignored my mind and spoke prophetically. The word spoke of how the man had been married for three years to a woman twenty years his junior. Under his love and care, she had blossomed in her personality and had changed considerably. She had grown from a mousy introvert into a more confident and outgoing personality. This had changed the dynamic of their relationship to a point where he was becoming less confident of her love and more convinced that she would leave him for a younger man. Into that situation, the Lord spoke a beautiful word of comfort and reassurance that lifted his spirit immeasurably.

> *All prophecy flows from intimacy*

Very often, a real battle is waged within our life between our mind and our spirit. Our mind wants to be in control, but God has created our spirit to know Him and move with Him. This is why peace, quiet, and rest on the inside are so vital to a healthy spiritual life.

Some people are "feelers" in the prophetic. We feel people's pain, joy, excitement, or other emotion. We feel things from the heart of God. Some people are "seers." We see in pictures and have dreams. We live a life of metaphor and symbolism. Some people are "hearers." Sometimes, we can move in all three. It is a good thing not to get locked into one methodology. Try to have a variety of ways to receive and deliver prophetic words. After all, God Himself is full of infinite variety.

Deal With Frustration

Frustration can be an enemy — or an ally — of any prophetic ministry. If left unchecked, it colors our thinking, infects the word we have, and gives us a jaundiced perspective on the life of the church. If we are to represent God's heart and be good servants, we must learn to master our frustration. We need the understanding and the grace of God to move our hearts rather than our own irritation and dissatisfaction.

As dangerous as frustration is, it can also be incredibly fruitful. I'm not afraid of frustration because it is a vital part of a person's spiritual development. How we handle our, and others', frustration is important. Every one of us must handle our frustration wisely and righteously. We cannot shoot our mouth off and blurt out any thought that comes into our head. Instead, we must let frustration develop us. We may be frustrated with our ministry, but often God is in that frustration, trying to change the way we live.

> *Frustration is a sure sign that you need to change!*

MARTIN LUTHER

Lived: 1483 to 1546

Prophetic Synopsis: The man who changed Church history forever spent hours meditating on a particular piece of Scripture. It is clear from his own words that God spoke to him through it:

"As I meditated day and night on the words 'as it is written, the righteous person shall live by faith,' I began to understand that the righteous person lives by the gift of a passive righteousness, by which the merciful God justifies us by faith. This immediately made me feel as though I had been born again, and as though I had entered through open gates into paradise itself. God accepts Christ's righteousness, which is alien to our nature, as our own. Though God does not actually remove our sins — we are at the same time righteous and sinful — he no longer counts our sins against us. And now, where I had once hated the phrase, 'the righteousness of God,' I began to love and extol it as the sweetest of phrases, so that this passage in Paul became the very gate of paradise to me."

Saddened by the state of the faith and Church leadership, Luther nailed ninety-five theses on to the door of a church in Wittenberg, sparking the Reformation and the creation of the Protestant Church.

Key Comment: "The Church does not need any head other than Christ because it is a spiritual body, not a temporal one."

More: Read *By Faith Alone* by Martin Luther

Source: Martin Luther. *By Faith Alone.* (Tulsa Oklahoma: World Publishing, 1998).

Frustration has a cutting edge, like a double-edged sword. It is okay for us to be frustrated with where our church is, with what the vision is, with the number of meetings, and the rest of the complaints one hears regularly in church life. But we must recognize that there is the other edge to frustration: when we feel frustrated, it's probably because God is frustrated with where we are in our character. God is exceedingly direct. We feel frustrated, and then He reveals its source — a stagnant prayer life, a lack of worship, a decrease in love, a habitual sin. We want to talk about our frustration, but He wants to deal with the one we're causing Him. The Holy Spirit will speak to us in the midst of frustration about our personal walk with God.

At least frustrated people care about something. I would rather teach in a room of fifty frustrated people than five hundred apathetic ones.

Rejection is an issue that often walks hand-in-hand with frustration. When we feel rejected, we must open our hearts so that the love of God can flow in. Many prophetic people can feel rejected because they do not have any relationships of worth or value. Prophets are often accused of being weird, temperamental, emotional, and abnormal. In some places where there is a great ignorance of the role of the prophet, that type of behavior is seen as normal for prophetic people. This is a bit of an unfair reputation, as prophets have not cornered the market in abnormality; there are many non-prophetic ministries that seem to fluctuate between the oddball and the highly entertaining.

Prophecy is about restoring people's dignity and self-respect — to do so, we have to be restored ourselves. I hate the enemy because he strips that away from people. He *Your apathy is the goal of the enemy* steals dignity and self-respect and creates a sense of disillusionment in our hearts about ourselves. He creates a sense of "I'm not worthy, I'm no good, I can't do anything." He steals every shred of self-worth he can.

Perhaps no more obvious example of this exists than in the world of advertising. Looking spiritually at the ad industry leads me to believe it borders on the demonic a lot of the time, because it is geared to making people feel dissatisfied with their lives. That's the whole point of it: advertisers have to make people unhappy with an aspect of their lives, and if they can achieve that, there is a good chance that people will buy their products. Advertisers create dissatisfaction about our lifestyles, our figures, our looks, our clothes, our possessions, and countless other things. Into that vacuum, they put their own product, hoping to entice us to purchase it and fill the void that they created in the first place. They trade on our insecurities and our need to be loved and valued.

The enemy's strategy works on that same principle. He is geared to making us feel dissatisfied with who we are. He wants to separate us from God, the church, our friends, and any useful function we may adopt in furthering the Kingdom. If he can get us to hate ourselves and tell our hearts that we are of no account and, as such, it doesn't matter if we don't go to the meeting or pray or worship, then apathy will follow. If we allow apathy into our lives, then it will hold the door open to unbelief, condemnation, self-loathing, bitterness, anxiety, fear, misery, and selfishness. All these things spell passivity, a passive acceptance of life and a demoralized outlook on the things of God. The prophetic is geared to challenging this whole issue, as it is based in the truth of God's love, grace, kindness, and mercy.

Eyes Of The Spirit… Not The Flesh

Frustration can easily move us into "prophesying" what we see or understand in the natural. A lot of prophetic people make the mistake of looking for clues from people, trying to pick something up from how someone looks (*i.e.* happy or sad), body language, or other traits.

This is a very soulish act and produces "prophecy" on a soulish level. If we are going to move out in prophecy, God is the one person we have to be looking at and listening to. We must not try to pick up clues from people or circumstances. It never works and usually goes wrong. It leads us into the realm of the soul — the mind, will and emotions — where we can give Satan the opportunity to add to what is going on. What we get may sound spiritual but it is information, not revelation.

Even the greatest Biblical prophets had to learn this lesson. In 1 Samuel 16:6–13, we read of how Samuel had to reject all physical and cultural clues before he could anoint the next king of Israel:

> When they entered, he looked at Eliab and thought, "Surely the LORD's anointed is before Him." But the LORD said to Samuel, "Do not look at his appearance or at the height of his stature, because I have rejected him; for God sees not as man sees, for man looks at the outward appearance, but the LORD looks at the heart."

> Then Jesse called Abinadab and made him pass before Samuel. And he said, "The LORD has not chosen this one either." Next Jesse made Shammah pass by. And he said, "The LORD has not chosen this one either." Thus Jesse made seven of his sons pass before Samuel. But Samuel said to Jesse, "The LORD has not chosen these." And Samuel

said to Jesse, "Are these all the children?" And he said, "There remains yet the youngest, and behold, he is tending the sheep." Then Samuel said to Jesse, "Send and bring him; for we will not sit down until he comes here." So he sent and brought him in.

Now he was ruddy, with beautiful eyes and a handsome appearance. And the LORD said, "Arise, anoint him; for this is he." Then Samuel took the horn of oil and anointed him in the midst of his brothers; and the Spirit of the LORD came mightily upon David from that day forward. And Samuel arose and went to Ramah.

In a Middle Eastern culture like Israel, all family rights belonged to the oldest son. Obviously, Eliab was a strong, handsome young man with some level of authority, as Samuel immediately thought he was called to be king. But God wanted Samuel to look beyond the physical world and see into the hearts of these young men. God knew which brother had a heart like His, and which one would be able to stand the trials and tribulations to come.

Ignoring physical clues takes an incredible amount of spiritual discipline. At a meeting once, I gave an appeal for ministry that drew a large response. As I watched people come forward, I noticed an elderly man on crutches, a young, green-haired man with zippers and safety pins everywhere, and a stunningly attractive woman all come to the front.

> *To hear properly we must be intimate with God's heart.*

Eventually, after an hour of ministry, I found myself in front of the attractive woman whom I had noticed earlier. I asked her name and she replied in a very throaty voice. I stepped back into my spirit to hear the Lord and was stunned at His words: "Tell him I am not happy." We cannot mishear God in our spirit, but I could hardly believe this word. I asked the Lord what He meant, being conscious that my mind was sending out alarm signals of distress (which it usually does when I receive this kind of revelation).

"Son," the Lord spoke again, "his name is Richard, and I want you to tell him I know his name and that he must change."

I took a deep breath and looked at this person. There was no way to be sure; all the clues said she was female. I had to make a choice. I decided to live in my spirit. I brought a measure of peace to my mind, which was begging me not to do anything stupid. Fear and embarrassment harassed me in those few seconds, but I had to overcome them.

"Richard, God knows your real name and He is not happy with your lifestyle," I said. "You have to change."

Before I could add a word more, Richard let loose with a string of obscenities, hiked up his long skirt, and ran from the building — closely followed by several other females. No one knew who they were, and to my knowledge, they have not been seen since. Still, I periodically pray that God would complete His work in the life of a transvestite named Sylvia or Richard.

Relying on clues just isn't an option for those who want to prophesy maturely. In a U.S. meeting once, the Lord gave me a word for a man at the rear of the auditorium. He was dressed like a vagrant, an absolute down-and-out character.

God began to give me a word that this man would have hundreds of thousands of dollars to sow into the church, that through his work he was going to lead key businesspeople to the Lord, and that he would finance various projects in the community and the nation. I looked hard at him — he looked like he needed a handout. Adding to my dilemma was the fact that right behind him sat a man in a business suit, looking like a million dollars. The individual behind the vagrant looked like he was the executive of a multinational corporation.

I mulled it over in my spirit. My first instinct had been to give the word to what looked like the poorer man, but the clues screamed a different story. Had I mixed the two up? I couldn't get any peace about it, so I wandered away and gave a few words to others in the congregation. I came back to the vagrant and the businessman.

I'm going to have to go for it, I thought to myself. *Ignore the clues and trust the Spirit.* Sometimes, prophecy is just about being brave and launching out. I asked the vagrant to stand up and started prophesying to him. No one in the room seemed to know him, and I was convinced the whole crowd was thinking the same thing: "He's missed it. It's the guy behind him." The man wasn't giving me any help whatsoever; he stared at me, stony-faced. There wasn't a flicker of emotion or recognition to be had.

Some people don't give us any help, often because they don't know how to behave. They have never received a prophetic word before. They don't quite know what to do with themselves, and they are as embarrassed as we are. Sometimes people's faces are very mobile, and they give us a lot of help and encouragement, building our confidence. At other times, people are really trying to "psych out" the prophet. A word can be absolutely on target, but you would never know it by looking at the face of the recipient. I have even prophesied over people who have stared back at me with an insolent, "let's see how good you are" look on their faces. Prophets cannot trust people's faces for confirmation. Our own peace and rest in the Lord should be sufficient encouragement.

I prophesied over the vagrant and discovered later on that he was an extremely wealthy individual who liked dressing down. He had heard about the conference and decided to check it out. After I had given him the word, he sat down and I carried on with the meeting.

> *Your humility will de-stress you and…*

A few minutes later, I received a word for the man in the suit behind the vagrant. "The job you have just interviewed for is yours," I heard in my spirit. This added to my unsure feelings. On the surface, it seemed that the wealth word was for the suit, and the job word was for the vagrant.

As you can imagine, the enemy was stirring up as much confusion in me as possible. Everything on the inside of me was screaming, "You fool! You idiot! You've got it wrong!" I tried to look cool on the platform but I was full of anxiety in my soul.

I could do only one thing: humble myself before God. "Lord," I prayed silently, "I will face this situation honorably if I have missed it; I will repent and put things right with people. I will publicly apologize and make sure no one is damaged by any mistake I have made."

The enemy hates humility because he cannot penetrate it. Humility opens a door for God to touch our lives. As I quietly humbled myself on the platform, I experienced a peace and rest in the Lord. I gave the man in the suit his word, and watched with gladness as he and his family punched the air with delight. Later, I learned that he had been unemployed for two years and had been to his first job interview in months that afternoon. A week later, he was offered the job.

I was relieved and very grateful to the Lord. Prophetic ministry is never straightforward. It is ridiculously easy to make mistakes even after years of practice. People apply impossible standards to the prophetic office that they don't assign to any other ministry. I believe that if we relaxed the standards and allowed for more grace, we would actually have fewer prophetic mistakes and a lot more honesty and integrity in the gifting. Pressure is a great enemy of prophets; we are under immense pressure to perform and be super-spiritual. Christians sensationalize the gifting and create a hype and mystique around personalities that is, frankly, immoral and dangerous. We are called to be ourselves in the Lord, within our scope of function.

I do not have to be under pressure to be prophetic. I have to be myself in Jesus, and people can either cope with that or not. It is almost inevitable that we will thrill some people and disappoint others, depending on what is happening when we go to particular places.

Prophets must never move out in what they see naturally. We cannot lean on our own understanding. Instead, we have to draw out what God has already put in place. Sometimes, prophetic ministry stands with one foot in the past and the other in the future. We bring both of those extremes into the present to help people make sense of where they are right now.

... distress your opposition.

In 1 Samuel 1:12–18 we see how easy it is for a prophet to get something wrong.

> *Now it came about, as she continued praying before the Lord, that Eli was watching her mouth. As for Hannah, she was speaking in her heart, only her lips were moving, but her voice was not heard. So Eli thought she was drunk. Then Eli said to her, "How long will you make yourself drunk? Put away your wine from you." But Hannah replied, "No, my lord, I am a woman oppressed in spirit; I have drunk neither wine nor strong drink, but I have poured out my soul before the Lord. "Do not consider your maidservant as a worthless woman, for I have spoken until now out of my great concern and provocation."*
>
> *Then Eli answered and said, "Go in peace; and may the God of Israel grant your petition that you have asked of Him." She said, "Let your maidservant find favor in your sight." So the woman went her way and ate, and her face was no longer sad.*

Eli was not practicing his sensitivity to God, he was looking for clues. Hannah was sad and desperate. Her heart was broken. She was probably swaying in her grief and moaning in spirit. I know how that feels!

She was also passionately interceding before God along the lines of her vow. Eli heard none of that. He looked in the natural and then made a judgment on what he thought was her behavior. He thought she was drunk! It is so vital, beloved that we take our thoughts to a place of captivity in Christ-likeness.

> *We are destroying speculations and every lofty thing raised up against the knowledge of God, and we are taking every thought captive to the obedience of Christ, and we are ready to punish all disobedience, whenever your obedience is complete. You are looking at things as they*

are outwardly. If anyone is confident in himself that he is Christ's, let him consider this again within himself, that just as he is Christ's, so also are we. (2 Corinthians 10:5–7)

We prophesy out of our own vision, understanding and testimony of God. What we think about Him is the most important thing in the world (Revelation 19:10).

Response To Prophecy

Ignoring physical clues is not an excuse to throw out any concern for the person for whom we are prophesying. We must be sensitive and carefully consider the person receiving ministry. When we prophesy over people, we must learn to put margins into the word. Do not be anxious to gush out everything you have received; it is easier to add than to retract. We must not be so eager to prophesy that we fail to consider the needs of the recipient.

If we prophesy over an individual for even a few brief moments, we may speak several hundred words. What is this person doing while we are speaking? He or she is probably standing there in memory mode, frantically trying to remember every single sentence and phrase. Their memory will be selective — it will choose to remember the words that have an immediate application to his or her current circumstances. Only a small percentage will be retained; the rest will be deleted or distorted. The main part of the word could be about the future, but that may be lost. Later on, the individual may panic trying to remember. The enemy can even try and convince them that the forgotten pieces were the most important part of the prophecy. A sense of disappointment may settle on the receiver.

Even worse, a person may remember the bulk of the words but retain little or nothing of the spirit behind them. Prophecy communicates spirit-to-spirit as well as speaking to our minds. There is a spirit to prophecy that sets it above all other communications. Prophecy I received decades ago still has a spiritual impact on me. The spirit is eternal, and we can still hear the spirit language of the Lord down through the years. We can read the written transcript of a prophecy a thousand times, but if the Holy Spirit touched our spirits at the point of delivery, our hearts will retain the freshness and power of the original word as if it was just given.

All prophets need to act like a shepherd

If we are going to prophesy into people's lives, we need to be responsible. We need to either bring a tape recorder or notebook to capture the detail of the word and allow people to fully engage with it. A relaxed recipient is more likely to receive communication spirit-to-spirit, which is the goal of all prophecy. The individual can have the words recorded for later, but it's the actual spirit of what God is saying that will live with him or her and change their life.

This is one reason why I don't endorse "private" prophecy. While I do believe in "personal" prophecy — that is, a word individuals receive that is directly for their lives and circumstances — private prophecy is a distasteful practice. My American friends call it "parking lot prophecy," and it occurs outside the constraint of meetings or accountability. It lacks integrity and submission to leadership.

We must earn the right to minister into people's lives. If we are living in a godly fashion and are seeking to behave responsibly, we have nothing to fear from accountability. People must be protected, which is the role of a shepherd. It's important that people hear, understand, and can respond to what God wants them to do and say.

Recording Prophecy

Recording prophecy is an important discipline to get into. A large percentage of Scripture is recorded prophecy, written down as it was delivered. The priesthood had secretaries, the army had recorders who faithfully wrote accounts of orders and battles, and kings and prophets had scribes working with them as normal practice. The New Testament continued that tradition, as evidenced by the entire book of Revelation, and the many prophetic insights recorded in the gospels, Acts, and epistles.

Isaiah was told on several occasions to write things on a tablet and a scroll. For example:

> "Moreover the LORD said to me, 'Take a large scroll, and write on it with a man's pen concerning Maher-Shalal-Hash-Baz'." (Isaiah 8:1)

> "Now go, write it before them on a tablet, and note it on a scroll, that it may be for time to come, forever and ever." (Isaiah 30:8)

Jeremiah had an assistant named Baruch help him record all of his prophetic words to Israel and Judah (Jeremiah 36). These records played an important role decades later as the prophet Daniel meditated on them.

Scribes are everywhere in Scripture. Ezra was a gifted scribe, so recognized by the secular king Artaxerxes (Ezra 7) and by the godly leader Nehemiah (Nehemiah 8): "Ezra the priest, the scribe, expert in the words *of the commandments of the* LORD, *and of His statutes to Israel"* (Ezra 7:11). 1 Chronicles 27:32 notes that King David's scribe was his uncle Jehonathan, *"a counselor, a wise man, and a scribe."* In Exodus 34, God told Moses to write down the *"tenor"* of the covenant between Him and His people.

I carry a portable tape recorder and a supply of tapes wherever I go. I also have written thousands of pages in my journals. If a recording is not practical when I am praying for someone, I will insist that a third person be present to record the word and act as a witness. This not only increases accountability, but it allows the receiver to relax and engage God's Spirit in the word.

If you are not presently journaling the insights you are receiving from God, I strongly encourage you to begin to do so. This self-discipline shows that you are serious in taking care of God's words. It places a high value on them, communicating to the Spirit that you are listening carefully. It also enables you to further develop the revelation, as God can and will illuminate new pieces of it.

Journals do not have to be an elaborate or expensive exercise. Any type of book, format, and process is workable, as long as you commit to keeping it up. Some scribble, others type their thoughts. Some draw, others write poems. The form is unimportant: it is the content that matters. When God speaks to you about something, write it down. When He shows you a picture or highlights a Scripture, record it.

Weeks, months, and even years later, you will be encouraged to see how far God has taken you in the spirit, and how many things He has shared with you have come to pass.

Conclusion

We are all on a journey into the heart of God, and it is a trip that should be enjoyed. We should love the way God speaks to us, and love the way He speaks to others. There is nothing like giving a gracious word that opens another human being to suddenly seeing God for themselves in a new, or improved, way. Having a burden for people is about sharing God's burden for them.

Some days, we will have words of incredible power and rich significance, and we'll think: this is what it's like to really prophesy. On other days, we'll wonder if we can even spell the word prophecy! Some days, we'll get bizarre and outrageous things that we will have absolute faith for. Other days, we'll get similarly "out-there" things that we just won't have the faith to buy into. Our confidence will have wavered.

The Exercise Of Prophecy

The gift of prophecy doesn't change, but our level of faith does. Some days, our faith is present in huge proportions, and other days, it is the size of a mustard seed.

I was once on an airplane with an individual who was absolutely disparaging Christianity. He essentially told me that it was stupid to be a Christian. He spoke so loudly to me that the entire plane could hear him. My flesh just wanted to slap him, but I tried to retreat into my spirit instead.

"God," I prayed, "give me something to shut him up." The man blathered on: religion is a crutch, there is no God, there is no supernatural. "Give me something, Lord," I prayed. "Show me something."

All the Lord showed me was a picture of a small dog with three legs. It was a Jack Russell terrier, white, except for a black ear. Its name was simply Jack.

"Oh no," I groaned in my spirit. "Give me something better than that."

As he railed on about Christianity, I prayed for him. Finally he stopped and I attempted to strike up a more normal conversation. Eventually I steered the conversation around to his life… job, family and finally pets.

"What's your favorite animal?" I asked. "Horses, cats, dogs?"

"Oh I like dogs very much" he said.

"Do you like big dogs or small dogs?" I asked.

"I hate big dogs, but I like small dogs."

"Like a Jack Russell?" I inquired.

"Yeah," he said.

> *Prophecy is an adventure and all adventures have risk*

With each question, I was building my faith in the word God had given me. He likes small dogs, he likes Jack Russell terriers — I decided to just launch the word and go for broke.

"When you were six-years-old, you had a Jack Russell terrier named Jack," I said. "It was totally white, except for one ear that was completely black. When you were six, the dog was involved in a traffic accident and it had its left, hind leg torn off. When you got the dog to the veterinarian, you prayed in that waiting room. You said, 'Dear God, if You save Jack, I will serve You.'"

We looked at each other as tears streamed down his face.

"James, please don't tell me God doesn't exist," I said. "The same God who saved your dog has been looking out for you, and maybe right now is your chance to meet up with who He is."

On days where our faith isn't present, we need to ask questions. Every question we ask builds up a little more faith until we can go for it all. The Holy Spirit loves questions; we just have to be creative asking them. On the days when our faith is diminished we can still dialogue with Him. The Holy

Spirit isn't bothered by a little faith because He knows that just a mustard seed is enough to move mountains. A joy comes when we start small in faith and grow into fullness. I had little faith when I received that picture of Jack, but it grew as I asked a few questions.

If God allows life to be tough on us on certain days, it's for a reason. He wants to develop our gift and teach us how to be confident in Him.

Notes

Notes

Notes

The Exercise of Prophecy

Reflections, Exercises, and Assignments

The following exercises are designed with this particular chapter in mind. Please work through them carefully before going on to the next chapter. Take time to reflect on your life journey as well as your prophetic development. Learn to work well with the Holy Spirit and people that God has put around you so that you will grow in grace, humility, and wisdom in the ways of God.

Graham Cook.

What Constitutes Maturity?

Prophetic maturity is concerned with displaying sound wisdom and knowledge alongside good practice and accountable, teachable behavior. It is connected to the development of Christlike characteristics and demonstrating the values and temperament of the Holy Spirit. Within the context of this chapter you must be willing and able to develop these attributes as a sign of your growing maturity:

- Demonstrate that you understand the life and nature of God for you, and your willingness to behave as Christ would in your current circumstances. It is clearly evident that you are cultivating a greater perception of God's essential goodness in your own life?

- Pursuing love as a primary source and response in your life. Are you known as someone who models love as a prime value? Actively demonstrating high levels of grace and kindness? Is your personal humility very much to the fore particularly in difficult situations?

- Regarding your temperament and personality, are you able to exercise the fruit of self-control? Can you prophesy for the common good of the church? A mature person is able to move beyond their own frustration to deliver a clear word from the Lord that edifies the church and produces momentum in difficult circumstances.

- We operate prophetically in a war zone. We live on the battlefield between two kingdoms of light and dark. We will have tribulation and opposition. It is essential that you can demonstrate how to move in the opposite spirit to what comes against you whether on a spiritual or human level. Do you have a strategy for difficult people? Maturity is treating your grace growers well. It is knowing how to bounce back under attack and demonstrating that everything in life is useful for our growth and development.

- To earn the right to prophesy you must cultivate a good methodology in using the gift. Maturity in prophecy is the ability to deliver a burden and achieve God's objective even when under pressure in your own life. It is in your capacity to inspire people to move from problem to solution with your encouragement.

- Real maturity lies in answering with your lifestyle and gifting the following question: Can you be trusted? Accountability is always best when provoked from below rather than needing to be imposed from above. Mature people seek out the next level of accountability that is required for the anointing that they desire to move in.

What Constitutes Immaturity?

Immaturity develops through a constant failure to learn the lessons of life and spirituality. Bluntly, we are tested on everything we are taught. Grace comforts us when we fail the test; truth prepares our hearts to take it again. When carnality does not decrease, wisdom does not grow and we are challenged again to put on Christ.

If we are dishonest about what we are learning we will only react to events and people rather than respond to the Living God. It is one thing to trust the Lord, it is quite another to be trusted by Him! Within the context of this chapter you must face up to the challenges of ongoing immaturity. Here are the possibilities for your consideration:

- Examine your own heart for signs of unforgiveness, holding grudges and feelings of bitterness and resentment towards others. How much do you blame others for your own shortcomings? Do you withhold love, acceptance or approval when you don't get your own way?

- When we are present/past in our own relationships we often manifest rejection. This may lead to us being a loner, who has difficulty in building relationships. Our prophesying can be clouded by our personality. How much does your own past influence your present/future relationships?

- A past that has not responded to grace may lead us into a place of being harsh, negative and judgmental. If our lifestyle is not synchronized with the message of grace, love and forgiveness then our prophesying will not reflect the nature of God. Our sense of frustration will challenge the message to be negative rather than channel us to be positive. Do you habitually see the negative before the positive? Have you developed the anointing to see the second image God is releasing? Is your outlook, temperament and prophetic output more centered in the Old Covenant rather than the New?

- How well are you doing at working through your current issues? Are you defensive when faced up with personal truth? Can you be questioned about your lifestyle? To whom are you accountable and do they have the experience and maturity to challenge who you are/are not in the Spirit? The most common form of immaturity is evasive behavior; an unteachable spirit; an independent mindset; and spending all your time with people that you can control or easily dupe.

- Prophesying the problem without a solution is immature and dangerous. Without a sure sense of objective we cannot give words that release and empower others to improve and go further. When we have not taken issue with our own life we display a hypocrisy towards others that is rooted in lack of grace. When we are not edifying we may be pulling someone down. How well do you inspire, encourage, edify, comfort and empower people with your gift?

- What tests have you passed recently and how has that victory been thoroughly established? What tests have you failed and what impact is that defeat having on your relationship with the Lord; your faith and your prophesying?

AN ASSIGNMENT

Think of a person around your life at this time, particularly one that you do not know very well.

Read and meditate on Psalm 37:3–5 on their behalf. Ask the Lord to touch your heart with His compassion and intentionality for that person.

Without just quoting the scripture:

1.   How would you encourage this person to trust the Lord and stay in a place of faith?

2.   How does the Lord want them to delight in Him?

3.   Is there a specific desire that God wants to fulfill?

4.   What can you say that would cause them to re-commit their heart and trust to God at this time?

5.   Using the scriptures and questions as a guideline, write a card to this person providing specific encouragement into their current life experience of the Father.

GRACE GROWERS

We all have difficult people in our lives whom the Lord uses to develop our character, personality, ministry and lifestyle.

1. Identify the people with whom you currently are finding it difficult to love and build a relationship. Make a list.

2. What is it about these people that you find the most difficult? How do they affect you?

3. What is their perception of you? Is it accurate (even partially)? If so, how?

4. What particular fruit of the Holy Spirit do you need to develop to be with them and to love them effectively?

5. What is God teaching you and changing in you?

6. **NB.** Do the above steps 1–5 for each person on your life.

7. How can you make the first move towards these people?

CASE STUDY:
MATCHING PROPHETIC DELIVERY WITH CONTENT

The delivery of a prophetic word must match its content. One cannot grab someone by the throat and prophesy love and peace; likewise, a prophecy about warrior strength cannot be properly prophesied in an airy whisper. The context must match the content.

Below are a few prophetic words I have given to individuals enrolled in my prophetic schools (I have changed the names for privacy reasons). In this exercise, read the prophetic word and answer the questions following it.

Prophetic Word

Donna, what I see in the Spirit is you standing under a waterfall. The water is cascading onto your head — the whole waterfall is about the peace and the rest of God. The Lord says He is going to drive out of your brain the capacity to worry, to be anxious, to be fearful, to feel inadequate, to feel insecure, all those things. There is a peace and a rest of God coming to you that is so remarkable, it will change your very personality. In these days, there is a peace so strong, so profound, and so powerful that nothing will be able to make you anxious again. There is a laughter rising up, because the Lord says, "Sweetie, you've cried enough." The Lord says that you were always meant to go through life with a grin. And now He's going to come to you to teach you how to live everyday under His smile. You're going to learn what it is to be precious to God because that's how He sees you. You don't feel precious a lot of the time, but He says to you, "I think you're precious, and because I'm God, what I think matters more than what you think."

The Lord says, "Life is still going to be life for you. There are still going to be difficulties and ups and downs for you — the difference is going to be on the inside of you." You're not going to be up and down, up and down, up and down; the Lord is going to give you a straight, even road to walk on. It's called peace. The Lord says that it's in His heart for you to become one of the most peaceful people of your generation. This rest and peace will bring you to a place of favour with God where you're going to get revenge on the enemy for everything he's ever done to you. Your peace is going to reach out and heal people because a prophetic anointing is going to grow in your heart with a confidence

Reflections, Exercises, and Assignments

and a certainty. Around you will be a peace, and within you will come a peace. Pressure will come from the outside, but the Lord says that peace will be an equalizing pressure on the inside. He is going to drive out of your head the capacity to worry, to be anxious, to be afraid.

You're standing under a waterfall of peace. So everything inside you is heading into a place of peace, serenity, tranquility, and calm. This is your journey in these days, and the Lord says, "From this moment, every situation you encounter will have peace with it." He will teach you how to access that peace — and when you do that on a regular basis, confidence is going to come, faith is going to come, and then the prophetic is going to rise up inside of you.

Answer the following questions:

1.   What is the crux (focus) of this word?

2.   What is the emotion and plan God has for Donna?

3.   What would be the best way to deliver this word? What tone of voice would be best to use? What body language and position should be used?

4.   After delivering the word, what would you pray over her?

When peace is the objective, we have to embody it. In my ministry, I love prophesying peace, because I end up feeling just as peaceful as the thing I'm seeing. I can't let something like peace flow out of me without it actually coming in and touching me. It's like a prophetic aftertaste; there's always a bit that flows back into the prophet's own life. When we prophesy in peace, we have to say it in such a way that everything — the way we speak, the way we stand, the way we look — has to flow towards that objective.

The Exercise Of Prophecy

LECTIO DIVINA

Lectio Divina (Latin for *divine reading*) is an ancient way of reading the Bible — allowing a quiet and contemplative way of coming to God's Word. *Lectio Divina* opens the pulse of the Scripture, helping readers dig far deeper into the Word than normally happens in a quick glance-over.

In this exercise, we will look at a portion of Scripture and use a modified *Lectio Divina* technique to engage it. This technique can be used on any piece of Scripture; I highly recommend using it for key Bible passages that the Lord has highlighted for you, and for anything you think might be an inheritance word for your life (see the *Crafted Prayer interactive journal* for more on inheritance words).

Read the Scripture:

If I speak with the tongues of men and of angels, but do not have love, I have become a noisy gong or a clanging cymbal. If I have the gift of prophecy, and know all mysteries and all knowledge; and if I have all faith, so as to remove mountains, but do not have love, I am nothing. And if I give all my possessions to feed the poor, and if I surrender my body to be burned, but do not have love, it profits me nothing.

Love is patient, love is kind and is not jealous; love does not brag and is not arrogant, does not act unbecomingly; it does not seek its own, is not provoked, does not take into account a wrong suffered, does not rejoice in unrighteousness, but rejoices with the truth; bears all things, believes all things, hopes all things, endures all things.

Love never fails; but if there are gifts of prophecy, they will be done away; if there are tongues, they will cease; if there is knowledge, it will be done away. For we know in part and we prophesy in part; but when the perfect comes, the partial will be done away.

When I was a child, I used to speak like a child, think like a child, reason like a child; when I became a man, I did away with childish things. For now we see in a mirror dimly, but then face to face; now I know in part, but then I will know fully just as I also have been fully known.

*But now faith, hope, love, abide these three; but the greatest of these
is love. (1 Corinthians 13)*

1.   Find a place of stillness before God. Embrace His peace. Chase the
unhelpful thoughts out of your mind. Calm your body. Breathe slowly. Inhale.
Exhale. Inhale. Exhale. Clear yourself of the distractions of life. Whisper
the word, "Stillness." Take your time. When you find that rest in the Lord,
enjoy it. Worship Him in it. Be with Him there.

2.   Re-read the passage twice. Allow its words to become familiar to
you. Investigate Paul's definition of love. What images does it bring to your
spirit? What do you see? Become a part of it. What phrases or words especially resonate with you? Meditate especially on those shreds of revelation.
Write those pieces down in your journal.

3.   Read the passage twice again. Like waves crashing onto a shore,
let the words of Scripture crash onto your spirit. What excites you? What
scares you? What exhilarates you about this revelation of the love of God?
What are you discerning? What are you feeling? What are you hearing?
Again, write it all down in your journal.

4.   Write the theme of this passage in your journal.

5.　Does this passage rekindle any memories or experiences? Does it remind you of any prophetic words you have given or received? Write those down as well.

6.　What is the Holy Spirit saying to you through this Scripture? Investigate it with Him — picture the two of you walking through it together. Write those words in your journal.

7.　Read the passage two final times. Meditate on it. Is there something God wants you to do? Is there something He is calling you to? Write it down.

8.　Pray silently. Tell God what this passage is saying to you. Tell Him what you are thinking about. Write down your conversation together. Picture yourself and the Holy Spirit as two old friends in a coffee shop, chatting about what God is doing.

9.　Finally, pray and thank God for His relationship with you. Come back to the passage once a week for the next three months. Read it and let more revelation flow into you. If you feel compelled to, craft a prayer based on this passage for yourself, your family, your friends, or your church. Pray that prayer until you feel God has birthed it in you.

Notes

Notes

Notes

Notes

MODULE TWO

THE PROCESS OF PROPHECY

The Process of Prophecy

WHAT YOU WILL LEARN IN THIS SEGMENT:

- How to come to God so that our prophesying is clean and pure.
- The power of meditation to reveal Presence.
- All joy belongs to the Father. It's who He is and therefore who we are too!
- The importance of stillness in waiting on God.
- Being renewed in the spirit of your mind.
- The spiritual life is powerfully possible when your soul comes under the rule of your spirit.
- Hearing and praying given huge impetus to knowing God's will.
- Process is the key to life in the Spirit. It is the process that makes us rich not the outcome.
- Pursuing love as a prerequisite for moving in prophecy.
- Prophecy restores people's dignity and self respect.
- Sensitivity to the Lord is the basis for all prophecy.
- The simple steps of moving in prophecy.
- Prophecy is released when we acknowledge a burden for an individual or a group of people.
- Living form your heart not your head.
- How to receive revelation not just information.
- The power of enlightenment in seeing from the heart.
- All knowledge leads to an actual experience of truth.
- Your perception is linked to your destiny.

The Process of Prophecy

WHAT YOU WILL LEARN IN THIS SEGMENT:

- Your will is the vehicle for the spirit.
- Praying with God not towards Him.
- Developing joyful routines that touch God's heart.
- The relationship between prayer, power and process.
- Pray like a bridge not a widow. Begging is not favor!
- To receive closure on the past and develop a present/future relationship with the Lord.
- There is always a new "you" emerging!
- The three phases of revelation.
- The simple power of expectation.
- Operating in the flow and the ebb of life in the Spirit.
- How vision and dreams work and their purpose.
- Moving in what you see.
- Developing the relationship between prophecy and scripture.
- Hearing the whispers of God.
- Becoming attuned to the faint touches of God.
- Impression engages the heart of the person prophesying with the Holy Spirit.
- Everything comes from God and returns to God.
- Developing quietness is a key to being prophetic continuously.
- Developing the rhythm of your own fellowship with the Lord.
- Starting where you are and giving what you have.

The Process Of Prophecy

I F PROPHECY, LIKE A WEB site, had a list of 'Frequently Asked Questions,' this one would top it: "When I'm moving in prophecy, how can I tell if it's me, the Lord, or the enemy?" I've been asked that question many hundreds, of times over my thirty years in prophetic ministry.

It is a legitimate question. We are human beings, subject to pain, disillusionment, hurts, dreams, aspirations, longings, and desires. We sort, delete, distort, and repackage the mound of information we receive every day. Our humanity can conspire against us and color a prophetic word with a different hue than God intended. We can give into the power of "me."

We can also come under the influence of the enemy, either directly through bitter, unresolved issues in our lives, or indirectly through bad attitudes and a lack of good relationships. It is possible for a frustrated person to speak prophetically their own thoughts and opinions, mixing them with the words that God is really saying. The enemy can inspire that to happen and people could be moved by a spirit other than the Lord's, but this usually happens only when people have buried their hurts and rejection in real anger. Their lives become fertile ground for enemy activity. Alternatively, the enemy can use our unyielded thoughts and impulses, and as we speak out of our own soul, he can move in behind our words to cause mischief.

With these issues in mind, it is no wonder so many Christians fear polluting a prophetic word. How do we give a pure word of prophecy that glorifies the Lord, has no tinge from our hearts, and has no influence of the enemy attached? Further complicating this question is the issue of faith. Sometimes we may not be operating in complete certainty and we have to prophesy as far as our faith allows.

One thing can guarantee the purity of our prophecy — a large dose of humility. A humble spirit ensures that we will not seek to do anything to dishonor the Lord Jesus, discredit the ministry, or disrupt the body of Christ.

In this life, we either humble ourselves or we get humiliated. We either fall on the rock or it falls on us. Humility is not a natural characteristic in any of us. No one is born with it. Our relationship with God builds as we submit our lives, thoughts, and perspectives to Him. Our aim is to always live our lives in the best way possible, so that the Holy Spirit is made welcome in us. *"Create in me a clean heart, O God, and renew a steadfast spirit within me,"* as David sang in Psalm 51:10–11. *"Do not cast me away from Your presence, and do not take Your Holy Spirit from me."*

If we prophesy in humility and make a mistake, the Lord will give us grace to face the issue and put things right. Mistakes are inevitable as we learn how to move in the supernatural. That is why Paul was so clear in 1 Thessalonians 5:19–21 — *"Do not quench the Spirit. Do not despise prophecies. Test all things; hold fast what is good."* We need to be able to sift and separate the good from the bad, the misguided, and the misinterpreted.

With the help of the Holy Spirit, we must ensure that we live our lives in the best way possible. There must be no part of us that does not belong to Jesus. Our lifestyle must be full of rejoicing, meditation, prayer, healing, waiting on God, love, and expectation.

Rejoicing Always

Rejoicing is a key ingredient in moving in the power and presence of God. Many Christians have been conditioned to think that they enter God's presence with prayer. But Scripture is clear that thankfulness is the door to His presence — *"Enter into His gates with thanksgiving, and into His courts with praise. Be thankful to Him, and bless His name,"* says Psalm 100:4.

It is not a coincidence that rejoicing precedes prayer without ceasing. Our stillness is dependent on our gratitude. Whatever happens, we must thank God for the set of circumstances we are in. I'm not saying that we must thank God for something horrible that has happened: Christians are not called to be masochists. However, we can thank God that He is always with us.

> An always rejoicing heart is the key to listening to God

Rejoicing in God gives us the opportunity to hear Him. When we enter His presence with thanksgiving, we open more of ourselves to His voice. *"In everything give thanks; for this is the will of God in Christ Jesus for you,"* Paul

AIMEE SEMPLE McPHERSON

Lived: 1891 to 1944

Prophetic Synopsis: Born in rural Canada, Aimee accepted Christ at age seventeen in a revival meeting led by Robert Semple. Months later, she married Semple and traveled with him to China to spread the Gospel there. Upon their arrival in Hong Kong, however, both contracted malaria. Aimee was a few months pregnant when Robert died.

Alone, terrified, sick, pregnant, and just nineteen, Aimee called out to God. "Morning after morning of the month that followed, I would wake up with a scream as my great loss swept over me," she said. "Then the Comforter would instantly spring up within me until I was filled with joy unspeakable, and my hot, dry eyes would flow with tears of love and blessing." Aimee eventually gave birth to a little girl, worked hard, and made enough money for the two to return to America.

After remarrying, God called Aimee to preach. For months, she wrestled with that call. She had another child, and eventually had a nervous breakdown.

As she laid in her bed, not sure if she was going to live or die, Jesus appeared to her and said, "Go preach My Word." Aimee made excuses as to why she couldn't, but Jesus was adamant: "Do the work of an evangelist. The time is short, I am coming soon." The moment she accepted the call, God healed her.

Eventually, Aimee moved to Los Angeles and planted a church. She arrived in 1921 with just a tambourine and ten dollars, and opened a 5,300 seat church — debt-free — a year later. The walls of her church were lined with the crutches, wheelchairs and canes of the people God healed. Her illustrated sermons were copied by Hollywood: she rode in on a motorcycle once, and hired dozens of animals on another occasion. During the Great Depression, she set up a food bank and free store, helping 1.5 million people.

Key Comment: "All I could do was say one word when I prayed: Jesus!"

Sources: Stanley Burgess and Gary McGee, editors. *Dictionary of Pentecostal and Charismatic Movements*. (Grand Rapids, MI: Zondervan (9th printing), 1996). Roberts Liardon, *God's Generals*. Tulsa, OK: Albury Publishing, 1996).

wrote in 1 Thessalonians 5:18. When we want to know God's will for a situation, we begin by giving thanks.

Probably two-thirds of the rest of the world would change places with us in the west in a heartbeat, no matter how poor our lifestyle. To many, we are rich beyond their wildest dreams. Count your blessings; there are so many things to give thanks for. If we struggle with being grateful to God for what He has given us, chances are we will be ungracious to people in how we live our lives. It is disciplines like gratitude, thanksgiving, praise, and worship that keep the presence of God fresh and alive in our hearts.

This is a fundamental spiritual truth that can re-shape and re-ignite our personal time with God. By entering His presence with praise, not petitions, we learn how to adore God. Our hearts become full of constant, continuous worship. We are people called to be happy in God; if we don't have joy in our relationship with Him, how can we expect anyone else to?

As a Christian, who would you rather be represented by: the most miserable individual on earth, or the happiest person in the world? This is the very choice God faces! Nobody wants to be represented by someone who is glum and miserable. Adoration helps us remain happy in God.

Meditation: Loving God With Your Mind

I love having quiet times with God. There is nothing like experiencing God's love, touch, and blessing in stillness with Him. His job is to be our Lover; ours is to be His beloved. I love letting God touch me. He draws me into Him, erasing all of the striving, pressure, frustration, and frantic pace of life.

Meditation is about finding our rhythm with God. When we couldn't have cared less about Him, God couldn't have cared more. Before we knew Him, He took the initiative and reached out to us. *"We love Him because He first loved us,"* says 1 John 4:19. We responded to what He did, and He answered our response. Like a dance, we went back and forth — and we still do. God moves, we move. The Father works, we work. The Holy Spirit engages, we engage. Everything we do flows out of our relationship with God. Meditation provides us with the inward anointing to reveal the Presence of God.

All of life in the Spirit flows from the inside/out. Coming from the inner man of the Spirit, through the soul as a vehicle of expression which uses our body to demonstrate to the outside world who we really are in the Spirit.

Meditation is a fabulous spiritual discipline that enables us to see in the Spirit. It is the eyes of our heart being enlightened so that we can know (i.e., understand and experience) who God is for us. (Ephesians 1:18).

Prayer is the process of finding out what God wants to do and then asking Him to do it. Meditation is an important precursor to that effort. Before we pray, we ought to meditate, read, think, listen, and be still. Reading the Bible does reveal the will of God to us because confidence and prayer go together. By meditating on the Word of God, the way I pray is shaped.

Several months ago, our church leadership team read Romans 8:35–39 together:

Who shall separate us from the love of Christ? Will tribulation, or distress, or persecution, or famine, or nakedness, or peril, or sword? Just as it is written:

"For Your sake we are being put to death all day long; We were considered as sheep to be slaughtered."

> Spirit life flows from the inside out.

But in all these things we overwhelmingly conquer through Him who loved us. For I am convinced that neither death, nor life, nor angels, nor principalities, nor things present, nor things to come, nor powers, nor height, nor depth, nor any other created thing, will be able to separate us from the love of God, which is in Christ Jesus our Lord.

The difficulty is that our emotions can become more time for us than the gospel if we let them.

Emotions can be as strong and as hard to arrest as a runaway horse. We can place more power and emphasis on them than the revealed word of God in scripture.

"I feel really disconnected from God", we say. However we fail to see that against what the Lord says in scripture. "I will never leave you nor forsake you". "I am with you always". "Nothing can separate you from My love!"

Reading a passage like the above can infuse Christians with confidence. What a great thing to pray! Nothing can separate us from the love of God: by meditating on it, this truth embeds itself deep within our spirits. Our minds become renewed through the power of God's love. We give our inner being the opportunity to access the Holy Spirit and be changed.

In Psalm 46:10, God gave us an important instruction: *"Be still, and know that I am God."* Stillness releases a capacity in us to receive truth at a

Meditation: Loving God With Your Mind

deeper level. *"Now may the God of peace Himself sanctify you completely; and may your whole spirit, soul, and body be preserved blameless at the coming of our Lord Jesus Christ,"* Paul wrote in 1 Thessalonians 5:23–24. *"He who calls you is faithful, who also will do it."* Learning how to cooperate with the Holy Spirit in the midst of problems and difficulties is vital. Without that help, we miss the wealth of our spiritual journey.

It is perfectly possible to bring ourselves to a place of peace. It is a simple discipline. Having practiced this for thirty years, I can now bring myself to peace in any situation within ten seconds. I have learned how to retreat back into my spirit and find the peace of stillness that meditation births in me. It has become simple for me, like using a computer or driving a car. Without stillness, our experience of God is limited. Stillness is a precursor to rest in the Lord, drawing us into a continual experience of His presence.

Put simply, we have to hear God's silence before we can listen to His voice. A silence exists in God that is so knowing, so healing, so releasing, and so embracing, that all kinds of things can be communicated to your heart. The silence is almost deafening: *"Deep calls unto deep at the noise of Your waterfalls; all Your waves and billows have gone over me,"* as the psalmist sang (Psalm 42:7). That capacity to enter stillness can release an unbroken communion with God and bring us into a place of being God-conscious.

The Lord does not cause the difficulties in our lives but He does know how to take advantage of opportunities!

God uses problems and issues to teach us how to be still. God uses every issue in several different ways because He is constantly at work in our lives. All too often we pray, "Lord, set me free from this," when He wants to work on five or six attitudes, conditions, and character issues in our life. "I'll set you free eventually," God says, "but I'd like to cover half-a-dozen of these things first. If you cooperate with Me, the benefits of this problem are going to be significant."

In the Spirit, every problem comes complete with its own provision attached. God is so kind that He will not let you experience an issue without His provision coming with it. Every problem is designed to bring us into something new in our experience of God. He allows in His wisdom what He could easily prevent by His power.

Meditation helps us discover that provision, by reminding ourselves of how reliant we are on God. In recent times, meditation has become a dirty word in some Christian circles because of its connection to the New Age and eastern religions. However, meditation has been a part of humanity's relationship with God for thousands of years. The Psalms, for example, are a series of meditations, and are full of humans expressing their need to meditate.

When we consider deeply the things of God, we are meditating. When we reflect on His work in our lives, we have begun to meditate. It doesn't hurt to sit down and think about Jesus and meditate on the type of person He is. For me, I am constantly drawn back to how kind God has been to me. He is the kindest, happiest, and sunniest person I have ever met. I believe that when we get in contact with Heaven, we will hear laughter. When we really come into the presence of God, tremendous joy, well-being, and peace flood our lives.

Joy is who God is; where He lives from; and what He does. He lives in perpetual, everlasting and eternal joy. In His Presence there is fullness of joy. The Father does not give us joy. He gives us Himself. He is absolute joy personified. The atmosphere surrounding God is always joyful. We need to anchor our souls in the person of God and embrace His uninhibited delight in all things.

> *Every problem comes with it's own provision attached.*

When we rejoice it is because we have entered the place of His joy and delight. We center ourselves in His joy. We breathe it in. We smile because we live under His smile. We rejoice because He is delight and delightful.

Whenever we encounter the Kingdom we are lovingly confronted with the God who loves to celebrate! We come under the influence of His innate joyfulness. When life is tough then we have permission to count it all joy! (James 1:2,3).

Joy is meant to overwhelm every negative emotion. "Sorrow and sighing may last for a night but joy comes in the morning". (Psalm 30:5]. When joy is present no negative emotion can flourish. Jesus was acquainted with grief (Isaiah 53:3) it was not a close traveling companion. We need to be restored to the joy of our salvation… the delight and pleasure of our first major contact with the Lord. Joy keeps all experience in God… fresh. New every morning is God's goodness and compassion (Lamentations 3:21–23). Life in the Spirit is daily renewable and joy is always a part of God's day for us. It is His plan for us to be joyful on a constant basis. "These things I have spoken to you, that your joy may be full"! [John 15:11).

Several years ago, at a church weekend, I became aware of a man who had been going through an awful, miserable time. In a meeting, I felt compelled to lay my hands on him and pray for him to be refilled with the Holy Spirit. He fell on the floor and laughed for about half an hour. He really laughed; we couldn't do anything. The meeting went haywire, as God's joy

Meditation: Loving God With Your Mind

took hold of him and the rest of the room, and we laughed and laughed and laughed. Through his joy, God began to fill the rest of us.

In recent years, I have seen some disturbing counterfeits of this, with some people charging big fees to bring the joy of the Lord into churches. I believe strongly that the joy of the Lord cannot be called up like some genie out of a bottle. It is not a spiritual manifestation that comes at the request of man. It is the by-product of the indwelling presence of God as He sovereignly and graciously causes rivers of living water to rise up within our hearts. The joy of the Lord comes from within.

> The Father surrounds Himself with joy.

Meditation can be a long process. Sometimes, I have spent several weeks on one particular passage of Scripture. When God is speaking to me clearly about something, there is not much point in reading something else. This is the underlying principle behind the *Lectio Divina* exercises we have included in this manual: we have to become disciplined in exploring the truth God is entrusting us with.

It is amazing how God uses meditation to share His heart with us. Years ago, the Lord spoke to me about working in the Caribbean. My flesh was fully saying "Yes and Amen" to that idea! Following that revelation, I enjoyed a private, ongoing joke with God about my "island ministry in the sun." Even as I spent years in the rain and the draughty cold of backstreet British churches, I chuckled with God: "One of these days, Lord, You will give me my desert island ministry." For several months, God spoke to me about the Caribbean. Other people would give me prophetic words about it. It seemed like just a matter of time.

One day, while speaking at a prophetic conference in London, I met a man, quite by chance. I had just completed a seminar and was sitting quietly during a coffee break in the office of the senior pastor. The pastor had left me and another visitor alone together. At the time, I was exhausted and only really thinking about coffee and rest. The man and I struck up a conversation about the conference I was leading. I gave him a brochure, thinking he was a local man who might wish to attend the event over the next few days.

Instead, the man said he wanted to stage a similar conference at his home church. It was at that point that I discovered that Dr. Noel Woodroffe led a church in Trinidad. He asked me if I would come and speak at his event. To be honest, I thought he was just being polite. However, a few months later, Noel sent me a plane ticket and my long-standing joke with the Lord was over. Noel was only at that London church for a few moments, but it was long enough for the two of us to meet and forge a friendship.

The Process Of Prophecy

All of us have experienced situations where completely unforeseen things have happened and altered the course of our lives in different areas. It's good to sit down once in a while and think back on what God has done for us in the past several years. It's good to meditate on our own life, and God's role in it. God Himself does this in Heaven, according to Malachi 3:16:

> *Then those who feared the LORD spoke to one another, and the LORD listened and heard them; so a book of remembrance was written before Him for those who fear the LORD and who meditate on His name.*

Waiting On God

Meditation is all about waiting on God, and giving ourselves the time and space to be in communion with Him. This is not an unfocused event, but carries a deep sense of purpose: we want to be open to hearing God's voice everywhere. I constantly carry a notebook with me because God speaks to me in the most peculiar places. I haven't found a shower-proof notebook yet, but I'll buy one the day they are invented!

Sometimes waiting on God means letting God know that you actually love Him, that He's important to you, and that you take pleasure in who He is. There are times when we will wait on Him and nothing will happen. That's okay, for if God does not speak initially, He will always speak eventually. We need to be ready when He does.

Waiting on God is born out of a spirit of quiet and stillness. We have to calm the clamoring thoughts within our minds and hearts. Meditation and waiting on God go hand-in-hand; one often births the other. It fills our minds with thoughts of God and we become God-conscious. Into the quiet, God drops His words like the morning dew, refreshing our souls and spirits.

Conquering this discipline in private will deepen your public ministry. I once asked a professional tennis player how he dealt with one-hundred-mile-per-hour serves coming at him.

"You come to a place in your reactions where you're expectant of the ball coming across the net," he told me. "You have to develop an inner quietness, a watchfulness, and slow down your heartbeat so that the tennis ball looks like a football coming at ten miles per hour. You need that kind of mental capacity. Your reaction, physical ability, and knowledge of how your opponent plays all combine together and you see things ahead of time."

> *Rest is a weapon!*

The player was not a Christian, but his explanation translates perfectly into the world of the prophetic. Being in the presence of God slows down our heartbeat. It slows down our reactions and calms us on the inside. The louder it is on the outside, the quieter we must become on the inside.

My ability to quiet myself before God has allowed me to hear His voice in the most pressure-packed circumstances. Many years ago, I was in a Pentecostal church. There was a time of worship that was absolutely excruciating to be a part of. I was squirming in my seat and apologizing to God because I couldn't join in. I knew the songs — I just didn't think they should be sung that way.

"Lord, I'm really struggling with this worship," I prayed. "I'm sorry. To be honest, we've had fifty minutes of mindless singing and I'm really quite bored."

"It's alright for you, you're only visiting this place," I heard God whisper back to me. "I have to be here every week."

The pastor concluded the singing with a time of "waiting on the Lord." After a few moments, an elegantly-dressed woman stood up, came to the microphone, and said the Lord had given her a vision.

"I see a penguin, halfway up a flagpole, with a carrot in its ear," she said. I wish I could make something like that up, but it is literally what she said. I sat still on the platform and waited, with everyone else, for an interpretation. Suddenly, I realized that everyone was staring at me and expecting me to interpret this mess!

I sat there with a mental picture of a penguin, carrot in ear, clamoring up a flagpole. It made no sense, and God wasn't showing or telling me anything about it. The main leader walked across the stage and knelt beside me.

"What's the Lord showing you?" he whispered.

"Nothing," I replied.

"Well, what do you think of the vision?" he tried again.

"I think you should tell her to stop eating cheese before coming to church — it's nonsense," I answered. "I mean, carrots and penguins and flagpoles? It's nonsense."

The pastor got indignant. "She's our most spiritual sister!" he said. "You need to go and give the interpretation."

"But there isn't one," I protested.

"There must be one," he said. "She's given the vision."

"I think you ought to discipline her," I replied. It was as though we were speaking two different languages. In the end, I had to go to the front and tell everyone that there was nothing supernatural about the vision. The whole place was silent as she jumped up and stormed out of the room. A whole group of people followed her, including the pastor. When things had settled down, I did some teaching.

After the meeting, I was called into the pastor's study and disciplined. It turned out that she was the biggest giver in the church and could do anything she liked, even give an oddball prophecy. The church lived in unreality.

Unreality occurs where Christians are not operating out of rest and peace, but live according to the whims of the external pressures they face. It sparks a form of mental gymnastics where revelation cannot penetrate. The mind is the enemy of the spirit — and the spirit is where God deposits His revelation. It takes faith for our conscious mind to accept the things our spirit tells us.

The Heart Precedes The Mind At All Times

Sometimes, God asks us to do something unreasonable, and our minds try to talk us out of it. The mind deals with information, and the spirit with revelation. It can be difficult for those two elements to coexist. But we must submit our mind to our spirit, as counseled in 1 Corinthians 2:14 — *"But the natural man does not receive the things of the Spirit of God, for they are foolishness to him; nor can he know them, because they are spiritually discerned."* We can only discern a prophetic word in our spirit.

We must return to the roots of our inherent spirituality and begin to believe as the early Christians did, who practiced their walk with the Lord.

When we become Christians we did not invite Jesus into our head: Faith is primarily an affair of the heart not the mind. Our mind will undoubtedly play its part but not from a place of logic but spiritual intuition because we must all daily "be renewed in the spirit of our mind" (Ephesians 4:23).

We received salvation from a fragment of the truth. We did not know the whole bible nor the whole history of Jesus. Someone and something touched our heart and we opened up to the claims of the Kingdom.

Our heart needs less data than our mind. Our spirit receives revelation our mind can only process information. When Jesus walked on water half his disciples were terrified thinking it was a ghost. Peter said "if it's you Lord bid me come". Jesus did not throw Peter an instruction manual on how to walk on water. He just smiled enigmatically and said one word. "Come", was all He said and on the strength of that one word Peter walked on a substance he had no business being on, except that he had permission.

The mind acting alone will always require more information. It will have more questions and will want everything dotted and crossed before it makes a decision. The problem with that is that God will not explain Himself. He does not make proposals for our approval.

The heart is designed to respond to revelation, the mind is not. When we are renewed in the spirit of our mind it is because it has come under the rule of the heart regarding revelation.

The heart responds to God's word in revelatory form. The mind follows the heart and our mind is empowered to think through the "how to" of God's instruction. The command instruction to obey comes from the heart.

The way that we come into salvation is the way that salvation is sustained. As Jesus is established in our heart by the Holy Spirit we are also taught how to think as He thinks. Our mind must be under the rule of our heart or we are rendered useless for believing the impossible. The mind by itself can only rise to a possibility of something miraculous. We give mental assent to something without acknowledging the reality of it in spiritual terms.

It is our heart that recognizes the voice of God and sees His imprint on a situation. Our heart rises to the probability that something amazing is about to occur. We believe.

Repentance is not just about thinking again, it is about turning our thinking away from mere logic to having the mind of Christ. True repentance is a wonderful invitation to think as Jesus would think about the issue or situation in front of us.

Only the heart can receive revelation

If our spirit does not win the battle for primacy with the soul then our faith will always be at the mercy of our logic. A logical, analytical mind will always talk us out of a supernatural experience. It is not difficult to tell who is a soulish Christian for they always need reassurance. Their head is in charge of their spirituality so faith always gives way to logic and reason. The possibilities of the Holy Spirit coming into our lives with His wonderful cheerfulness and abounding confidence is always much reduced when intellectualism rules our faith.

Of course I realize that we need great thinkers and key intellects in the Kingdom, but never at the expense of faith, childlike trust and the creative imagination so vital to a life being led by the Spirit.

Our hearts must increasingly come to a new place of enlightenment where we can see in the Spirit.

> *In Him, you also, after listening to the message of truth, the gospel of your salvation — having also believed, you were sealed in Him with the Holy Spirit of promise, who is given as a pledge of our inheritance, with a view to the redemption of God's own possession, to the praise of*

His glory. For this reason I too, having heard of the faith in the Lord Jesus which exists among you and your love for all the saints, do not cease giving thanks for you, while making mention of you in my prayers; that the God of our Lord Jesus Christ, the Father of glory, may give to you a spirit of wisdom and of revelation in the knowledge of Him.

I pray that the eyes of your heart may be enlightened, so that you will know what is the hope of His calling, what are the riches of the glory of His inheritance in the saints, and what is the surpassing greatness of His power toward us who believe. These are in accordance with the working of the strength of His might which He brought about in Christ, when He raised Him from the dead and seated Him at His right hand in the heavenly places, far above all rule and authority and power and dominion, and every name that is named, not only in this age but also in the one to come. And He put all things in subjection under His feet, and gave Him as head over all things to the church, which is His body, the fullness of Him who fills all in all. (Ephesians 1:13–23)

Promise. The Holy Spirit comes to each believer to enable them to real-ize, receive and inherit every promise that the Father has set aside for them. Our faith grows exponentially as those promises become a reality and we learn progressively to live in the favor of God in the face of Jesus Christ.

In that context for life it is so vital that "the eyes of our heart are enlight-ened". It is part of our inheritance in Christ that we perceive all of life from the Father's perspective. Knowing what the Lord thinks about any issue is a normal and necessary part of our relationship with Him. The role of the Holy Spirit is to make us aware of how the Lord is thinking and also to release to us in visual form the insights and intentions of the Father. We have eyes to see and ears to hear all that Father would impart to us. This is such a tremendous, close and intimate relationship that we have with Jesus. There is no value in ignorance when our destiny is confidence. "They that know their God shall be strong and do exploits," (Daniel 11:32).

The mind receives information

We are learning to live from our inner witness of the Holy spirit and His Presence in our lives. He is fully aware of Heavens plans and lives to make us just as conscious and familiar with the Father's intention. The Holy Spirit is a brilliant teacher who seeks to develop our understanding and practice of seeing from the heart and living in a place of sensitivity. On every level He instructs us in righteousness, which is right living across all the spectrum of lie, particularly in the matter of faith and obedience.

There is no substitute for sensitivity and obedience as the driving force of childlike trust and mature faith. We are compelled to become sensitive; finely tuned, susceptible and responsive to the Father's nature. Our heart will develop an acute sense of perception that is delicate and powerful. This is an awareness not rooted in mere head knowledge but is an actual spiritual, emotional, physical and mental experience of God. The Father overwhelms all our senses and faculties in His pursuit of fullness in our lives. Fullness is concerned with touching every part of our being and releasing us to have great awareness of the love and joy of the Lord.

> God speaks through our heart to our mind

The Holy Spirit will give us "a spirit of wisdom and revelation" so that our knowledge of God does not get stuck at the mental level. Knowledge in this context is always tied into an experience of God rather than just an intellectual notion of Him. Knowledge that does not lead to a deeper relational and spiritual experience of God is not worth the knowing. Our mind is touched but our heart is unchanged.

We are enlightened so that "we will know" what the mind of the Lord is and how to experience His thinking over us. The first commandment is to "love the Lord your God with all your heart, and with all your soul, and with all your mind," (Matthew 22:37).

This involves loving the Lord with everything that we are and have within ourselves. Our mind comes last in the order of loving simply because it can never be first. The mind can only follow the heart, it must never lead. When the mind leads we are reduced in our capacity to experience. It is our heart that has opened up to Jesus. It is our heart that has received His life and Presence. It is our heart that is the doorway to an ongoing experience of His life.

> When our heart perceives, our mind can know

After our heart; that is the very centre, the spirit, the inner man of our life in God has been born again. We now live from the inside out. Our soul comes under the rule of our inner man. Our will and our emotions are governed by intimacy and sensitivity to the nature of God. In that context our mind is set free to love the Lord and to enjoy His thoughts.

Wisdom and revelation enter our spirit and our thinking and our mindset is renewed and enables us to live at a higher level of thought and perception. Wisdom is superior to knowledge. Wisdom is a Christian context in the understanding of how the Father sees; how He thinks, and how he likes to do things. It is through wisdom that we develop a knowledge of God and

His ways. Knowledge emanating from wisdom is the perception of thought leading to an experience of God's nature and a way of behaving that is consistent with confidence that produces faith.

To love God with your mind is to be drawn into an invited experience of knowing His thoughts. I love the way God thinks! When we allow ourselves to think as He does our minds cease to be a battleground and instead become a place where we love the Lord and His thinking. Meditation, the act of deep thought, becomes a place of worship and intimacy with the mind of Christ. We are designed to practice intimate thinking with the Lord Jesus.

All our thoughts therefore lead us to joy and the Presence of God. Our mind, following our heart, is now enabled and empowered to support the heart with love and intimate thinking. Thus are we consistently renewed in the spirit of our mind so that we are consumed by Christ's mindset.

> *Truth only sets us free when it becomes an experience!*

This is true enlightenment! It can only occur as the eyes of our heart are opened and made aware of the greatness of God. We are never overwhelmed by life when we are undone by the majesty of God's lovingkindness. Enlightenment makes us luminous in the glory of God's nature. We see the light about everything and our hearts are made light. We walk in the light of His thinking, intentionality and loving intimacy. He lifts up the light of His countenance upon us (Psalm 4:6). What a poetic and beautiful description of smiling!

He causes His face to shine upon us (Psalm 80:3, 7, 19). His very graciousness is a wonderful tonic leading to total peace and blessing (Deuteronomy 6:22–27).

From the place of wisdom and revelation our heart is enlightened and enlarged to live in a place of simplicity, sensitivity and trust … so that we will know … who God is for us at any moment.

Meditation is not just a place of deep thought. It is also a place of deep worship and intimate contemplation of the nature of god. Out from that place of internal rest and stillness we hear the word of the Lord and our thinking is corrected.

This is one of the laws of life in the Spirit … when God speaks from His heart we can never respond in our head. He is not looking for mental assent but a heart response. He does not seek our logical agreement or permission. We must respond in the medium of the message … heart to heart.

The Father always communes twice over an issue, speaking directly and indirectly. When our heart has received, responded and obeyed His word then our mind is flooded with revelation releasing strategies and tactics of how to move forward in our obedience. Faith grows by hearing and hearing by the word of God (Romans 10:17). Our trust and sensitivity to the Holy Spirit promotes obedience which creates movement and momentum. Faith is active. Our mind needs to become responsive.

This is precisely what being led by the Spirit means! Our mind serves our heart. Knowledge serves faith and our will is serving our obedience causing us to have greater experiences of God in the context of our current circumstances.

This is a critical discipline for us to recover at this time, otherwise what the Father speaks to us will make no sense. A heart response opens the mind to receive all the possibilities. If we respond to God's heart only with our head then logic and reason will close the door to the supernatural. We will be reduced to only having options in the natural world because the possibilities of heaven will be shut out.

> *Your mind must serve your heart or you cannot fully know God*

When the eyes of our heart are enlightened our sensitivity to the Holy Spirit enables our creative imagination to begin to see what God is saying. This is so vital if we are to believe all that the Lord has in store for us. Our assignment in the Kingdom is in direct proportion to our identity in the eyes of the Father.

Moses had to lead over a million people from bondage to a tyrant into freedom, and then into full release as a nation in their own territory. In order for this to occur he had to see himself in a particular way. The Lord needed Moses to step up into a higher place of awareness so that his heart could operate at a higher dimension of faith and power.

In that context the Lord speaks these remarkable words to him in Exodus 7:1:

> *Then the LORD said to Moses, "See, I make you as God to Pharaoh, and your brother Aaron shall be your prophet.*

If you do not see it, you cannot become it. Identity must be visualized before it can be realized. If Moses does not see this high place of living then he will be forced to speak to Pharaoh from a lower state of being. He will be reduced to asking for favors, just like all the rest of the people at Pharaoh's court. Faith is then diluted to supplication instead of command. It is vital that Moses speaks to Pharaoh from this heightened sense of who he is in the Lord. Moses has to come at Pharaoh from a higher level

> *If you don't see it, you cannot become it!*

of identity than Pharaoh himself possesses. Anything less and the assignment is not possible. "See!… I have made you as God to Pharaoh. In other words by the time that the Father has finished with Pharaoh, he will only be able to view Moses in his limited understanding of things. That is… Moses must be some sort of God in human form. Ironically this is the spiritual perception that Pharaoh has been taught to have of himself. This means then that the king of Egypt is about to meet more than his match at this level! Pharaoh has massive authority and will only respond to someone who demonstrates more.

We see the same truth about visual perception in Joshua 6:1,2:

Now Jericho was tightly shut because of the sons of Israel; no one went out and no one came in. The LORD said to Joshua, "See, I have given Jericho into your hand, with its king and the valiant warriors.

See! See in your heart that I have given you Jericho, its king and the best of his battle hardened warriors. The heart response is to "see" what the Lord is proclaiming over you and to return that image to the Lord in confession and declaration. "Lord thank you that you have made me this person already in the Spirit. I confess that my life and current experiences are therefore all geared to cooperating with the Holy Spirit to enable what you see to become my absolute present reality. Therefore I declare that my will is given over to you that the person you see in me shall emerge in this day for such a time as this". Or as Mary put it succinctly "behold the bondservant of the Lord, be it done to me according to your word" (Luke 1:38).

Everything in Christ Jesus is Yes and Amen! God's heart says "Yes"! In matters of the heart between you and the Father, reason must take its cue from divinely inspired imagination moving in trust and faith. The only time God will speak to your reasoning is when you have sinned. Then He says: "Come now let us reason together, though your sins be as scarlet, yet they shall be as white as snow" (Isaiah 1:18). Even here He invites us to "see", by using pictorial language. Mostly the Father invites our hearts into an experience of trust.

Trust in the LORD with all your heart and do not lean on your own understanding. In all your ways acknowledge Him, and He will make your paths straight. (Proverbs 3:5–6)

The Heart Precedes The Mind At All Times

When our heart produces trust, our mind is empowered to understand in the way that God requires for that particular moment. If our heart does not let us down then we always have confidence before God (1 John 3:21). What our heart imagines under the Holy Spirit, your faith can realize.

> But just as it is written, "THINGS WHICH EYE HAS NOT SEEN AND
> EAR HAS NOT HEARD, AND which HAVE NOT ENTERED THE HEART
> OF MAN, ALL THAT GOD HAS PREPARED FOR THOSE WHO LOVE HIM."
> For to us God revealed them through the Spirit; for the Spirit searches
> all things, even the depths of God. (1 Corinthians 2:9–10)

What God has prepared for us cannot be seen or heard until it has entered our heart. Our inner man is enlightened and then we see the purpose of God and we are opened to hearing on a deeper level. Our identity is out of alignment with God's essential nature until we see Him as He is. He builds everything out of what we have seen.

When Jesus asked the question "Whom do people say that the Son of Man is?", He was essentially asking "How do they see or perceive me?" What you think about God is the most important thing in the world. That perception is driven by what you see that He is for you. Simon Peter received a spiritual perception of Jesus that changed his name and his personal identity (Matthew 16:13–20). When we fail to see, then our identity is out of harmony with God's perception of us and our inheritance will be unclaimed.

This is the most vital part of prophecy. When we prophesy we encourage people to see who they are in Christ. We restore them to an affair of the heart. We build up their confidence and their ability to know the heart and mind of God. All prophetic people are ambassadors of reconciliation, restoring people to their rightful identity. Prophecy restores the heart.

A lifestyle of heart led responsiveness to the Holy Spirit is the essence of the prophetic gift and ministry. This type of sensitivity to God's Name and Nature is the heartbeat of prophecy. Approaching the heart of God in prophecy is therefore about ruling in life through the heart. We recognize that our heart is the door that Jesus is knocking on continually (Rev-

> Your perception is
> linked to your destiny

elation 3:20). When we open that door in each situation then we have an experience of God in fellowship that is ongoing and powerful in its intimate nature. Our mind is incredible at establishing the truth that our heartfelt experience has opened up to us. Heart and mind working together will enable us to be transformed in life. The issue is such a paradox is always about primacy. A paradox is two apparently conflicting ideas contained in the same truth, *e.g.* we have to die to live; give to receive; be last to be first. These are all paradoxes. Opposing truths acting out of alignment not competition. The church is both a body (fluid, changing, flexible) and a building (rigid, unchanging and inflexible). The church is both/and, not either/or. The description of the apostolic ministry is both agricultural and construction in metaphor. One is organic, the other is organized. We need both, but the order is critical. We can only build the church by growing people, thus the organic has primacy.

The prophetic gift moves in concert with apostolic purpose and divine intent. The key word in prophecy is always edify. Prophecy takes us from a poor perspective of God and self into a much richer outlook on life, so that we are built up in the natural and the spiritual dimension together. All prophecy has its roots in edification, exhortation and comfort. Words that are hard to say must come from this foundation so that people have the opportunity to be built up in their revelation and experience of God.

We have to come to a place where our spirit is a witness to what God is saying. Then we can release our mind to fall in line behind the word, begin the process of understanding it, and eventually speak it out. Our minds will often clash with the revelation we have received. It will try to constrain us, telling us not to speak out the word we have heard. It may seem illogical. To combat that, we need to learn to move in the peace and relaxation of God. We prophesy as far as our faith will allow us to.

Soul And Spirit

It is very important that we understand the discipline of how to live with God because everything flows out of our relationship with Him. What we think about God is the single most important thing in the world — it is the revelation that will drive our life and provide the channel through which our prophetic gift and ministry will flow.

> Your will is the vehicle for the Spirit

We are probably all aware that man is essentially two parts: soul/body and spirit — what the Bible often calls "the outer man" and "the inner man." In God's design, He intended the Holy Spirit to dwell and mingle with our spirit.

The soul is made up of mind, emotions and will, and must take its instruction and authority from the Spirit of God. In Scripture, it is spoken of frequently as being something over which we have to gain and exercise authority. *"Therefore we do not lose heart,"* Paul wrote in 2 Corinthians 4:16.

"Even though our outward man is perishing, yet the inward man is being renewed day by day." Up until the time of salvation, our soul rules unopposed in our life. We live a life unconnected with our spirit until God intervenes. We make our own decisions, reigning and ruling through our soul. We do what we want, living to please ourselves most of the time. We become self-centered and our love is often conditional.

At the moment of salvation, our spirit comes to life but our whole ability to live that life for other people or for ourselves is still dominated by the soul. At salvation, an internal battle begins. God breaks in, we are born again, and our spirit is revitalized. Now the battle for supremacy begins.

There is a law that emerges within us at the moment of salvation. Salvation is not a one-off occurrence — we have been saved, we are being saved, and we will be saved. Salvation is a process of sanctification. Sanctification is about bringing everything within us under the rule of God so that joyfully, in everything that we are and have, we are becoming His. The spirit begins to exert this pressure from within, but the soul doesn't want to give up its rule over us.

If our will is not the vehicle for the spirit, then our emotions will try and run the show. However, our will has an insatiable appetite to be in the presence of God, so our will is the vehicle for life in the spirit, not our mind and emotions. As our will comes under the rule of the spirit, our soul learns how to submit joyfully to the Holy Spirit.[2]

When our soul power is broken, we come into extreme joy. The soul power has to be broken or we cannot serve God effectively. The soul, if unconquered, is always affected by external things. So life in the spirit is about learning how to live from the inside to the outside, not the other way around.

When we live in our soul, we are always waiting for God to do something. When we learn how to live in our spirit, we are our own revival. When we learn how to live in the spirit, we don't need a move of God coming from outside, we have one on the inside of us. This is what Jesus meant when He told the Samaritan woman at the well, "If you drink My water, you'll never have to be thirsty again."

---

2   For a more full explanation and impartation of this particular discipline regarding soul and spirit please read the journal *"Towards a Powerful Inner Life,"* available at www.brilliantbookhouse.com.

Tongues

Speaking in tongues, for those people who have the gift, is a very important part of our devotional life and our relationship with God because it edifies our spirit and renews our mind. I love tongues because I can pour out my heart to God in whatever situation I'm in, even if I'm in pain or I'm exhausted. I have an expectation that when I speak in tongues, God will break in and do something. I don't want to use this gift unless I have expectation for I know that the two go together.

There are times when I want to have ten minutes of adoration of Jesus, where I can sit quietly and pour out my heart about how much He means to me. When we enter that time of praise, our reactions to the circumstances around us change. We begin to respond to things in a godly manner, revering Jesus. It is the opposite spirit to which the world operates under. It is the very essence of Jesus' life: "Pray for those who use you, bless those who persecute you."

How do we know that we are being led by the Spirit? The only effective way is by gauging our reactions to situations around us. If something difficult is happening, and our reaction is one of peace, joy, thankfulness, gentleness, and humility, we are being led by the Spirit. If what comes out of our mouth is something altogether different, the chances are we are being led by the flesh. We know we are being led by the Spirit of God by the kind of character that we are manifesting in given situations. Moving in the opposite spirit is very, very important to us, and of extreme importance to God. Speaking in tongues builds up a reservoir inside of us, helping us to top off the well within. It keeps us unblocked and in communion with God.

Unceasing Prayer

Prayer is absolutely vital in our preparation to prophesy. Prayer and prophecy are inextricably linked in terms of the communication process. Both involve listening before talking. In my own prayer time, I usually find myself somewhere in the spiritual paradox between wonderful and frustrating, joyful and pained, confident and uncertain, anointed and unanointed. Fortunately, all of those feelings are the same to God: prayer is prayer. When my daughter was thirteen, she described prayer perfectly to me: "Some days, you get in the elevator and zoom to the penthouse suite. Other days, you take the stairs." Either way, prayer is an interesting journey.

> Pray with God —
> not towards Him!

Most of us don't listen enough before we pray. When I pray something, I listen straight away, just in case God tells me I can have what I asked for.

Sometimes we pray more than we need to because we never hear God say, "Yes." Wherever we pray, whatever we pray, we must get into a habit of immediately listening.

Often, we listen best when we are reading. If that's the case, we ought to read the Bible before an extended, set-apart time of prayer. The Holy Spirit can and will impress on us something from Scripture. Perhaps God gave us two ears and one mouth so we would listen twice as much as talk.

Prayer, in its simplest form, is finding out what God wants to do and then asking Him to do it. When we don't listen before we pray, we end up presenting God with options instead of a request. We'll pray whatever comes to mind instead of entering into communion with Him. Our internal, clamoring agenda gives God a multiple choice prayer. "Please Lord, do *A*. Unless *B* is Your will. Or *C*. But *D* would be great, too," we pray. By practicing stillness, and communicating with Him throughout the day, we can better hear and understand His heart for our issues.

Prayer is praying with God not to God. It is praying with the answer not to try and find one.[3]

God is very different from us. God is always still and often silent, but He punctuates that silence with words. This makes every word God speaks an event, because He has an inherent creativity in the power of His Word. In Genesis 1:3, He said, *"Let there be light,"* and there was light for the first time. His first recorded message was an incredible event, and one sung about for thousands of years after — *"By the word of the LORD the heavens were made,"* says Psalm 33:6. John 1:1–5 gives another glimpse of the creative power of God's word:

> *In the beginning was the Word, and the Word was with God, and the Word was God. He was in the beginning with God. All things were made through Him, and without Him nothing was made that was made. In Him was life, and the life was the light of men. And the light shines in the darkness, and the darkness did not comprehend it.*

Human beings, on the other hand, punctuate words with silence. We're always talking and rarely quiet. This makes our silence an event. We're usually quiet only for the purposes of reflection, or if we're searching something out.

The great thing about God is that He doesn't have to talk to communicate. Just a look can be sufficient. The Bible says that Jesus turned and looked

---

3   For a more full explanation of this joyful discipline please read the journal on Crafted Prayer available at www.brilliantbookhouse.com.

JOHN G. LAKE

Lived: 1870 to 1935

Prophetic Synopsis: Surrounded by death and illness all his life (eight of his fifteen siblings died young), Lake was desperate for God to heal. In the 1890s, Lake heard about John Dowie's healing rooms, and took his brother to one: the man was healed. Later, he took his sister, who suffered from cancer, to Dowie. She was healed too. In 1896, Lake's wife, Jennie, contracted tuberculosis, and she was healed as well.

Ten years later, after seasons of prayer and fasting and being mentored by Dowie, Lake prayed for a woman with rheumatism. God filled the room and His power fell on Lake like warm rain. He heard the Lord say to him: "I have heard your prayers. I have seen your tears. You are now baptized in the Holy Spirit." The woman was healed.

The Lakes went to South Africa and planted more than 600 churches. When Jennie died, John returned to America and settled in Spokane, Washington, opening a series of healing rooms.

In six years in Spokane, 100,000 healings took place — that's forty-five every day! A Washington, D.C. doctor declared Spokane the healthiest city in the world. A Better Business Bureau committee investigated one hundred healings and concluded: "We soon found out... you did not tell the half of it."

Lake could put his hands on a person and the Holy Spirit would show him what was wrong. He could go into a hospital, speak to a patient whose condition baffled doctors, pray, and discern exactly what their ailment was.

Key Comment: "The currents of power began to rush through my being from the crown of my head to the soles of my feet."

Sources: Stanley Burgess and Gary McGee, editors. *Dictionary of Pentecostal and Charismatic Movements.* (Grand Rapids, MI: Zondervan, 1996). Roberts Liardon, *God's Generals.* (Tulsa, OK: Albury Publishing, 1996).

at Peter and broke his heart. God can speak to us through His love, His joy, and even His presence. We just have to carve out time to spend in that quiet place with Him. The more disciplined we become in every moment of our lives, the more dialogue we will engage Him in.

A discipline does not have to be a heavy or onerous duty. It is a joy if we choose to see it that way. It describes a joyful routine that does our hearts good. Like brushing our teeth in the morning or our first sip of coffee each day.

All daily routines need to be joyful otherwise the stress of it can unbalance our approach to life. The Holy Spirit is so brilliant at playing the enjoyment game, it is what makes fellowship with Him a complete delight!

Before the Lord called me into my current ministry, I was the business development manager for a large training and recruitment company. My life was a hectic round of business deals, management problems, employment research, government negotiations, training sessions, event organizing, and strategic oversight. There were times in those busy days when I would tell my secretarial staff that I needed ten minutes of undisturbed rest. I would retreat into my office, close the door, and sit quietly, thanking God, listening to Him, asking Him for His perspective, and praying for His help. Many right decisions came out of those short bursts of prayer. While I can't say I always heard God specifically in those moments (although sometimes I did), He did shape me in those times. My track record at the company, together with my continuous promotion among the staff, indicates that the Lord influenced me far more than I actually knew. Those prayer times kept my heart free from ungodly pressure — they were like a spiritual lifeline for me.

> *Spiritual discipline is a joyful routine that does our heart good*

Prayer can come in seasons. When I wrote *Developing Your Prophetic Gifting* all those years ago, I was in a season of my life where God answered many of my prayers immediately. What once took days or weeks to be prayed through suddenly took minutes. I was learning to hear God more clearly, and my expectation in terms of listening grew. My prayers were full of faith because I knew God was listening and acting.

Obviously, prayer is not just about being in request mode before God. He isn't Santa Claus, after all. The wonderful thing about prayer is that we can talk to God about anything and everything, wherever we are, whatever we're thinking, or whatever we're feeling. We have the freedom to open up our spirit and go places with God. I specialize in short prayers: "Lord, help this person," I'll ask Him during the day. "Father, remember my friends out there in Africa," I say. I keep the flow of prayer going, holding open a channel of communication between the two of us. The best way for someone to enter the secret place with God is to never leave it. By stepping back into our inner man and working at being peaceful and restful, we can develop deep, constant communication with Him.

A life of unceasing prayer allows us to continuously talk everything through as it comes into our lives. We can mention things to God immediately and constantly. It happens conversationally; we just run the things in our heart by God, as we would a good friend. Our fears, our shortcomings, our hopes, our dreams, our concerns, and our joys can all be brought to God in unceasing prayer.

Such a lifestyle releases our soul to be at peace because we have committed to God everything that is happening in our lives. He has a stake in all of it. Our spirit — the part of us that communicates with God — influences our soul positively when we engage with God constantly. When we talk about every situation with God, things are put into an eternal context. It makes us less prone to anxiety, worry, fear, and idle speculation. Instead, we are watching for God to do something incredible in, and through, us. The Apostle John knew this principle, and instructed us in it in 1 John 5:14–15:

> *Now this is the confidence that we have in Him, that if we ask anything according to His will, He hears us. And if we know that He hears us, whatever we ask, we know that we have the petitions that we have asked of Him.*

Prayer is a matter of continually asking the Holy Spirit to break in and speak. When was the last time you asked the Lord for some encouragement? If it has been a while, try it right now. "Father, I need some encouragement. Please would You do something, please would You say something, please help me."

Prayer, Power, Process

Living constantly in the presence of God can heal us of our old wounds, and even our physical illnesses. Emotional, spiritual, mental, and physical needs are all the same to the Father. We know that God is able to heal instantly, but there are also occasions when He heals us over a longer period of time. We can be healed both immediately by His power and gradually through our relationship with Him. At times, the Lord is

Confidence is rooted in who God is for us… now

developing our capacity to walk in power and authority. On these occasions, when under the guidance of His will, we pray the prayers of authority and faith and we see immediate results. At these times, too, our prayers are accompanied by a specific gift of faith, healing, or miracles, and we can be amazed at how Heaven comes to earth in those moments.

Still, there are other times when we enter a process of healing that seems to be in line with God's desire to redevelop our relationship with Him. We are not ill or wounded because our relationship with God lacks depth. God Himself is not mean to us; He does not deny healing for the sake of building relationship. Rather, the Father simply uses what is available to touch and deepen us in difficult moments.

In all our situations, the love of the Father is profound enough to upgrade our image of Him, that we may know His nature and lordship in a more realistic manner.

Healing through relationship is a process because the Lord is developing our patience, endurance, and steadfast trust. It is the keeping power of God that increases our faith and brings us to a new level of perception, relationship, and, ultimately, revelation. He nurtures us as we pray in faith and learn to abide in the shadow of His wings. He does not always deliver us from the valley, but He does always walk through it with us.

God is our keeper and loves His role in watching over us and teaching us to abide in confidence.[4] We learn to trust the Father as we actively listen to the One who ever lives to make intercession for us (see Hebrews 7:25), and learn to walk with the Comforter. It is vital that we allow the Holy Spirit to develop this particular role in our lives. We can be weak and find God's strength through comfort, as well as through joy.

In the valley, in the process of restoration, renewal, and finding physical, mental, emotional, or spiritual health, we learn how best to fight. In this instance, the weapons of our warfare are thanksgiving, praise, trust, and rest. Sometimes we inherit the promises of God immediately, but, at other times, it comes through faith and patience.

> *Freedom is about always being free!*

Even if God's power is not demonstrated immediately, His Sovereignty will always come through progressively. Power and process is designed by God's will. If it is process that He chooses to heal us in, we must wait gladly on the Lord and remain attentive to His voice and bound to His loving nature.

---

4   For a more full understanding of this powerful truth Graham's journal on God's Keeping Power would be valuable study on building a relationship with God's intentional nature. Available on www.brilliantbookhouse.com.

Words of knowledge may come through others about our circumstances. Sometimes these words are accompanied by another gift of faith, healing, or miracles, and we are set free. If not, they are God's encouragement for us to continue praying and believing in the process of life. The prophecy may carry the certainty of God's ultimate will, giving us confidence. We can craft them into a prayer to use daily, knowing we are praying God's will and therefore the answer to our dilemma.

Freed from the tyranny of our current condition, we are now released in heart and mind to pursue the other purposes of God in our circumstances. What else does He want to do apart from our ultimate healing? Is our healing a part of our wider restoration and renewal? Is the Lord taking us into a deeper place of abiding love and intimacy? He knows the plans He has for us, in every situation, to give us a future and a hope! What is He planning in that beautiful heart that loves us so amazingly? What grace will come our way, what wisdom and insight may open the eyes of our heart?

This is the path and the process of enlightenment which enables us to fully know God and to be known, as we read in Ephesians 1:15–23. We use what we are exploring and discovering to pray with certainty and to formulate our own psalms of thanksgiving. David's intentional, written-out praise — or as we now call them, the Psalms — were what enabled him to become a man after God's own heart.

Intimate Prayer

A few years ago, God began to speak to me about a new kind of prayer He was about to release to us. Paradoxically, this new method is actually an ancient way of prayer, one in which God's faithful servants like David and Paul flourished. These heroes of the faith learned how to pray exactly what God willed for a person, and saw His answer unfold before their very eyes. This type of prayer can transform Christians from living in a persistent widow mindset (Luke 18:1–8) into living in joyous, bride-like intercession.

> *Pray like a bride, not a widow*

As the Bride of Christ, we carry incredible favor with God. This favor is similar to the favor Queen Esther found in the eyes of her king. I believe God is taking many Christians into a new season of intimate, bride-like prayer. Real warfare in the Kingdom of God is always concerned with the battle for intimacy. This is a time to come off the battlefield and enter a new place of intimate petition. Many intercessors have become too exhausted and too burned-out to continue praying the way the Church has been advocating. As we learn to become conformed to God and His nature, and be transformed in our minds and personalities, He will teach us to look beyond the natural into the supernatural realm and see the Kingdom of Heaven at work in every need. It will no longer matter what life, people, or even the enemy throw at us, because we will understand that God is at work all around us.

I believe God is raising up an army of Esthers, an army of bridal intercessors, and it is a time to come off the wall and rest in the throne room presence of God — in our secret place in Him. It will be difficult for some people to come out of ministry and move into the discipline of resting in God, but the discipline of rest must be entered. This is a time of laying down ministry to gain fresh intimacy.

Don't pray with importunity, like the widow before the unjust judge in Luke 18, but pray with delight and favor. Don't just pray against the enemy, but also let your delighted prayers cause the King to stir Himself and come down. God's anointing will cause you to intercede with joy so that His glory will fill the earth. What is the glory of God? In Exodus 33:18–19, when Moses asked God to show His glory, God said He would cause His goodness to pass before him. One of the glories of God, therefore, is that He is good!

Begging is not favor!

As bridal intercessors, it will be our joy and delight to pray for the goodness of God to come down so that the Church can learn that we really do overcome evil with good. The Holy Spirit will give us a new strategy for prayer and perseverance; one that contains delight and laughter, and is full of ardent and passionate love, bathed in fresh worship, and birthed out of a deeper intimacy.

As we come and petition the Lord out of this place of closeness, He will be pleased to speak His favor and blessing into our hearts. Not only will our prayers move His heart and hands, but the words we receive from Him will be like a balm of Gilead across the nations, and churches will rise up in fresh favor. The attention of the Church will be taken off the enemy and put on God.

Pursue Love

Historically, the biggest failure in the prophetic has been a lack of love in prophets' hearts. In 1 Corinthians 14:1–5, the Apostle Paul addressed that very shortcoming:

> *Pursue love, and desire spiritual gifts, but especially that you may prophesy. For he who speaks in a tongue does not speak to men but to God, for no one understands him; however, in the spirit he speaks*

KATHRYN KUHLMAN

Lived: 1907 to 1976

Prophetic Synopsis: Separated from her husband, and having just lost her fledgling ministry, Kathryn Kuhlman was desperate for God in the mid 1940s. After praying for several days, she was touched by the Holy Spirit: "Four o'clock that Saturday afternoon, having come to the place in my life where I surrendered everything, I knew nothing about the fullness of the Holy Spirit. I knew nothing about speaking in an unknown tongue. I knew nothing about the deeper truths of the Word," she said. "That afternoon, Kathryn Kuhlman died. If you've never had that death to the flesh, you don't know what I'm talking about. When you're completely filled with the Holy Spirit, when you've had that experience as they had in the upper room, there will be a death to the flesh, believe me. I surrendered unto Him all there was of me, everything! Then for the first time, I realized what it meant to have real power."

Kuhlman's ministry exploded as the power of God followed her everywhere. When a woman was healed of a tumor while she preached, she turned her attention to healing. Hundreds, and then thousands, were healed as she shared the power of the Holy Spirit. She became very gifted in giving words of knowledge regarding illnesses: "How does one know the woman over there in such and such a dress is being healed? I don't know. If my life depended on it, I could not tell you. I do not know but the Holy Spirit knows."

In 1965, Kathryn moved to Los Angeles and held meetings in the Shrine Auditorium. She preached there for ten years, filling the 7,000-seat room almost every night. She became famous. She preached five hundred times on CBS television. Magazines like Redbook, People, Time, and Christianity Today did stories on her. She went on all of the popular talk shows, including Johnny Carson, Mike Douglas, Merv Griffin, and Dinah Shore. She met movie stars, singers, TV actors, and even Pope Paul VI.

Key Comment: "His power is under His authority — not ours."

Sources: Stanley Burgess and Gary McGee, editors. *Dictionary of Pentecostal and Charismatic Movements.* (Grand Rapids, MI: Zondervan, 1996). Roberts Liardon, *God's Generals.* (Tulsa, OK: Albury Publishing, 1996).

mysteries. But he who prophesies speaks edification and exhortation and comfort to men. He who speaks in a tongue edifies himself, but he who prophesies edifies the church. I wish you all spoke with tongues, but even more that you prophesied; for he who prophesies is greater than he who speaks with tongues, unless indeed he interprets, that the church may receive edification.

"*Pursue love,*" Paul said. That's the best piece of advice I can give anyone seeking to move in the prophetic: pursue love. Most people, when they're learning about prophecy, jump into the Old Testament first, looking at how the great prophets prophesied. However, a huge difference exists between the Old Testament and New Testament styles.

In New Testament prophecy, it is vital that we pursue God for all we're worth. God is love, therefore we cannot pursue God if we do not pursue love. "*Beloved, let us love one another, for love is of God; and everyone who loves is born of God and knows God,*" says 1 John 4:7. When we pursue God with all our heart, one thing should be happening — we should become more and more in love loving to the people around us.

Our heart will be changed to accept everyone, even people we previously couldn't stand being around. "*Love your enemies, do good to those who hate you, bless those who curse you, and pray for those who spitefully use you,*" Jesus taught in Luke 6:27–28. Even more astonishing than His teaching was the fact that He did just that: He loved people who hated Him. "*Father, forgive them, for they do not know what they do,*" He prayed in Luke 23:34 as the men crucifying Him cast lots for His clothing. If we are pursuing God, everybody around us is a potential target for God's love. No one is safe from the love of God.

> To pursue love is to be caught by it first!

The reason God put us in the circle of people we're with in our workplace, neighborhood, and church, is so that He can pour out His love through us. And the nastier they are, the more God wants us to love them.

In the prophetic, love needs to be our foundation. There is nothing worse, and I know this from experience, than being in a roomful of people, all of whom are waiting for a prophetic word, and you haven't got any love in your heart. It is a lonely, awful place to be. Most of the prophets I know who have had nervous breakdowns have done so because they had no real depth of love for people in their heart.

The only pressure we ought to be under is the pressure to be loved by God, and to love others. I have found that the safest place to be in ministry.

When I am surrounded by the expectancy of hundreds of people, and I have nothing to say, and I don't know what God wants to do next, being loved by Him creates a peace inside myself. It is a safe environment because all I can do is stand there and let God love me.

To be successful long-term in ministry, we have to understand how to be loved by God. When God's love touches a human being, it changes things on the inside. We can only pursue what has apprehended us. God made love His first commandment because it is His biggest value. He commands us to love because He commands it of Himself. He demands what He most wants to give. It takes God to love God. Only God can love God well. He gives to us first the very thing He most wants from us. "We love Him because He first loved us" (1 John 4:19). Our chief delight is to respond to the love of God and to return it to Him.

Everything originates in God (John 3:27) therefore everything comes from Him; it runs through Him and goes back to Him (Romans 11:35–36). What God commands, he is first to bestow. His initiative draws our response. Love is always available.

Everyone aspiring to move in the prophetic must have their hearts conditioned by love. Learning to be loved on a daily basis is our biggest lesson. Accepting and allowing the love of God to penetrate our heart, soul, mind and physical strength is a lifelong pleasure. To be still in His love. To rest in His love. To find joy and delight in God's loving nature. To be wrapped in His love and the majesty of His grace. To be free to give love to anyone, regardless of circumstances.

To speak from the platform of God's love is an awesome pleasure and a very real responsibility. The chief role of a prophet is to make God radiant in His people. My prime ministry after worship is simply to reach Christians for Christ. As prophetic people, our experience of God's love makes us aware of what He is doing in the hearts of those we minister to. God puts us between His heart and someone else's, and we can become a conduit for God's love to flow to someone. Love teaches us to see what God is seeing, to feel what God is feeling, to bless what God is blessing, and to do what God is doing.

New Beginnings

Prophecy can restore people's dignity and self-respect. It can give them hope again. But to do this, we must be steeped in God's love. We are either living in the present/past or the present/future in our relationship with the Lord and one another. Some relationships are stuck in the past because they are connected to memories and encounters that were either traumatic or eventful.

Our mind and emotions play the same tapes over and over until it becomes a normal part of our background conversation. Current mind-sets have been overcome by memory. It is our head noise that ruins the present. Some of our memories can be wonderful and yet can still keep our relationships in the past if we have not upgraded them for some time. The phrase "we must catch up one day" is one that we all use to signify that our relationship needs to become more current.

The best relationships have a present to future application. A "now" and "not yet" feel that provides the sense of a shared journey, an exploration of life. We live in the present with a strong sense of our and others potential. We are all a mix of visible traits and hidden capabilities. The latter may only emerge when the proper circumstances arise. Until then they are dormant and may only be recognized by the prophetic.

> *God is present–future in His relationship with us*

The Father lives with us and occupies the space between the potential we have and the actual that He views in our future. A prophecy is spoken from the future back to the present. That does not yet make it real or substantial. Free will is involved. Prophecy relates to the possibility not the inevitability of fulfillment because the will of the individual/group has to be engaged in cooperation with the Lord in order for the word to come to pass. "Be it unto me according to your word" is a sure sign that Mary fully intended to cooperate with the Father regarding the birth of Jesus.

Sometimes people are trapped into reliving or reenacting their past in current relationships. Prophetic ministry needs to enter that place gently, lovingly and firmly to extricate the individual from a present/past lifestyle. Prophecy in this context has an objective to restore people's dignity and self respect.

The best way to extricate people from the past is firstly to show them their future. Everyone has to have something to reach out for in life.

Not that I have already obtained it or have already become perfect, but I press on so that I may lay hold of that for which also I was laid hold of by Christ Jesus. Brethren, I do not regard myself as having laid hold of it yet; but one thing I do: forgetting what lies behind and reaching forward to what lies ahead, I press on toward the goal for the prize of the upward call of God in Christ Jesus. Let us therefore, as many as are perfect, have this attitude; and if in anything you have

EVAN ROBERTS

Lived: 1878 to 1951

Prophetic Synopsis: At age twenty, Roberts had a prophetic vision that changed his life. In it, he saw the moon, full and bright, with an arm stretching from it into Wales. Immediately, he knew that God was about to touch his country, bringing 100,000 people to the faith.

It wasn't just visions Roberts experienced. One Friday night, he had been deep in prayer: "It was communion with God," he said. "Before this I was afar off from God. I was frightened that night, but never since. So great was my shivering that I rocked the bed, and my brother, being wakened, took hold of me, thinking I was ill."

Roberts had another powerful vision, just before the Welsh Revival hit: "I had a vision of all Wales being lifted up to Heaven. We are going to see the mightiest revival Wales has ever known — the Holy Ghost is coming soon, so we must get ready."

He was right; God used him to move in Wales in a powerful way. Thousands were healed. Roberts' prophetic gift became so finely tuned that he could tell the nonbelievers in a room and preach directly to them. "The revival in south Wales is not of men, but of God," he said. "He has come very close to us. I have been asked concerning my methods. I have none. I never prepare what I shall speak, but I leave that to Him. I am not the source of the revival, but only one servant among what is growing to be a multitude. I wish no personal following, but only the world for Christ. I believe the world is on the threshold of a great religious revival, and pray daily that I may be allowed to help bring this about."

Just as he prophesied, 100,000 Welsh people came to Christ in six months.

Key Comment: "Ask and it shall be given unto you. Practice entire, definite faith in God's promise of the Spirit."

Sources: Stanley Burgess and Gary McGee, editors. *Dictionary of Pentecostal and Charismatic Movements*. (Grand Rapids, MI: Zondervan, 1996). Roberts Liardon, *God's Generals*. (Tulsa, OK: Albury Publishing, 1996).

a different attitude, God will reveal that also to you; however, let us keep living by that same standard to which we have attained. (Philippians 3:12–16).

Pressing on is made more possible through the influx of prophecy. People need to forget the past. "The former things have passed away, now I declare new things. Before they spring forth, I proclaim them to you" (Isaiah 42:9).

The prophetic must put us in mind of a future time in regard to our present. When our mind is able to cover the ground between our present and the future then we are free to move on in the things of God. If our mind is only back tracking to the past there can be no momentum.

> *Prophecy is the language of promise revealed*

"Do not call to mind the former things or ponder things of the past. Behold I will do something new, now it will spring forth. Will you not be aware of it?" (Isaiah 43:18–19).

Prophecy makes us aware of the future and it therefore has the capacity to call us up and out of something.

Prophecy can put us in touch with the romantic part of God's nature regarding His love for His bride who is the Beloved of His heart. Prophecy calls us to the next stage of life and the next phase of relationship with our Beloved Jesus.

My beloved responded and said to me, "Arise, my darling, my beautiful one, and come along. For behold, the winter is past, the rain is over and gone. The flowers have already appeared in the land; the time has arrived for pruning the vines, and the voice of the turtledove has been heard in our land. The fig tree has ripened its figs, and the vines in blossom have given forth their fragrance. Arise, my darling, my beautiful one, and come along!" (Song of Solomon 2:10–13)

It carries the language of promise. Love moving to the next chapter of experience. Hard times are over and new things are appearing. The Lord leaves us in no doubt of His affection for us. This is so much the heart of all true prophecy. The restoring of dignity and self respect is essential to the individual moving into a stronger relationship as the beloved of God. Prophecy causes us to arise and come away into a deeper relationship as the beloved. The Lord wears His heart on His sleeve, always visible, always tangible. He is so tactile in His affection for us.

When people have been damaged, it is the future that can release them from the past. The present is merely rerunning memory tapes and is therefore more prone to repeating scenarios from the past. The future alone calls people up to a new beginning. Prophecy tells us that God is with us (present) and also moving in advance of us (future). He will help us. He will deliver us. He will not fail us.

> *The LORD is the one who goes ahead of you; He will be with you He will not fail you or forsake you. Do not fear or be dismayed." (Deuteronomy 31:8).*

There is always a new "you" emerging! The Father loves to change us from one degree of glory to another. His love for us is transformational. He loves to create new from old. He is astonishingly brilliant at the process of transformation. He uses prophecy to create movement and momentum to take us out of the Egypt of our current circumstances into the Canaan of His promise and affection.

Prophetic people have this same affection and excitement in their heart. It shows in how they view people; the message of hope they carry; and in the way they present that message and deliver the heart of the Lord. What an amazing gift is prophecy! What an amazing burden the Lord wants to give us. It is a burden, a passion for freedom and to see God's beloved becoming more captivated by His deep love and longing.

> *Only the future can release us from the past!*

Prophetic input is an invaluable aid in the development of our identity. What is emerging in you right now? Who are you becoming? We all change. Prophecy provides us with the means to connect ourselves to the heart of God regarding our future and our destiny. It provides continuity in the affection of God. "I am with you always". No matter how the road ahead may challenge the journey, the Lord is unchangeable towards us. He is a constant, our North Star.

Three Phases Of Revelation

Generally, there are three parts to revelation. A word of knowledge often opens people up, while a prophetic word fills the gap created. Finally, a word of wisdom can give instruction on what to do next. These three elements work together to form the broader prophetic gifting.

A word of knowledge is simply revelation about something that has happened that the prophet could have no way of knowing, except supernaturally through the Holy Spirit. Sometimes, a word of knowledge can lift people right out of the pit of despair. On other occasions, God uses it to build a series of steps so people can walk out of the pit themselves. It is the prophet's job to know the difference, and to know what God wants to do in the word of knowledge He gives us.

Words of knowledge, because they are so personal, can be intensely powerful. I remember prophesying over a man named Michael. God gave me a burden for him, but he was a complete wall. I was breaking up on the inside, but he looked like he was totally together.

"Father," I prayed internally, "what's the best way of speaking to this man's wall? If I just give him a word, it will rebound off of him. How do I reach him?"

Almost immediately, I felt the Holy Spirit tell me to ask him about his dad. I put my hand on Michael's shoulder and asked him about his father. Suddenly, unexpectedly, almost unbelievably, the wall fell. Michael choked with

> *Prophecy is not just what we say, but how we say it*

tears and began to sob. It was as if God pressed a button in his heart, one only He knew existed.

"Michael," I said, "I have a picture of you when you were six years old. Your dad has made a kite for you. He made it in his shed at the bottom of your garden, and he spent a long time on it. Your dad was a perfectionist and he gave you the kite for your birthday. It wasn't really what you wanted but you liked it. Still, your response wasn't what he wanted — he wanted you to be excited about it after all the hours he had put in on it. You went outside to try it, but you were kind of clumsy as a child. I see you tripping over your own feet and putting a hole through the kite. Your dad was livid; he stood you up against a wall and began to tell you a number of negative statements." I recounted some of those phrases to him and watched as he completely broke down. The dam had broken in his life through the word of knowledge.

At that point, people around us began to jump in with words of encouragement and Scripture that fit with what I was saying. I quieted them down because I knew there was more God wanted to take hold of. Sometimes, in our humanity, we want to rebuild a person too quickly. When there's a crack in a wall, God may want to scoop more than just the surface out. Prophetic people need to look at the whole battle, not just the first shot.

After a few minutes, Michael began to calm down. During that time, I had been praying and asking God what He wanted to do next. At the age

MARIA WOODWORTH-ETTER

Lived: 1844 to 1924

Prophetic Synopsis: Maria Woodworth-Etter was barely a teenager when God spoke to her: "I heard the voice of Jesus calling me to go out in the highways and hedges and gather in the lost sheep." Still, Maria married a man who did not believe in women in ministry. Five of their six children died young, even as God continually called Maria to preach.

All of the death and all of the wrestling with God pushed Maria into the Bible. She read every word, trying to find some meaning for her life. As she read, she saw examples of women — like Mary, Deborah, Esther, Miriam, Hulda, Anna, Priscilla and others — being used by God to do unbelievable things.

One day, Maria looked up from the Bible and prayed: "Lord, I can't preach. I don't know what to say and I don't have any education." At that instant, God gave her a vision that electrified her life: "I thought I would go through a course of study and prepare for work, thinking the Lord would make my husband and people willing in some way to let me go out and work ... The dear Saviour stood by me one night in a vision and talked to me face to face ... Jesus said 'You can tell people what the Lord has done for your soul; tell of the glory of God and the love of Jesus.'"

Woodworth-Etter did exactly that. At age thirty-five, she began her ministry, preaching, prophesying, and healing the sick. She was famous for falling into Spirit-induced trances while speaking. She would simply stop moving, and God's presence would fill the room as people waited for her to "come to." Her gift of healing was so incredible that she was twice charged with practicing medicine without a licence.

Key Comment: "Let us not plead weakness; God will use the weak things of the world to confuse the wise. We are sons and daughters of the Most High God. Should we not honour our high calling and do all we can to save those who sit in the valley and shadow of death?"

Sources: Stanley Burgess and Gary McGee, editors. *Dictionary of Pentecostal and Charismatic Movements.* (Grand Rapids, MI: Zondervan, 1996). Roberts Liardon, *God's Generals.* (Tulsa, OK: Albury Publishing, 1996).

of six, a curse had been put on this man's life. Being a victim as a child followed him into adulthood.

I then had a second word of knowledge for Michael. I saw him in a room with three other men. These men were all shaking their fingers at him, telling him "You've missed it, you're out of the will of God, you're going to lose your way, you're going to be ineffective."

The Lord showed me that he had been part of a leadership team that disagreed over what they felt God was calling them to do. The three men didn't want to go where Michael was suggesting. The men wanted to play it safe; Michael wanted to take a risk for Christ. My heart went out to him. While God is completely safe as far as His character and love goes, He is a risk-taker in vision. He is not safe in who He calls or what He wants to do. He asks us to accomplish the impossible.

In that instant, God showed me how He wanted to reach out to Michael.

"Michael, God wants you to know you haven't missed it," I whispered to him. "Those three men were wrong. What they told you four years ago was wrong. God says, 'Son, you haven't missed it.'" This time, the dam burst at an even greater level. We almost needed to mop the floor, he cried so hard. As he wept and wept, I turned him over to the people who had words of affirmation and comfort.

Prophets must listen to the heartbeat of God at all times. We can never assume that He is finished working in a person. God loves to lavish His love on people, pouring Himself into them. What He wants is for us to pursue love for each person we meet. We are not called to pursue our own gifting or ministry, but to pursue the love of God for ourselves and other people. By learning how to be sensitive to the Holy Spirit, we learn how to be sensitive to those around us.

> *True prophecy binds up the enemy, not people*

After finishing with Michael, we felt that God wanted to do something in the rest of his family. We asked Marion, his wife, to come up to the stage. The whole room was euphoric — they could see and feel the presence of God. After the two words of knowledge for Michael, I knew logically that his wife would have suffered with him through the past several years. It wasn't prophetic; it was common sense.

I asked God if there was anything He wanted to help her through. The time with Michael had been so powerful that my spirit was wide open to what God was saying. His whisper felt like a shout in my bones. He showed me that twelve years before, she had a traumatic experience while giving birth to their only child. She had severe post-natal depression, went through a period of mental instability, and had spent eight years on medication. Plus she has problems with her self-image. To be honest, that was more than I wanted to know. What could I do with that kind of information? I couldn't just relay it and totally humiliate the woman. It would have destroyed her.

"What do I do, Father?" I prayed. "How do I handle this?" In my heart, I knew it was important that she speak because she was going to have to be part of the process of healing. God wanted to bring healing to the very roots of who she was.

"Marion," I said carefully, "that was a really traumatic birth you had twelve years ago, wasn't it?" She began to cry almost immediately. I asked the Lord to show me how she was feeling so I could put things in a way that would release her, not shatter her. "God knows how you felt at the time — alone, frightened, misunderstood. You couldn't break out of the spiral you were in. Lots of people prayed for you and gave you Scriptures, prophesies, and when you didn't get any better, they blamed it on the demonic."

It was like peeling an onion; every layer brought her closer and closer to healing. I kept away from the issues that would have humiliated her, but she knew that God knew them. The people around her hadn't understood her pain. They had judged her based on the surface instead of getting inside the pain she had felt.

That day, all I did was what those Christians around her should have done all those years before — asked God to let me inside her pain. The loss of knowing her first child would be her last and the grief of being misunderstood and judged.

"Do you think you could let go of all that?" I asked her. "Could you forgive the people who didn't understand?" She began to forgive, even as I asked God for a word of prophecy. Until that point, I had been operating out of the word of knowledge. Now I wanted to see if God had something for her future.

> *Prophecy confirms what God has done, is doing, and will do!*

"I want you to tell her she was healed four years ago," the Lord said to me.

"Really?" I replied. "What do you mean?"

"The enemy has robbed her of her healing for four years," He said. "She has been healed — she just has to acknowledge the truth."

"Okay," I said. "How did You heal her?"

"I healed her when those men blasted her husband," God explained. "He went right down the tubes for almost nine months and was completely depressed. She saw the pain and grief he was going through and made a conscious decision to take herself off the tranquilizers. She ran the house

Three Phases Of Revelation

again, kept everything in line, prayed, and was a strong partner to him during that awful period. I allowed some things to happen in her husband's life because it was the point where his wife was healed. But she has been under this low self-esteem for so long that she has never acknowledged the fact she is doing well. From the day her husband began to slide, she has carried the family. Graham, she doesn't need prayer for healing, she needs to be told, 'You're healed, and this is the evidence.'"

I looked at her and said, "Marion, God has given me a word for you." As I recounted what God had shown me, the lights went on in her mind like they do when one enters a dark house and flips a switch. She finally saw the evidence of God's healing.

"The enemy has got a part of your mind convinced that nothing has happened," I said, "but the reality of your life bears out something much different."

A grin spread across Marion's face as her spirit witnessed to what God was saying.

"Yeah, yeah, you're right," she said. "I am healed." At that precise moment, things broke loose in the spiritual realm. She was healed by acknowledging the truth of what the enemy had hid from her. She was delivered and restored. Suddenly, she had all of the power, strength, worth, and value in the world. Scales had dropped from her eyes and she could see that God had done something incredible.

The prophetic is not about the prophet, but about God and putting His love into people's hearts. We must never parade what we know in the spirit. The essential quality after love that we need is humility — a desire to have only Christ be seen in us. Prophets must think through their styles and find one that does not distract from the power of God's message. Sensitivity to the Lord is the basis for all prophecy.

Operating In Prophecy

Having a desire to prophesy is half the battle, as Paul taught in 1 Corinthians 14:1 — *"Pursue love, and desire spiritual gifts, especially that you may prophesy."* In some situations, I have been tired or hungry and not in the mood to prophesy. At those moments, I have heard God tell me to "stir up my spirit."

"I'm tired," I say.

"Son, have a desire, because if you have a desire, I can work," He answers. Before I know it, I have forgotten about the fatigue and I am doing what

God wants. We need to look for prophecy, expecting and wanting it to be a part of our lives.

Desire leads us to the next attitude every prophet needs: expectancy. If we are going to move in any spiritual gift, we need to have a sense of expectation. I expect God to do something today. I don't want to live an hour without expectation. There is nothing worse than realizing, on Friday night, that we have drifted through a whole week without having a meaningful conversation or moment with God. When I wake up in the morning, I want to have an expectation that God is going to do something that very day.

Expectation is all-important. The heroes of the faith listed in this book all expected God to do something with them. Expectation was the common thread in all of their lives, even though their ministries spanned two millennia and a dozen different cultures. They believed God would speak to them, and through them, every day.

Expectancy is the lifeblood of moving in the Spirit. We are all pregnant with purpose. When we live as divine carriers of the life of Christ then we develop an attitude, a mindset and a heart response that flows from that inner life source.

The secret place of our spirit always acts as a womb to birth in us the seed of the next part of our life journey and ministry. What new thing is growing in you today? What partnership with the Holy Spirit is required to bring that expectation to full term and delivery?

Several years ago, I believe the Lord spoke to me about moving in the gift of prophecy everyday. He was trying to grow in me a greater expectation in the Holy Spirit. I haven't been perfect in that call, but the practice of expectancy has sharpened the gift and broadened my vision for the prophetic considerably.

> *Move in what you have permission for and prepare for the next thing God is birthing in you!*

When I want to move in prophecy, I believe that God can speak into a situation. I expect God to speak into a person's life. This leads into the next step in operating in the prophecy: believing that God is going to speak through us. "Lord, anoint my eyes, ears, and mouth," we pray. With our minds, we should believe we have the mind of Christ, as Paul wrote in 1 Corinthians 2:16. If I have the choice, I want to dismantle my way of thinking and adopt God's instead. I want to think how Jesus thinks, because God's Spirit knows what is in God's mind, and that same Spirit dwells in us. Total wisdom, total knowledge, total understanding are available from God to us, and I want to tap into them.

After desire and expectation comes a specific burden for someone, some-where, or something. When we expect God to use us to prophesy, we look around for the person whom God wants to touch. Before opening our mouth, we need to pray for that individual, asking God for His burden for them. Prophets must be concerned for that person: "Lord, please speak to her… and if I can help that process, I am willing." Nothing in the prophetic is scarier than having someone prophesy over you without feeling an ounce of concern or love for you.

It is burden which reveals God's heart. When we have a burden for something and we're praying, the Holy Spirit enables us to begin to put that into words. We start to feel that God wants to say and do something. This brings us into a sense of conviction, and it is conviction which produces expression. When we're convinced that God wants to say something, the desire, will, and means to express it all fall into place.

The expression can vary. Sometimes, I may pick people out in a meeting setting and ask them to stand. Other times, God may get me to pick people out, and I will ask them to come to the front of the room. At this point, I may not have received any prophetic words for them, but I have a sense of burden and expectation that God wants to do something. I call them out while asking God, "what do You want to do?" As I pray over the first person, the gift begins to flow, and God does something amazing.

We take that kind of risk because we expect God to move. We expect Him to show up. Therefore, when we go into places with expectation, there is a high probability that we will move in the prophetic gift. We need to antici-pate what God wants to do and choose to work with Him to accomplish it.

God gives us a burden about things because He wants to speak and act. As far as He is concerned, a burden is a declaration to us that He wants to speak through us and use us in this situation. He has chosen us to work with Him because He has a burden for that particular person. This is a rare, and welcome, privilege for any of us.

> *Expectation is: It's going to rain, sell your umbrella!*

Again, those steps are: desire, expectation, burden, conviction, and expression. We can stir up the gift of prophecy by having the right motives. When we want to see a person blessed, healed, restored, and released, we are sharing the heart of God. We have put ourselves into the place where God can use us.

All of us can prophesy; the gift of prophecy is resident in each of us. We may not be called to be prophets, but every one of us can prophesy, and I hope we will seek that gift out more.

Starting Where You Are

Prophets need to allow God to push them into the revelatory. Sometimes, it is good to start at a low point. If we have had a difficult day, it is not wise to start with a massive prophetic word. We ought to start where our level of faith is at and build from there.

> God is the same in and out of season

Praying for people is a wonderful way to build our own sense of expectation. Once we start praying for someone, it is a short jump into the prophetic, because the two disciplines use the same faculties. When we ask God what we should pray, the Holy Spirit answers us. Suddenly, our spirits feel as though we should be praying something else, and we jump from prayer into the prophetic.

On days where our expectancy needs to be built up, we should not allow ourselves to be placed under incredible pressure. We should start small. If we feel low, start low: God doesn't mind, and He will build us up. In the twinkle of an eye, He can lead us into revelation.

We must start where we can. The last meeting we were in may have been a high point of revelation, but that doesn't mean we can come in at the same level every time. Sometimes we do, and sometimes we don't. A lot can happen between meetings. We need to allow God to push us into the supernatural.

I once met with thirty pastors in Germany, and delivered an incredibly detailed, personal prophetic word to each of them. It was a high point of anointing: as soon as I finished with one, I picked up with another. The Lord was phenomenal that day — it had nothing to do with me.

The next morning, I was exhausted after a terrible night's sleep. Suddenly, I didn't have faith for anything any more. So I started from scratch, just praying for people. I know that as long as I can pray, I can prophesy. My faith may be low, but it is never a problem for God.

We cannot maintain the high spots. There is a reason why Jesus led the disciples off the mountain after the Transfiguration. We can't live at that high level all the time. Our role is to be ourselves, and to be loved by God. As long as we are loved by Him, we can feel a burden for someone else.

We cannot operate from a continuous flow of the Spirit. For every flow there has to be an ebb in our experience.

What we do in the ebb is just as important as what we do in the flow. We learn Lordship in the valley and the mountain. He is Lord of every life experience. Nothing prevents Him from being God. We must experience Him in the depths as well as the heights. We must learn to be a contribution when everything is against us.

When I prophesy out of my own low places of life there is no diminishing of power. The Spirit is the same. The release of anointing and the impact of the Spirit may be different but no less real and full of truth. Humility comes to our aid at times like this. Be sure to keep your life on the altar. The Lord will set fire to the sacrifice we offer Him.

We don't always have to hear God in the moment, either. He can speak to us ahead of time about what we will face, who we will meet, and what we should do. Once, while preparing for a tour of America, God gave me almost two hundred prophetic words for people before leaving England. I wrote them all down in my journal — what people would be wearing, the color of their hair, their glasses, even where they would be sitting. He had messages for each of them.

At one point in the tour, I felt terrible. I hadn't slept well for a few nights, and had come to a church which was bursting with expectancy. Of course, I felt like death warmed over. My faith, my confidence, my life: it was all on the floor. As all eyes turned to look at me, I just told God I could pray for one person, and hopefully that would build enough faith in me to pray for another. "What should I do, Lord?" I asked.

"Just read to them out of the book," He said. I opened up my journal and looked around the room. Sure enough, the first guy was there, wearing a dark blazer just like God had shown me. So I picked him out and prophesied. Over that conference, I think I did all of the people out of that book. God had provided for them and for me because He is relentlessly kind. He knew the warfare that would surround me on this particular tour and made arrangements beforehand to be with me in the pressure and support my personal fragility. That's His nature.

How Does Prophecy Come?

All of us have a distinctive language with God, and a unique way of how revelation comes to us. As we grow in the prophetic, we learn how our own gift manifests itself most often.

VISIONS. Sometimes, revelation comes through visions, pictures, or even moving scenes. Many of us have probably had a picture that has sparked something in us. Generally, there are two types of vision.

First, there is the *unremarkable vision* that uses everyday things around us, and maybe even uses our own understanding of things to speak prophetically. In Jeremiah 1:11–12, we witness this kind of vision: *"Moreover, the word of the Lord came to me, saying, 'Jeremiah, what do you see?' And I said, 'I see the branch of an almond tree.' Then the Lord said to me, 'You have seen well, for I am ready to perform My word.'"* When God asked the prophet what he saw, Jeremiah looked around and noticed the almond tree branch. It was a perfectly common and ordinary sight, totally unremarkable. However, the interpretation, timing, and specific need of the people combined to produce a positive and significant prophetic contribution.

There are times when we can use our own human knowledge with the picture we have been given. I was once in a meeting of several hundred people, about to speak, when the Lord directed me to a young woman in the middle aisle. I asked her to stand up, and as she did, God showed me a picture of a hazel tree. I knew the type of tree because my father and I had been landscape gardeners. All I had was this picture, so I asked the Lord, "What do You want to say?" There was nothing. I started in with what I knew: "I'm seeing a picture of a hazel tree," and began to describe its properties from what I could remember from my training.

"It's got beautiful flowers and fruit," I said. "It can grow almost anywhere, it's resistant to disease, and its bark and flowers can be used for medicinal purposes as a tonic or a sedative that brings comfort from pain. It's very hardy and resilient."

> *God's super compliments our natural*

As soon as I came to the end of that statement, I knew what God wanted to do. "That's how God sees you," I continued, "He thinks you're beautiful and that you're going to bear good fruit in your life. You mustn't be worried that you're no good; you're tough and able to resist the enemy. You'll grow in almost any situation." As I moved prophetically, she cried and her friends cheered and laughed.

I finished prophesying, prayed for her, and taught my seminar. At the end of the meeting, she came to me.

"Thanks for what you said. You don't know this, but my name is Hazel," she told me. Apparently, that same afternoon, she and her friends had been drinking tea, and Hazel had been in a bad mood. "Hazel. Stupid name, Hazel," she had said. "Why couldn't I have been called by a prettier name? I hate it, and I wish I could change it."

God, in His incredible sense of humor, had picked her out and given me a vision of a hazel tree. "Excuse Me," He was saying, "but I chose your name. I gave it to you, and I gave it to you for this purpose." She told me that she had cried because she realized that her name had been given to her for a reason. When she was in the womb, God had named her Hazel. What a powerful word from a perfectly ordinary and common source.

Second, a vision can be *supernatural*, rather than unremarkable. Acts 10 recounts the story of two men. One was a Greek who was devout, kind, trustworthy. God chose to reveal Himself to this man in a sovereign way. The other man was a Jew who was loud, impetuous, and racist. God wanted to put Cornelius and Peter together, but how? How could He unite them when they were separated by such a religious, national, and cultural divide — especially in the heart of one man who had been taught separatism from birth?

God chose to minister a supernatural vision to Peter in order to unlock what had become a form of national prejudice in his heart. He was given a vision of a sheet lowered from Heaven, holding a full variety of edible species. A voice said, *"Arise, Peter, kill and eat."*

> *Do not look to the past for signs of God when He is doing a new thing*

Peter's first reaction was typical for his life: "I can't do that because these things are unholy, unclean, and I've never done that sort of thing in my life." God's voice boomed: *"What God has cleansed you must not call common."* It happened three times, leaving Peter totally bewildered. What on earth did the vision mean? He had no interpretation for it, but while he was meditating on it, the Holy Spirit gave him some instructions.

"Behold three men are seeking you," the Spirit said. *"Arise therefore, go down with them, doubting nothing; for I have sent them."* Peter went with the men to Cornelius's house, preached the Gospel, watched as the Holy Spirit fell on those men, and saw a completely new kind of church be born.

Sometimes we can get pictures that have a prophetic interpretation. Some are diagnostic in the sense that they give us information about things. Others may lead us into a word of knowledge, telling us something that has happened or is currently under way. When we receive a vision like that, our first step is to ask, "Father, in light of this, what is it You want to say?" Do not speak out the first thing you receive, because it may be diagnostic and could result in us prophesying a problem, not an answer.

If we practice the art of waiting quietly, perhaps just for a few moments before we open our mouth to prophesy, we may glorify God more in the delivery and save ourselves some considerable heartache. Most mistakes in prophecy occur because we rush in with what we believe God is saying while He may still be speaking.

We can also receive revelation through *moving pictures*, like a movie screen. We will see a portion of a scene, like the one I recounted earlier in this book of the adulterous husband, his redheaded secretary, and the Connaught Hotel. I saw them walk into the hotel together, check in, receive a room key, and get into the elevator. This was a moving picture.

The Purpose of Visions:

It is not my intention to do more than give a thumbnail sketch at this moment regarding visions. In a later book in the series we shall look at the phenomenon of visions, dreams, dark sayings and mysteries in greater detail. If you wish to follow up your understanding of visions, the following are some useful scriptures.

- To bring encouragement. To stir up hope regarding the promises of the Lord. Genesis 15:1–6.
- To proclaim the calling of another. Luke 1:22.
- The revelation of hidden things and interpreting of dreams. Daniel 2:19.
- To bring good news. Luke 24:23.
- For the sake of guiding people and instructing them on unfamiliar paths. Acts 9:10.
- To change a cultural mindset. Acts 10:9–16.
- To declare the will of God in mission. Acts 16:9–10.

> *When we know the purpose of something we can see the power in it*

DREAMS. Some people receive revelation through dreams. I don't sleep much, and I don't seem to dream. In fact, I can remember only two dreams in my life, but they were both very significant.

Numbers 12:6 provides a Biblical precedent for prophetic dreams: *"Then He said, 'Hear now My words: If there is a prophet among you, I, the LORD, make Myself known to him in a vision; I speak to him in a dream.'"* The Bible is full of examples of how God speaks in dreams. God spoke to Pharaoh in a dream only Joseph could interpret. The same thing happened with Nebuchadnezzar, and only Daniel could understand it. Joseph had a dream about Mary: the angel said, "Marry the girl!" That dream changed his mind because he was doubtful about the pregnancy before it (Matthew 1). The so-called three wise men were warned in a dream to avoid King Herod. Later on, Joseph had another dream instructing him to take Mary and Jesus to Egypt. These were very practical, very prophetic dreams.

Dream interpretation is a gift produced by meditating on the dreams we have had, and asking God for His take on them. *"Daniel had understanding in all visions and dreams,"* says Daniel 1:17. One of my closest friends has a gift of interpreting dreams. If you are a dreamer, you need to write down your dreams, and work through them with God. Open them up for comment and prayer — they may be for you or for someone else. It may or may not be relevant, and a few weeks down the road, you may want to put it on the shelf. Get in the habit of writing things down; treat a dream as you would a prophecy.

The Purpose of Dreams.

These scripture references may be helpful in determining a deeper purpose for dreams than has been outlined here. A future book is planned to look at this in some detail. However these are the scriptures to get you started on your journey of understanding dreams and interpretation.

- Proclamation regarding a future event or promise. Genesis 28:12–15.
- To declare guidance and provide interpretation. Genesis 31:10.
- Declare a purpose. Genesis 31:24.
- To prepare us for the future, using foreknowledge of an event or circumstance. Genesis 40:5.
- To provide warnings of future events. Genesis 41:1–7.
- Releasing confirmation to encourage another. Judges 7:13–14.
- Future pronouncements. Daniel chapter 2.
- Future revelation. Daniel chapter 7.
- For encouragement in difficult circumstances. Matthew 1:19–21.
- To expose the purpose of the enemy. Matthew 1:19–21.

There are obviously more. The storyline around these instances will help to provide a framework for the context in which to understand each element.

SEEING WORDS. Revelation can also come by seeing one or two words over people. I have seen words such as "faith" and "healing" appear on someone's forehead. Those words alert us that God wants to say something and that He has marked a person's life with something He wants to reveal.

When we see a word, we can step back into our spirit and ask God what He wants to say. Into that quietness, God can drop a prophetic word. That first vital word activates our spirits; usually, it triggers a conceptual understanding of what the Holy Spirit wants to say. For example, seeing the word, "healing," over someone can cause us to ask questions such as:

> *We grow by asking questions*

- Is it healing for themselves?
- Is it healing for a family member or someone close to them?
- Does it indicate a healing gift will operate in their church?
- Is the Lord moving the individual into a healing gift?
- Is the Lord calling forth a full-on healing ministry?

As we ask the Lord questions in our spirits, the concept of where and how healing will be released will become clear. We can then aim the word in the right direction.

It is the same principle with less definitive words such as "peace." A prophet believes that the Holy Spirit wants to speak a genuine word of peace into the life of an individual. Where? How? Why? Peace into what area? What turmoil exists that needs peace to overcome it? Is it peace for financial worries, employment difficulties, relational problems, health issues, or something else? Where do we aim a word like that? To what area does the Lord wish to bring peace?

Our hearts must be on the same wavelength as God's, or we lose valuable perspective and power. The Bible teaches us that we have a High Priest, Jesus, who can be touched by the feeling of our infirmities. He is in tune with our feelings. In prophecy, we are seeking to communicate the spirit of the word, not just an abstract concept. A prophecy should impact a person's spirit, not just his or her mind.

Sometimes God uses a sentence or phrase that we picked up elsewhere and for some reason stays in our mind or memory. The Holy Spirit may use it as a catalyst when He wants to speak to someone. It could be something we read, heard on TV or the radio and the Spirit brings it back to our remembrance.

One sentence I heard when praying for a woman was "Carry on doing on earth what in heaven you are famous for". It obviously begs the question: "What is she famous for in heaven?" I saw a picture of her dancing in a living room setting. The Father showed me that she had danced as part of her devotional in worship but now she was older had discontinued this form of private intimacy. The Lord wanted her to know that He loved it; she blessed Him by doing it and He wished for her to continue.

> *God loves both the revealed and the proceeding word that He speaks!*

SCRIPTURE. The Bible can be an aid to prophecy. The Holy Spirit makes scripture come alive to us in a variety of ways. By personal messages; specific instruction; the revealing of God's essential nature; the process of truth and good teaching on the doctrines and tenets of spirituality and faith. He loves to prophetically inspire us also and will use the bible to lift a curtain on an aspect of our future relationship and walk with God. He will use scripture to act as a catalyst for the prophetic word to present a particular message to someone. Often I have given prophecy from a passage of Scripture. Verses pop into our hearts, and suddenly the prophetic spirit begins to move on it.

I prayed for a man once who worked within a very politically-motivated group. People hated him because he was a Spirit-filled Christian. The knives were out; people were altering his work, hiding memos, and being obstructive in every possible way. They wanted him out and a friend of theirs in. The pressure on him was building, and he began to wonder if he was even supposed to be at his job.

As we prayed, God gave me Psalm 35. When I read it, I felt stirred up because it was all about fighting against the enemy, taking hold of the armor, believing that God is our salvation, having angels on our side, and turning those against us into confusion and dishonor. I put the Bible down and prophesied out of that psalm.

A short time later, several of his main antagonists were prosecuted for fraud, drug abuse, and mismanagement of funds. They were fired. Three Spirit-filled Christians took their place. That prophecy was a vital word to stand, fight, and see the salvation of God come.

IMPRESSIONS. God is at work in the small things as befits someone who absolutely has no ego, just a compelling sense of who He is and what He wants to be for His people. He loves the big picture but knows that the real power in something always lies in the attention to detail. He invites us into His world through the small things.

He never announces Himself. He tells you that He will come and invites you to wait for Him. Most of our inherent spirituality is waiting on the Lord. It is in learning how to attend on Him. This is not passive waiting only. We can wait on God on the busiest day. It is a subtle lifting of the heart in thanksgiving or worship.

Love the cheeriness of the Holy Spirit!

It is the beautiful habit of rejoicing, finding joy in the Father in everything. It is in the practice of God consciousness in our thinking. Allowing our heart to be filled with the wonder of Him. In living a simple life of astonishment at His continual goodness. It is in developing a certainty in the kindness of God. It is loving the laughter and cheeriness of the Holy Spirit. It is in being wrapped in the power of grace that is in the Lord Jesus. Eyes filling with tears at the thought of His sacrifice. It is in

SMITH WIGGLESWORTH

Lived: 1859 to 1947

Prophetic Synopsis: Few evangelists have pushed the kind of religious buttons Smith Wigglesworth pushed. His methods seem bizarre, but the fruit from his life and ministry are profound.

Wigglesworth's wife, Polly, was a powerful preacher, but Smith was painfully shy. He hated to speak in public, until the day the Holy Spirit got a hold of him. In 1907, he received the gift of tongues and was a changed man. As he preached that first Sunday, his wife was stunned: "That's not my Smith... What's happened to the man?" What had happened was a touch from God: "God once said to me, 'Wigglesworth, I'm going to burn you up till there's no Wigglesworth left; only Jesus will be seen.'"

His message was simple. "There are four principles we need to maintain: First, read the Word of God. Second, consume the Word of God until it consumes you. Third, Believe the Word of God. Fourth, act on the Word of God." It was the way he acted on the Word of God that offended religious-spirited people. The stories of his healings are legendary.

There was the time he kicked a deformed baby across the stage. When the child landed, it was whole. Another time, a frail, crippled woman came up for prayer. Wigglesworth was impatient with her so he commanded her to walk. The woman stumbled around for a few moments, until the evangelist walked up behind her and pushed her. She fell forward into a run and Wigglesworth followed her up the aisle, shouting "Run, woman, run!" She ran all right — right out of the building, but completely healed! On another occasion, Wigglesworth punched a man — wearing a hospital gown — who was suffering from cancer. When he got up, he was healed. "I don't hit people, I hit the devil. If they get in the way, I can't help it. You can't deal gently with the devil, nor comfort him; he likes comfort," he said

During his ministry, Smith Wigglesworth raised twenty-three people from the dead, including his own wife. He attributed his success to one person: God. "I know the Lord laid His hand on me. Filled! A flowing, quickening, moving flame of God."

Key Comment: "Only believe. Fear looks, faith jumps."

Sources: Stanley Burgess and Gary McGee, editors. *Dictionary of Pentecostal and Charismatic Movements.* (Grand Rapids, MI: Zondervan, 1996). Roberts Liardon, *God's Generals.* (Tulsa, OK: Albury Publishing, 1996).

cherishing the life; the freedom and the dependency on His Name and Nature.

There are many ways to remain in abiding in the Lord. To dwell, stay and remain in the place of love favor and expectation of His Presence. Into this lifestyle the Father drops His still small voice caressing our hearts with a whisper. His touch is powerful yet so faint we could easily miss it if we are not practicing His Presence.

An impression is a finger touch from God. It is an inkling, a notion, a tiny idea in the back of our mind or the forefront of our heart. It is a rabbit trail that leads to a goat track which becomes a pathway leading to a street, then a road which develops into a highway which becomes a freeway and the interstate right into His throne room.

God loves Jerusalem but chooses to begin something in a Bethlehem. He loves a huge palace but births something in a stable. He likes king size four poster beds but loves to put something precious in a cows feeding trough. He is easily overlooked.

When we contemplate hearing from God we can think of angels as messenger spirits; prophets with all the drama that unfolds around them; signs as big as a billboard. We don't think of whispers; faint touches; notions and ideas that form in the quietness of our hearts. We don't understand the pleasure that God finds in whispering. The joy that He has in a slight caress of our heart.

When we practice the joy in waiting on Him our hearts become attuned to the slightest possibility of His coming. He comes like a lion, not in roaring with power, but in stealth. A velvet whisper of sound so slight only your own stillness can detect it. One time in Africa I was in a hide at night with a hunter guide, waiting for a lion to show up at a kill. Armed with a night

Impressions engage our hearts with the Lord

sight we waited through a cold African night. We had chained part of a fresh buffalo kill in the lower branches of a tree. For hours we waited. My eyelids grew heavy. Several times my friend nudged me back to wakefulness.

I soaked my bandana in water scrubbing my face, willing myself to stay awake. At the moment I was convinced our vigil had been fruitless my guide whispered in my ear. "He is here!"

I looked through my night sight binoculars and could see nothing. I knew my guide would not point him out to me, that was not our agreement. I wanted to seek the lion out for myself. I wanted to develop the patience in waiting, the stillness in being watchful. I looked carefully. Using each square foot as a grid, I tested everything; looking for something that looked right but did not belong. Listening is like that. Isolating a certain sound from all the noises of life.

I saw the grass moving ever so slightly and realized it was in contradiction to the wind. I looked in the top part of the grass and eventually could see a shadow and then finally the tip of his ear as he settled down a few yards from the kill. He was testing the wind himself, looking for something that did not belong. I held my breath, willing my body into the comfort of stillness. We waited for what seemed like an hour or so but in reality was about twenty minutes. Suddenly he was there! In full view, huge, majestic, wild.

I drank in the sight of him. I gorged on his form, watching him eat. His strong teeth tearing at the meat. The sounds of his eating filling the night. Then just as suddenly, he was gone. An empty chain and flattened grass the only witnesses to his every having been present.

The sound of his coming and going were so slight that his visitation took on dream form.

So like God. Silent, present, still... to people who train themselves in quietness, worship and peace. The Father loves stillness and quietness. The Holy Spirit is so patient and diligent to train us in peace and the art of tranquility. The calm joyfulness that waits with simplicity. He will come.

An impression in this context, is an arresting thought, that says STOP, WAIT, CONSIDER THIS! It is a flag on the play of life that says stop, go back, you have missed something. It is an inner conviction that god is near, that He is brooding over our circumstances. We feel His peace before we hear His sound. It is a witness within that provokes us to wait. We tune in knowing He will speak. His voice can be strong or faint that does not matter. The important thing is we have tuned in through our inner quietness.

Impressions lead to experiences that may use our emotions. Sometimes I have looked at someone in the spirit and have had a sense of looking back whilst feeling pain or anguish. Silently I can breathe out my inner question to the Holy Spirit. "What happened in the past that was so traumatic for him?" Then I wait for the next piece; and the next; and the one after. Each piece of revelation the Holy Spirit releases can arrive in our heart with a progressively stronger sound carrying with it a powerful conviction not only about the diagnosis but also about the intentionality of what the Father has for this individual... now!

Moments of release and power can be so huge that they are out of all proportion to the initial reception, the first whisper.

Sometimes too, the initial contact and the final release are both slight, faint and seemingly innocuous. There seems to be no impact on the individual we minister to in prophecy. We may as well have just read out a shopping list over them. There is no visible reaction or response, just… nothing.

(The temptation here is to go further in prophecy than you should; just to get a response. Now you are prophesying for yourself; for your own reputation. So that others present can see your anointing).

People respond differently to prophecy. Whilst some respond verbally and visibly others may do a passable imitation of a brick wall!

Some people show you nothing, it does not mean that nothing has happened. Several days later we discover that the impact was absolutely enormous! Alternatively we find out later that everything is amazingly different but there was no evidence of power and breakthrough. It was all like a silent movie but unmistakably the hand of God. He seldom works as we would wish. I have learned just to ask for His Presence, never to dictate how He should come.

Sometimes I have felt myself looking forward and feeling joy or peace. I realize that the Lord is about to release something in the gap between where a person is currently and the person that is emerging next in their relationship with the Father.

The Lord uses impressions relationally. It is one of His ways to engage our hearts in conversation and dialogue. We ask questions so that we may explore His heart for this person. It is in what we feel that God is feeling for this individual that the real power of prophecy is earthed. God uses our hearts to indicate the passion of His intentionality. Every human being has three major needs. The need to be loved; to belong; and to be significant.

Impressions connect with our emotions

Prophecy becomes an impartation when we feel what God is feeling for someone. The strength of His intentionality as seen in Jeremiah 29:11 becomes the driving force behind the prophecy we release.

> "For I know the plans that I have for you," declares the LORD, "plans for welfare and not for calamity to give you a future and a hope. Then you will call upon Me and come and pray to Me, and I will listen to you. You will seek Me and find Me when you search for Me with all your heart. I will be found by you," declares the LORD, "and I will restore your fortunes and will gather you from all the nations and from all the places where I have driven you," declares the LORD, "and I will bring you back to the place from where I sent you into exile."

The goodness of God initiates something wonderful in our hearts. His intentionality is thrilling! When we connect with it, our hearts soar and we are compelled to call on His name. Intentionality breeds faith. We are designed by the Creator to respond to His advances. It is in our DNA. It is part of our Christlike nature that the Holy Spirit is developing in us. When we feel the weight of the Father's intention, we want to be intentional too! As He is, so are we in this world.

His intentions towards us are incredible. His delight and desire for us, sets us free to pursue Him. We all want to be with people who want to be with us. We joyfully go where we are celebrated. God's intentionality forms a desire in me to call on Him; to come, pray and listen to Him because I know that I am so welcome!

The Lord originates everything!

My capacity to become wholehearted is never generated from my own efforts. We receive from the Lord what He most wants us to become!

Or WHO HAS FIRST GIVEN TO HIM THAT IT MIGHT BE PAID BACK TO HIM AGAIN? For from Him and through Him and to Him are all things To Him be the glory forever. Amen. (Romans 11:35–36)

Every good thing given and every perfect gift is from above, coming down from the Father of lights, with whom there is no variation or shifting shadow. (James 1:17)

John answered and said, "A man can receive nothing unless it has been given him from heaven. (John 3:27)

Yet for us there is but one God, the Father, from whom are all things and we exist for Him; and one Lord, Jesus Christ, by whom are all things, and we exist through Him. (1 Corinthians 8:6)

For as the woman originates from the man, so also the man has his birth through the woman; and all things originate from God. (1 Corinthians 11:12)

For by Him all things were created, both in the heavens and on earth, visible and invisible, whether thrones or dominions or rulers or authorities — all things have been created through Him and for Him. He is before all things, and in Him all things hold together. (Colossians 1:16–17)

For it was fitting for Him, for whom are all things, and through whom are all things, in bringing many sons to glory, to perfect the author of their salvation through sufferings. (Hebrews 2:10)

No longer do I call you slaves, for the slave does not know what his master is doing; but I have called you friends, for all things that I have heard from My Father I have made known to you. (John 15:15)

In this is love, not that we loved God, but that He loved us and sent His Son to be the propitiation for our sins. We love, because He first loved us. (1 John 4:10, 19)

Everything originates in God! We are His beloved. Only God can love God. It takes God to love God. The love of God comes to our hearts as part of a great cycle of intentionality. We receive His love; it touches; affects; influences and changes us. Then we give back to the Lord the very love that He gave us in the first place.

We are empowered by the Holy Spirit to fulfill the first commandment simply because the Father Himself lives by the very same principles! We love Him because He first loved us. Everything comes down to us as a gift and we then give it back to God. In creation God uses the action of rainfall soaking the earth and then returning to heaven as the process of evaporation where clouds are replenished. Everything with God is cyclical, including the times and seasons.

Prophecy fits in with this cycle. It announces what the Lord will do and reveals our part in the process. Impressions are about asking questions and relating to the Holy Spirit in the moment.

Never launch out on an impression. Instead take it before God and allow the larger process to unfold in more revelation. If we move out too quickly we release blessing in measure rather than fullness. It is when we ask questions that the rabbit trail becomes a bigger pathway leading to a more powerful encounter.

The Holy Spirit is teaching us how to relax in God's intentionality, then how to respond to His advances. In prophecy we make people aware of God's intention and then enable them to receive and respond. Impressions are primarily for the giver not the receiver of prophecy. They bring us into a relationship with the Father that releases His heart, passion and total intention. We are moved by His nature. We are impacted ourselves and we seek to move out of what we are discovering of the goodness of God in the face of Jesus Christ.

Being Quiet Is Key

In 1 Kings 19:11–12, we read an interesting story of God interacting with his prophet, Elijah:

Then He said, "Go out, and stand on the mountain before the LORD." And behold, the LORD passed by, and a great and strong wind tore into the mountains and broke the rocks in pieces before the LORD, but the LORD was not in the wind; and after the wind an earthquake, but the LORD was not in the earthquake; and after the earthquake, a fire, but the LORD was not in the fire; and after the fire a still, small voice.

The voice of the Lord is like a whisper at times; it can be so soft that we strain to hear it. That's why being still and quiet is so important to prophecy. In the peace of God, revelation flows. There have been times when I have been so at rest that I've heard the whisper of God, turned to a person near me and said, "Can you hear that?" It's like He spoke out loud. If we have stillness on the inside, even the whisper of God sounds loud to us.

Too many Christians have no idea about the quietness of God. I remember working with some men in America for the first time. We were at a conference together, and I was just getting to know them. They were nice guys, and we sat in a hotel restaurant, talking and laughing. It was an ordinary, light-hearted conversation. After a while, they looked at me and said they had a word for me.

They laid their hands on me and yelled at me in perfect, King James English. They almost rubbed my head bald. They pushed me all over the place, shouting so loud they were spitting in my face. They were sending me to some country, somewhere, in their prophecy. It was awful.

"What are you doing?" I asked, stopping them in mid-sentence.

"What do you mean?" they said.

"What are you doing?" I repeated.

"We're prophesying over you," they said.

When we relax into God's intentionality we can respond to His advances

"I know that," I replied, "but I don't understand the funny language. Why were we having a conversation on one level and then we start praying and you speak in old King James English? Why are you trying to give me a migraine? And I had a shower this morning… why are you spitting all over me? I'm not deaf, but you're shouting at me. Please, I'm not trying to be rude or anything. I'm always ready to learn but I just don't understand this. Why do you have one way of speaking in life and another in ministry?

They couldn't think of a reason why. I kept going: "Okay, why put my head in a vice? Is there a reason? Because that was pretty painful. I have indentations on my skull." Again, they had no reason behind their actions.

"Why has your voice level gone up fifty decibels?" I continued. "It's unhygienic to spit on someone. I really appreciate your ministry but maybe you could change your approach. This one has left me really struggling and I can't understand a word you're saying."

I would have loved to have seen those three men come to my church in Southampton, UK, where I was living at the time. The place would have been rolling in laughter at the rudeness of their methods. My friends and church family would have howled.

After the prophecy, we had a conversation about it. I think we always need to de-mystify the prophetic. One of the problems with revelatory people is that they try to elevate it to an almost mystical connection with God. But God is sometimes so ordinary in His approach that we miss His voice.

Samuel almost missed God's voice in 1 Samuel 3. He heard the voice of God and thought it was Eli. Three times he heard the voice of God, and three times he thought it was Eli. Finally, Eli understood what was going on. *"Go lie down,"* he told the boy in 1 Samuel 3:9, *"and it shall be, if He calls you, that you must say, 'Speak, LORD, for Your servant hears.'"*

God's voice is ordinary and non-religious. There is nothing spooky about it. When we are speaking prophetically, we should invest our words with the heart of God. Our language should be normal and understandable, and as common with our usual style of conversation as possible.

> Father likes to come through the ordinary

A large percentage of prophecy is stating the obvious. God loves us, He cares for us. We shouldn't apologize if the word we have doesn't feel fresh or exotic. Prophecy can be like an old Scripture you've read a thousand times — you become used to it until God reinvigorates and brings it to your attention in a new way. When we look at a word and dismiss it as boring or usual, we look at prophecy the wrong way. God wants every person to feel His love, and He will reveal to us the way to communicate that seemingly well-worn theme. People need to hear the obvious sometimes. God has a way of putting fresh emphasis on things they already know.

The Process Of Prophecy

A prophet is always being tested in ministry. Walk softly in the prophetic before God. If you're not sure of something, stay quiet. In the context of local church most prophecy can wait a day, if not a week. Take time to pray about it because you can always come back to it. Prophesy at the level of faith you have got. It is better to stop in prophecy than to go too far. It is always easier to add than to retract.

Rhythm Of Life With God

One of the wonderful things about life with God is the rhythm we develop with Him. In creation, there is a rhythm. Night follows day. The seasons change. Birds migrate and return. The tide comes in and goes out. God's rhythmic imprint has been placed upon the earth and heavens. Our senses are aware of the rhythm of the world around us — we can smell the air and know what the weather will be like. We're used to the rhythm of the climate.

With God, we are always responding to something He is doing. Early in the day, we can be drawn into what God is doing. We're like children. What's Mom up to? Baking? Great, we'll help. Likewise, our Father works and we work. We love God because He first loved us. It is all about the rhythm of His Spirit.

The Holy Spirit will apply pressure to move us into the love of God. Like the moon draws the tide, He draws us to the love of God. Things may get worse as He tries to bring us into His rest, but we can trust that it is part of the rhythm of life with God.

God always makes the first move, and we return the favor. His delight is to love us, and our desire is to love Him. When we understand, and live in, the rhythm of God, we come into ministry in a much safer way. I can't say anything unless God speaks first. There is no pressure on me; it's all up to Him. When God says something, and faith fills my heart, then I can prophesy.

Most days, I am not consumed about the ministry. It is not a high priority when I could be in the presence of God. But isn't that what true ministry should be? Ministry, especially the prophetic, is about relating to God and doing, today, what He wants you to do. It is about matching the rhythm of His life. When we love who He is, minister to Him, and flow in His presence, we can be confident that God will use us as He sees fit.

Give What You Have

If we practice the Presence of God then we never have to question the source of what we are hearing. Availability is one of the prime motivators of confidence. Because I wait on God my availability connects with His intentionality. I can stir up the gift that is within me, (2 Timothy 1:6) because I know that the Father loves to connect with people. I may not always have a prophecy but I will have advice, wisdom and a prayer to offer.

Everyone giving as they themselves are enabled is a key principle that covers all of life not just spiritual gifts.

"Every man shall give as he is able, according to the blessing of the LORD your God which He has given you. (Deuteronomy 16:17)

For if the readiness is present, it is acceptable according to what a person has, not according to what he does not have. (2 Corinthians 8:12)

But Peter said, "I do not possess silver and gold, but what I do have I give to you: In the name of Jesus Christ the Nazarene — walk!" (Acts 3:6)

We first give our will over to God. He works in us both to will and to do! (Philippians 2:12, 13).

The burden of the Lord is light and our partnership with Him is easy (Matthew 11:28–30). We prophesy from a place of rest, humility and peace. We give cheerfully because the Father is delighted with joy and rejoicing. (2 Corinthians 9:7). The Father is always attracted to His own nature in us. He loves love, peace, joy, patience and all the attributes of the Holy Spirit.

> The Spirit quickens the everyday things

When our heart is open to His nature even our ordinary words can be quickened by the Holy Spirit. Someone once described the supernatural as God's super on our natural. He loves to move through us. When we first begin to move in prophecy of course there is mixture. There is always mixture! It is more obvious when we are just getting started and more subtle when we have been on the journey for a long time. Teachers and preachers have mixture. Pastors and counselors have mixture in their advice. Intercessors have mixture in their perceptions and prayers.

The Holy Spirit is so capable of sorting these things out. We have no need of suspicion or mistrust. We trust the Holy Spirit to witness to the

God part and be kind about the other. "We know in part and we prophesy in part" (1 Corinthians 13:9).

False prophecy is not about getting it wrong. That is poor prophecy that arises out of our inexperience and lack of wisdom. False prophecy involves a deliberate and calculated attempt to lead people astray. Usually for some selfish purpose. Monetary gain; increasing a power base; sexual dominance. Sadly in all walks of life and ministry there are people who are not saved below the waistline; have a big ego above the neck line; and the only balance they are about is the one in their local bank account!

Tongues And Interpretation

Tongues is the language of men and angels (1 Corinthians 13:1). On the day of Pentecost many people heard messages in their own languages that men who had previously been fishermen, could not possibly have learned. These were the same men who had been arrested by the priests and the Sadducees (Acts chapter 4). They were found to be ignorant and unlearned (4:13) but had obviously spent time with Jesus.

On many occasions I have spoken out publicly and in a tongue that I had not learned. The interpretation was given by people in the congregation and conference, who had heard their own language coming out of my mouth. One man in South Africa heard me say in his language (Nigerian) that his mother was praying for him to come to Christ. Which he did in that meeting! In Kentucky, USA, I spoke in flawless Cherokee for several minutes and reiterated a prophecy about a man and his family coming into a season of blessing and prosperity. The man who interpreted the tongue had been given that same word several weeks before by his brothers wife. He had not believer her, so she told him to write it down and pray for confirmation. I guess he got that!

> *Tongues is the language of heaven spoken on earth*

Pursue love, yet desire earnestly spiritual gifts, but especially that you may prophesy. For one who speaks in a tongue does not speak to men but to God; for no one understands, but in his spirit he speaks mysteries. But one who prophesies speaks to men for edification and exhortation and consolation. One who speaks in a tongue edifies himself; but one who prophesies edifies the church. Now I wish that you all spoke in tongues, but even more that you would prophesy; and greater is one who prophesies than one who speaks in tongues, unless he interprets, so that the church may receive edifying.

But now, brethren, if I come to you speaking in tongues, what will I profit you unless I speak to you either by way of revelation or of knowledge or of prophecy or of teaching? Yet even lifeless things, either flute or harp, in producing a sound, if they do not produce a distinction in the tones, how will it be known what is played on the flute or on the harp? For if the bugle produces an indistinct sound, who will prepare himself for battle? So also you, unless you utter by the tongue speech that is clear, how will it be known what is spoken? For you will be speaking into the air. There are, perhaps, a great many kinds of languages in the world, and no kind is without meaning.

If then I do not know the meaning of the language, I will be to the one who speaks a barbarian, and the one who speaks will be a barbarian to me. So also you, since you are zealous of spiritual gifts, seek to abound for the edification of the church. Therefore let one who speaks in a tongue pray that he may interpret. For if I pray in a tongue, my spirit prays, but my mind is unfruitful. What is the outcome then? I will pray with the spirit and I will pray with the mind also; I will sing with the spirit and I will sing with the mind also.

Otherwise if you bless in the spirit only, how will the one who fills the place of the ungifted say the "Amen" at your giving of thanks, since he does not know what you are saying? For you are giving thanks well enough, but the other person is not edified. I thank God, I speak in tongues more than you all; however, in the church I desire to speak five words with my mind so that I may instruct others also, rather than ten thousand words in a tongue. Brethren, do not be children in your thinking; yet in evil be infants, but in your thinking be mature.

In the Law it is written, "BY MEN OF STRANGE TONGUES AND BY THE LIPS OF STRANGERS I WILL SPEAK TO THIS PEOPLE, AND EVEN SO THEY WILL NOT LISTEN TO ME," says the Lord. So then tongues are for a sign, not to those who believe but to unbelievers; but prophecy is for a sign, not to unbelievers but to those who believe. Therefore if the whole church assembles together and all speak in tongues, and ungifted men or unbelievers enter, will they not say that you are mad?

But if all prophesy, and an unbeliever or an ungifted man enters, he is convicted by all, he is called to account by all; the secrets of his heart are disclosed; and so he will fall on his face and worship God, declaring that God is certainly among you. What is the outcome then, brethren? When you assemble, each one has a psalm, has a teaching, has a revelation, has a tongue, has an interpretation Let all things be done for edification. If anyone speaks in a tongue, it should be by two or at the most three, and each in turn, and one must interpret; but if there is no interpreter, he must keep silent in the church; and let him speak to himself and to God. (1 Corinthians 14:1–28)

With all prayer and petition pray at all times in the Spirit, and with this in view, be on the alert with all perseverance and petition for all the saints. (Ephesians 6:18)

But you, beloved, building yourselves up on your most holy faith, praying in the Holy Spirit. (Jude 1:20)

These signs will accompany those who have believed: in My name they will cast out demons, they will speak with new tongues. (Mark 16:17)

Gathering them together, He commanded them not to leave Jerusalem, but to wait for what the Father had promised, "Which," He said, "you heard of from Me; for John baptized with water, but you will be baptized with the Holy Spirit not many days from now."

So when they had come together, they were asking Him, saying, "Lord, is it at this time You are restoring the kingdom to Israel?" He said to them, "It is not for you to know times or epochs which the Father has fixed by His own authority; but you will receive power when the Holy Spirit has come upon you; and you shall be My witnesses both in Jerusalem, and in all Judea and Samaria, and even to the remotest part of the earth."

And after He had said these things, He was lifted up while they were looking on, and a cloud received Him out of their sight. And as they were gazing intently into the sky while He was going, behold, two men in white clothing stood beside them. They also said, "Men of Galilee, why do you stand looking into the sky? This Jesus, who has been taken up from you into heaven, will come in just the same way as you have watched Him go into heaven." Then they returned to Jerusalem *from the mount called Olivet, which is near Jerusalem, a Sabbath day's journey away. When they had entered the city, they went up to the upper room where they were staying; that is, Peter and John and James and Andrew, Philip and Thomas, Bartholomew and Matthew, James the son of Alphaeus, and Simon the Zealot, and Judas the son of James. (Acts 1:4–13)*

For they were hearing them speaking with tongues and exalting God. (Acts 10:46)

And when Paul had laid his hands upon them, the Holy Spirit came on them, and they began speaking with tongues and prophesying. (Acts 19:6)

… and to another the effecting of miracles, and to another prophecy, and to another the distinguishing of spirits, to another various kinds of tongues, and to another the interpretation of tongues. And God has appointed in the church, first apostles, second prophets, third teachers, then miracles, then gifts of healings, helps, administrations, various kinds of tongues. All do not have gifts of healings, do they? All do not speak with tongues, do they? All do not interpret, do they? (1 Corinthians 12:10, 28, 30)

If I speak with the tongues of men and of angels, but do not have love, I have become a noisy gong or a clanging cymbal. (1 Corinthians 13:1).

Tongues is the language of heaven. It is the language of angels and the conversation of the Spirit. He loves to speak to us in our own language. Even more He loves to communicate to us and through us in a heavenly language that we can speak back to Him in prayer and in worship.

> The language of the secret place is the communication of God's heart to yours!

Tongues is the language of the secret place. It is the speech of intimacy. It is a lovers language. It is a warfare language also whereby we may speak out things in intercession that the enemy cannot understand. When we speak in tongues in this way we communicate directly to heaven which frustrates the spiritual opposition we face on certain days. The enemy loves to mess with our mind particularly when it comes to knowing what to pray. It is therefore particularly galling for him when I speak in tongues from my spirit, bypassing my own mind in the process. It is the secret language of heaven that originates in my spirit not my head. I am in direct contact with heaven so my faith rises as I pray this way. I encounter the Lord when I use my spirit language. The most amazing truth also is that I can ask for and receive an interpretation so that I may discover what I just prayed! A lot of my current crafted prayers have developed out of my secret language.

This is probably the chief reason why the enemy stirs up controversy about the gift of tongues. He hates it when the church prays in the will of God. He loathes secret languages that render him powerless to intervene. He is angry when we communicate directly with heaven over his head. He seeks control of our faith in order to sow unbelief leading to demoralization and prayerlessness. He welcomes prayer that begins in doubt and questioning. He does not want believers to pray with God but towards Him. When we pray in the Spirit, we are asking God to do what He most wants to do. Praying in tongues gives me incredible confidence because the Presence of God is in the language of heaven.

If there is anyway that the enemy can stir up fear or misunderstanding about this amazing gift then he will gladly take it. He tries to make out that this gift is really just a subjective emotional experience that overwhelms peoples senses, controls their will and makes them vulnerable in their thinking. He does not want people understanding that tongues is an actual language that we can use in the same way as our native tongue.

We use different tones, intonations, decibels, inflections and emotions in the same way we would our natural language. As with our usual language we have to choose to speak it out. Our will is the vehicle for all our experiences with the Lord. "He works in us to will and to do, for His own good pleasure". (Philippians 2:13).

When we speak in tongues our will is the vehicle that enables us to communicate in a language that puts us in direct connection with the heart of the Father. This is why Paul was thankful that he spoke in tongues more than anyone! (1 Corinthians 14:18). There is a strong link between the use of our heavenly language and our capacity to receive revelation.

Our flesh cannot move against us when we pray in the Spirit. Our mind can join the party but not spoil it. Interpretation makes our mind fruitful after the fact not before.

All languages must grow. What is true in the natural is true in the Spirit. Vocabulary must develop. Our communication must take on a more adult form. It is sad in the Spirit to hear someone using the same few words that they have always used when they could have developed their heavenly language as they did their earthly one.

When we first begin to communicate in this language to the Lord we receive key words and phrases just as we do in our usual language. Our supernatural language follows the same precedents as our natural one.

Language forms around syllables coming together. Words form as we speak and sentences unfold in the normal way. The difference is that the supernatural language arrives without our pre-thinking it. The Holy Spirit stirs us to speak but allows us to control the flow, intonation, inflection and the decibel level. We speak out of our heart where Christ lives. As with any language we must practice it continuously to become fluent.

> All language grows into a greater expression of creativity

I have spoken in tongues for more than thirty years (since 1972) and have not developed four heavenly languages with the help of the Holy Spirit. One is for my deepest moments of intimate worship, a love language that fills my heart with adoration of Jesus. I am surrounded by His Presence, filled with His peace and brimming over with His confidence. It's impossible not to smile with this language. The quiet joy of His Presence radiates His pleasure and I am undone by love.

Another tongue I have developed with the Holy Spirit is for warfare situations. I choose to fight. I want to live in the territory where the clash of two kingdoms is most pronounced. This particular language puts an edge on my faith as a sharpening stone would on a sword blade. It stirs me up to fight. It refreshes me so that I am not weary. We beat the enemy by staying fresh. I love warfare. I want to relish the fight. I want to be a New Testament version of one of David's mighty men (2 Samuel 23:8–39). This language makes me stand up on the inside. My inner man of the spirit comes to attention and readiness. This particular language of the spirit increases my faith and energizes my relationship with the Lord. I see His majesty. I am filled with a sense of His sovereignty. It leads me into high praise and laughter… lots of laughter. It is our joy to be confident in the Lord.

A third language I have really helps me with my lifestyle of meditation and contemplation of God. I love to open my bible and lay my hands on a particular passage and pray for some time in this contemplative prayer language. I am praying always for a spirit of wisdom and revelation to communicate with me in the knowledge of Christ (Ephesians 1:16–18). I adore loving God with my mind as well as my heart. Thinking deeply about God is a huge pleasure in my life. This particular language is so wonderful in enabling me to focus on the spirit of truth.

I love the Holy Spirit. His calmness and tranquility. I love His energy and incredible cheeriness. He makes me smile, giggle and laugh out loud. I love His place in my heart. He is such a genius at everything and so amazingly happy. He is an astonishing tutor who loves to proclaim Jesus.

My fourth language is my everyday conversational communication with the Holy Spirit. It's the one I use to ask questions; stay in divine connection; query what is happening; prepare my heart for various events; and to generally acknowledge the Father in my heart. I love to pray in English the prayers that the Father has placed in my heart. This is praying with God rather than merely to God. These prayers originate in my prayer languages. The Holy Spirit interprets them to my mind from my heart.

> *Explicit languages for a specific purpose*

When I sense that an interpretation is coming, I take a pen and paper and sit quietly. Words begin to form in my mind and I write them down. At times I may write key words and key phrases and then meditate on them for a while. Sentences begin to form, meaning opens up and the knowledge of what to ask for fills my heart with confidence. I am praying with the answer not to find one.

Other times I can write down the whole prayer verbatim. I cannot describe the joy of holding the answer to prayer in my hand before I have ever prayed for it!

A prayer language is the language of prayer as God speaks it. Jesus ever lives to make intercession (Hebrews 7:25) and the Spirit Himself intercedes for us with groanings too deep for words (Romans 8:26). Wouldn't you want to know what they are praying? Having a supernatural prayer language is a phenomenal asset. Being able to interpret that language so that we can pray with the Spirit and with understanding pushes our prayer life into a

> *There is no place in our vocabulary or lifestyle for impotence!*

place of power and pleasure. Is it any wonder that the enemy puts such controversy around these particular gifts? He is quite frantic to deny every believer access to such incredible grace and power. He has a vested interest in our powerlessness in prayer. The cessationist doctrine about the Holy Spirit and the gifts not being for the modern day church has been one of his most memorable and powerful ongoing victories over the church. It has rendered the church impotent in the supernatural and has enabled the New Age movement to flourish uncontested by the Body of Christ at large.

These days are changing however. The church is gradually returning to her supernatural roots. Churches that were once anti-charismatic have moved towards the Holy Spirit in recent years becoming non-charismatic (a huge change) and many are now quietly charismatic. In a post modern world the view of truth is very different. Everyone loves truth and seeks it, not necessarily in Christ. People appreciate my truth in Christ and want me to value their truth no matter where it is founded or rooted. The organ for receptivity of truth is no longer the ear. People used to come to church to hear the truth expressed in good preaching and teaching.

In a post modern world the organ for receptivity of truth is the eye. People want to see something. We live in a show and tell world. This is the perfect scenario for a church that loves to pray for the sick and believes in miracles. Signs and wonders are the currency of heaven. They are the keys of the kingdom which unlock every religion and philosophy known to man. Prophecy, tongues and interpretation allow us to gain specific access to people's hearts so that they hear what God knows about them. The secrets of their hearts are revealed

> God has a language for you that interferes with the enemy

(1 Corinthians 14:26). God knows the innermost dreams of every person. When a man or woman hear a person speaking in a tongue which is either a heavenly language or the language of the listener and their own dreams are being spoken… worship is the result. People come to faith and certainty quickly when the church moves as heaven would. On earth as it is in heaven is still the goal of God. To create an earth the same environment and conditions that heaven regularly enjoys!

Anything less than that is a sub standard gospel. Tongues and interpretation is a part of our empowering in the gospel. They are great tools for evangelism and people development. Prophecy is a great tool for discipleship and growing people. The word of knowledge and the word of wisdom allow the church to partake of the tremendous insights of heaven to a hurting and needy world.

On a flight to Hong Kong as we were boarding in London the Lord gave me a word of knowledge for the person next to me. This Chinese lady had lost several relatives in plane crashes and was paranoid about flying herself. I introduced myself, told her I was a Christian, relayed to her what the Lord had showed me and expressed confidently that the Father would heal her of her fear of flying. She was shocked and intrigued but readily agreed to receive prayer. She ate, slept, read and we talked during the long flight. Absolutely no fear! She accepted Christ. She had too much evidence not to!!

Tongues and interpretation aid our communication both to God personally and of God to others. They are great gifts for building people up in the Lord. We can pray and sing in tongues enabling our channel of communication in worship and intercession to remain open and functioning at a high level. They are a sign to unbelievers that God can know, understand and communicate at the right level with them. They are faith builders that enable us to establish our relationship with the Lord at a deeper level more continuously. They strengthen and confirm us in Christ. They allow us greater freedom and intimacy in our fellowship with the Holy Spirit. They seriously interfere with the plans and purposes of the enemy because we are no longer subject to his mind games. In fact we can play a few games of our own!

God Uses Everyday Objects

The Father loves symbolism. The scripture is full of pictorial language, parables, allegories and creative speech. He can and does communicate through physical objects.

> The word which came to Jeremiah from the LORD saying, "Arise and go down to the potter's house, and there I will announce My words to you." Then I went down to the potter's house, and there he was, making something on the wheel. But the vessel that he was making of clay was spoiled in the hand of the potter; so he remade it into another vessel, as it pleased the potter to make. Then the word of the LORD came to me saying, "Can I not, o house of Israel, deal with you as this potter does?" declares the LORD. "Behold, like the clay in the potter's hand, so are you in My hand, o house of Israel." (Jeremiah 18:1–6)

> The natural and the spiritual always combine in the Father's heart

God sent the prophet to the potter's house to both watch in the natural and hear in the Spirit. The Father uses the natural elements to speak prophetically in a symbolic manner. The Holy Spirit always interprets the will of the Father. The Lord loves to vary His methods of communication with us to teach us to be open to all forms and practices of divine connection.

> Then the LORD said to me, "Even though Moses and Samuel were to stand before Me, My heart would not be with this people; send them away from My presence and let them go! And it shall be that when they say to you, 'Where should we go?' then you are to tell them, 'Thus says the LORD: "Those destined for death, to death; And those destined

for the sword, to the sword; And those destined for famine, to famine; And those destined for captivity, to captivity."'

"I will appoint over them four kinds of doom," declares the LORD: "the sword to slay, the dogs to drag off, and the birds of the sky and the beasts of the earth to devour and destroy. I will make them an object of horror among all the kingdoms of the earth because of Manasseh, the son of Hezekiah, the king of Judah, for what he did in Jerusalem.

"Indeed, who will have pity on you, O Jerusalem, Or who will mourn for you, Or who will turn aside to ask about your welfare? You who have forsaken Me," declares the LORD, "You keep going backward. So I will stretch out My hand against you and destroy you; I am tired of relenting!

"I will winnow them with a winnowing fork at the gates of the land; I will bereave them of children, I will destroy My people; They did not repent of their ways. Their widows will be more numerous before Me than the sand of the seas; I will bring against them, against the mother of a young man, a destroyer at noonday; I will suddenly bring down on her anguish and dismay.

> The Creator will always be creative in how He communicates

"She who bore seven sons pines away; Her breathing is labored Her sun has set while it was yet day; She has been shamed and humiliated. So I will give over their survivors to the sword before their enemies," declares the LORD.

Woe to me, my mother, that you have borne me as a man of strife and a man of contention to all the land! I have not lent, nor have men lent money to me, yet everyone curses me.

The LORD said, "Surely I will set you free for purposes of good; Surely I will cause the enemy to make supplication to you in a time of disaster and a time of distress.

"Can anyone smash iron, iron from the north, or bronze?

"Your wealth and your treasures I will give for booty without cost, even for all your sins and within all your borders. Then I will cause your enemies to bring it into a land you do not know; for a fire has been kindled in My anger, It will burn upon you."

You who know, O LORD, remember me, take notice of me, and take vengeance for me on my persecutors. Do not, in view of Your patience, take me away; know that for Your sake I endure reproach.

Your words were found and I ate them, and Your words became for me a joy and the delight of my heart; for I have been called by Your name, O LORD God of hosts.

I did not sit in the circle of merrymakers, nor did I exult. Because of Your hand upon me I sat alone, for You filled me with indignation.

Why has my pain been perpetual and my wound incurable, refusing to be healed? Will You indeed be to me like a deceptive stream with water that is unreliable?

Therefore, thus says the LORD, "If you return, then I will restore you — before Me you will stand; and if you extract the precious from the worthless, you will become My spokesman. They for their part may turn to you, but as for you, you must not turn to them.

"Then I will make you to this people a fortified wall of bronze; and though they fight against you, they will not prevail over you; for I am with you to save you and deliver you," declares the LORD.

"So I will deliver you from the hand of the wicked, and I will redeem you from the grasp of the violent."

(Jeremiah chapter 15)

Jeremiah receives specific instruction which combine physical objects with symbolic acts that are imbued with prophetic significance and spiritual meaning. Buy a clay jar first. Take the key people of the day on a walk to a particular place and prophesy to them. Then Jeremiah has to specifically break the jar in front of these men and use that act to symbolically interpret the will of the Lord. This is the old covenant practice of prophecy that continues in the early church life and ministry. The Lord gives Peter a symbolic vision on three occasions in order to prepare his heart for what the Father wanted to do with the Gentiles (Acts 10:10–20). Agabus a modern day prophet used Paul's own belt to bring him a prophetic word about his future (Acts 21:10–11).

There are many, many references in scripture in all the prophetic books, where God spoke creatively with prophets using signs, symbols, objects and everyday occurrences to convey His will and His word. He moves easily in partnership with the natural world and the supernatural realm.

I once spoke to a church that had become moribund in their faith and approach to God. The Lord told me to buy a particular plant that had become pot bound. That is, its roots had filled the pot to such an extent that they had no further room to expand. If it remains in this pot the plant will die for lack of nutrients and growing space.

I was instructed to set a table at the front of the meeting and to bring a larger pot, compost and potting soil and lots of water. I brought two pot bound plants. Carefully removing one plant from its prison I showed the church the problem and the danger this plant was facing. Then I relayed to them the prophetic message of their own spiritual condition comparing it with the plant. Finally I took a hammer and broke the second pot freeing the plant from its confines and repotted it in a large pot prophesying all the time regarding what the Lord wanted to do with each individual life. Finally as I watered the plant the Lord gave a beautiful promise concerning the influx of the Holy Spirit to create new life and momentum. What followed as several hours of personal ministry as people repented and responded. When I first displayed the pot bound plants they were sick looking and unhealthy. By the end of the evening one plant was dead and the repotted one was bursting with health. The Father loves such imagery. He created us to be seers as well as listeners.

> Have fun and be amazed!

Many, many times I have seen the Lord intervene in peoples lives in this manner bringing release and new freedom to know Him and explore His will.

When we approach prophecy through the very heart of God we find an anointing to speak that communicates on several levels. We learn not to be one dimensional in our approach to conveying the word of the Lord. He is wonderfully creative and to represent Him well we need to be touched and established by His ingenious, imaginative and stimulating originality.

The Holy Spirit is amazing! Therefore it is our role to be amazed by the Father and to be gently nudged in the direction of the marvelous way that He communicates Himself.

Study this book and do the exercises and assignments in whatever order the Holy Spirit determines. Please, please, enjoy the process of learning, discovering and become more. You will be astonished at what the Holy Spirit will show you and also at His wonderful demeanor. He is so ready to help you. Have fun and be at peace.

Notes

Notes

The Process of Prophecy

Reflections, Exercises, and Assignments

The following exercises are designed with this particular chapter in mind. Please work through them carefully before going on to the next chapter. Take time to reflect on your life journey as well as your prophetic development. Learn to work well with the Holy Spirit and people that God has put around you so that you will grow in grace, humility, and wisdom in the ways of God.

Graham Cooke.

What Constitutes Maturity?

How we undertake a task tells an awful lot about us. Our identity, mind-set, experience and creativity are all evidenced in the life that we bring to each assignment. So too is our attitude, our demeanor, and our standing in God. Our identity comes to the surface when we engage in any enterprise. Our doing reveals the current state of our being.

Prophecy is a commitment of the heart to speak in a way that edifies, encourages and releases comfort. It is never casual, nor matter of fact. Prophecy is spiritual not logical. It is an affair of the heart and issues forth from a life that is fully engaged in experiencing the Lord. Prophecy that comes from God's heart will re-engage another's heart before God which will unlock their mind to be changed and renewed.

Heart prophecy is intuitive, creative and powerful. It raises everyone's sights so that they can see God more clearly and see themselves in Him. When people prophesy, we see who they are in Christ. Within the context of this chapter you must be willing and able to demonstrate these attributes as a sign of your growing maturity.

- God loves us with all His heart and His mind. It is vital that your mind is renewed in Christ and that your words carry the evidence of deep thought. Allow the Spirit to think in a powerful way in your own life situations. Know how the spirit of revelation works in life and ministry. The heart sees, and our mind connects with that revelation to create prophecy that is crafted and effective. Your prime place of engagement is with the heart of God, then the mind of God. Is your logic and reason preventing you from being and doing what the Father is seeing and saying? Heart prophecy is inspirational and transforming. We need the heart of the Father, the mind of Christ and the impetus of the Holy Spirit in each prophecy we bring.

- God is surrounded by joy. He abides in incredible happiness. Heaven is full of laughter, singing and joyous living. Our joy in life is meant to be full. Enjoy the prophetic and enjoy God's Presence. Do you have pleasure in stillness and being quiet? Do you make time simply to listen?

- Your confidence level in the goodness of God for you must operate at a high level to be consistent and continuous in the prophetic gift. We cannot visit confidence occasionally we must live there habitually. What you are in God, you transmit in prophecy. Authentic prophecy flows from a genuine experience that is current. Who are you in Christ?

- To pursue love is to run hard after God's heart. It is to get in His face everyday. Love grows by pursuit. What are you seeking for right now regarding the heart of God in your own life? Sensitivity to the Holy Spirit arises out of a heart that has been touched and is easily aligned with the Father. Everyone who connects with you should be touched by the Lord … is this true of you? What amazes, astonishes and astounds you about God? What does your present fullness consist of that gives testimony to Who God is for you? Your current life and experience of God drives your prophetic expression.

- Life in the Spirit is built on knowing Who Jesus is for you. Within that revelation of Him, identity is formed and attachment commences that leads us into a partnership that transcends mere ministry. Prophecy is not what we do, it is who we are. We become encouragement. We are comforters. We are builders who love to make God bigger. We adore growth and we are as jealous as God to see people do well in Him. In partnership we become unconscious stewards of His goodness and kindness and other people see it in us, and respond to the Lord. When people are around you, are they expectant of God? Do they connect with Who He is for them? Do they catch the spirit of His love, joy and peace?

- If your heart is fully attuned to the Father then you are a reconciliation ministry with power to restore. The world beats people up, the kingdom of heaven renews, refreshes and revives them. The Father is wonderfully creative in His ability to make all things new. Scripture is a visual revelation of the promises of God being fulfilled. Prophecy and Scripture have an excellent partnership that allows us massive freedom to be artistic, imaginative, clever, ingenious, inspired, inventive and original.

- If your heart and mind are renewed in Christ then you have access to the Creator within. God has never stopped being creative. Ask the Lord to engage with you creatively in prophecy. When your mind is renewed your imagination can serve the Lord.

What Constitutes Immaturity?

It is not what goes into a man's mouth that defiles him, it is what comes out. To prophesy the heart of God there must be a purity in our normal conversation and language. A fountain cannot issue forth sweet water and bitter. Your mouth is the expression of what is in your heart.

Are you holding grudges, resentment, unforgiveness? Do you enjoy sarcasm… are you good at making fun of others? Of course there is a light-hearted banter that exists between good friends. This is more than that and may lead to cynicism, mocking and derisive communication.

Prophecy is never casual but intentional. It has depth. Immature prophecy is crude, unprepared, unformed and childish. There is a difference between immature prophecy and inexperienced. The latter is new, green, unpracticed and comes from a life that is learning how to be familiar with the beauty of the Lord. It is unskilled in the art of using words to inspire and strengthen others but it loves the training.

Immature people never work hard at relationships. They do not listen and do not retain what they learn because they never practice it until it becomes intuitive and therefore established in their life. Immature people are usually pessimistic. They seldom take ground then hold it… so eventual defeat follows any gain they may make because they do not persevere.

Prophecy must be pure. There can be no mixture in motive. We cannot influence others for our own gain. We cannot use prophecy to make a point. Prophecy is not magic. It has to be followed up with obedience and surrender in the recipient. There is no breakthrough without follow through. Immature prophecy guarantees an outcome outside of obedience and renouncing of sin and error. Prophecy works with the Cross of Christ and indeed points to it.

When people are in sin, we need to see them through God's eyes in Christ. The prophetic word must lead them to a joyful capitulation to the mercy, forgiveness and purity of the Lord.

- Our lack of relationship with God will be seen and noted over a period of time. Immaturity is holding to a place of being double-minded so that we flip flop from a right way to a wrong way of thinking, seeing, living and being. We cannot entertain doubts and trust God. These two cannot coexist in the same space at the same time. One of them has to go and we get to choose. Likewise we cannot have anxiety and peace living together. Nor fear and love; callousness and compassion; meanness and kindness; exasperation and forbearance;

irritation and patience, to name just a few anomalies that can afflict us. Immaturity is either not choosing or choosing poorly. Mostly it is our lack of pleasure in Who God is for us that encourages such negativity. What are you displaying of the fruit of the Spirit? Anxiety speaks louder than words.

- When our soul is not under the rule of our spirit it is impossible to become continuously confident. Our soul, when in charge always seeks reassurance. We believe the worst not the best. In days of difficulty we do not express the luxury of hope. Hope is expectation of the goodness of God coming through on our behalf. Hope understands future grace, that knows that everything is more than covered by the goodness of God. I am free to make an honest mistake and the Father's love will cover it. An undeveloped life cannot carry the anointing over time and distance. If you want the anointing to be heavy then your heart must be light and your rest must be big. (Matthew 11:28–30). Rest is a weapon. Weariness is a liability. Is your soul or your spirit prominent in your life? The fruit of the Spirit is the prime indicator of spirituality. What are you modeling consistently?

- Some people have minds like a vacuum cleaner, they suck up any old rubbish. Immaturity is present when we fail to love God with our mind. Our thought life should aid our heart in worship not hinder it. When logic and reason mean more to us than wisdom and revelation then our knowledge of God cannot lead us into fruitful experience. The mind of Christ is intuitive not reasonable. The thinking of God is imaginative not logical. Prophecy reflects the way God is in His creative self. Walking around Jericho for a week saying nothing is illogical, so is shouting and expecting fortified walls to fall down! That was the prophetic instruction.

- We are immature when our knowledge of God has not led us into an experience of Who He is in the realm that we are discovering. When scripture reveals one thing and our lifestyle another, immaturity is the evidence.

- Indifference to peoples life condition is a form of adolescent immaturity. Whilst it is true that we each have giftings and callings that are inclined towards certain people groups, there will always be the times when we are moved with compassion for someone who may be outside our normal remit.

Reflections, Exercises, and Assignments

- To have no compassion is immature. It often can signal a preoccupation with self. Learning to see people through the eyes of God makes us present to the moment in a crowd of strangers! Seeing negatively is a sign of immaturity. So is speaking out continuously what you have not appropriated by experience.

- Do you know your own identity in Christ? Are you aware of your own inheritance? Immature people speak out as ones who are not fully engaged in their own journey of discovery. We may not be aware of the fullness of our destiny but we must be on the road to discovery and having experiences.

AN ASSIGNMENT

Think of a person around your life at this time who seems to be prone to anxiety and worry.

Read Luke 10:38–42

This is a human allegory about spirit and soul. It is about the paradox of Being and Doing. A paradox is two apparently opposing ideas contained in the same truth. In a paradox the issue is about both/and not either/or. When a paradox is under stress the issue is one of primacy... which is most important.

In this case primacy is dictated by "one thing is needful"... It is concerned with the discipline of beholding and becoming like Jesus. It is about the priority of right relationship.

1. What is the one thing your friend must do at this time?

2. What specific encouragement can you give that would inspire your friend to forsake anxiety for trust?

3. How would you give the word in a way that would enable them to resolve to change?

4. What particular promise do you sense that the Lord is wanting to release into this persons life at this time?

5. Write the word on a card and mail it. Alternatively write the word down for them but also speak it to them.

IMAGE OF GOD

We are all made in the image of God. How we perceive ourselves in Christ will seriously enable us to empower others in the Spirit.

1.   What must change in your own self image?

2.   What are the things you most dislike about yourself?

3.   What are the scriptures/promises that mean the most to you regarding your identity?

4.   What is the next thing that God wants to develop regarding your image?

5.   NB. You may have a list of things to change about yourself! Pick the top one and concentrate on that only… don't be worried over the others. We move ahead one breakthrough at a time.

6.   What is the antidote to that particular poor image?

7.   For example, If an inclination to worry is defining your image into being an anxious, fearful person then the antidote is confidence. Look up confidence in scripture and study it for the next few weeks.

8.   If you were to prophesy over an anxious person you would have an objective to release them into confidence. What would you write to them?

9.   Write to yourself, read it and apply it.

CASE STUDY:
MATCHING PROPHETIC DELIVERY WITH CONTENT

The delivery of a prophetic word must match its content. One cannot grab someone by the throat and prophesy love and peace; likewise, a prophecy about warrior strength cannot be properly prophesied in an airy whisper. The context must match the content.

Below are a few prophetic words I have given to individuals enrolled in my prophetic schools (I have changed the names for privacy reasons). In this exercise, read the prophetic word and answer the questions following it.

Prophetic Word

Brian, I sense that the Lord is about to come and reveal Himself to you as a warrior and as your King. There have been seasons where He has come to you as a Lover and a Father but now He is going to come as a King, as Captain of the Lord of Hosts. He is coming to you like this because this next season of your life is about you becoming more war-like. There is a warfare spirit that is going to come upon your life, your worship, your thanksgiving, and your praise. You're going to come to a whole new level of understanding the sovereignty, supremacy, and majesty of Jesus.

Every situation that comes into your life in the next season is to teach you about the sovereignty of God. He has a strength and power that He is going to pour into your life in these next days. It will cause you to rise up on the inside in warfare. There is a spirit of breakthrough in this next season in your life, where you'll learn about the power and capacity that's in you to break through for yourself. The Lord says all of your own situations are fair game: every situation that you're coming into is about you triumphing. It's about you breaking through and about you breaking out.

When you pray, when you intercede, God will take you to a place of proclamation and declaration. You will declare to the enemy, that he can go this far, but no further. There is an anointing upon you to come into the lives of others and say, "I'm drawing a line here and you're not coming across that line, because the Spirit of God forbids you. This is where it stops." There is an anointing upon you to cause breakthrough

Reflections, Exercises, and Assignments

in the hearts and lives of other people. Your whole prophetic spirit is about releasing captives — you will go against the oppressor, grab his hand, and unclench his fist so that he lets go of people. You will pull his hand away from people and declare freedom into people's lives. The Lord says that He has put a sword in your hand and everywhere you go you're going to hear the sound of chains hitting the floor.

Answer the following questions:

1. What is the crux (focus) of this word?

2. What is the emotion and plan God has for Brian?

3. What would be the best way to deliver this word? What tone of voice would be best to use? What body language and position should be used?

4. After delivering the word, what would you pray over him?

If the objective of a prophesy is to give strength and power, then you're not going to say it like this: "Um, I just uh, uh really sense that uh, the uh, um, the Lord really wants to um, uh, that He, uh, He really um, that the Lord wants to uh, come and uh He really wants you to um, be strong." This isn't going to breed confidence: it just leads the listeners to think, 'God, help him. Save him, do something, take him to glory, get him out of our sight, who is this poor child?' The objective is lost.

LECTIO DIVINA

Lectio Divina (Latin for *divine reading*) is an ancient way of reading the Bible — allowing a quiet and contemplative way of coming to God's Word. *Lectio Divina* opens the pulse of the Scripture, helping readers dig far deeper into the Word than normally happens in a quick glance-over.

In this exercise, we will look at a portion of Scripture and use a modified *Lectio Divina* technique to engage it. This technique can be used on any piece of Scripture; I highly recommend using it for key Bible passages that the Lord has highlighted for you, and for anything you think might be an inheritance word for your life (see the *Crafted Prayer interactive journal* for more on inheritance words).

Read the Scripture (1 Corinthians 14:1–5, 26–33, and 39–40):

Pursue love, and desire spiritual gifts, but especially that you may prophesy. For he who speaks in a tongue does not speak to men but to God, for no one understands him; however, in the spirit he speaks mysteries. But he who prophesies speaks edification and exhortation and comfort to men. He who speaks in a tongue edifies himself, but he who prophesies edifies the church. I wish you all spoke with tongues, but even more that you prophesied; for he who prophesies is greater than he who speaks with tongues, unless indeed he interprets, that the church may receive edification.

How is it then, brethren? Whenever you come together, each of you has a psalm, has a teaching, has a tongue, has a revelation, has an interpretation. Let all things be done for edification. If anyone speaks in a tongue, let there be two or at the most three, each in turn, and let one interpret. But if there is no interpreter, let him keep silent in church, and let him speak to himself and to God. Let two or three prophets speak, and let the others judge. But if anything is revealed to another who sits by, let the first keep silent. For you can all prophesy one by one, that all may learn and all may be encouraged. And the spirits of the prophets are subject to the prophets. For God is not the author of confusion but of peace, as in all the churches of the saints.

Therefore, brethren, desire earnestly to prophesy, and do not forbid to speak with tongues. Let all things be done decently and in order.

Reflections, Exercises, and Assignments

1.   Find a place of stillness before God. Embrace His peace. Chase the nattering thoughts out of your mind. Calm your body. Breathe slowly. Inhale. Exhale. Inhale. Exhale. Clear yourself of the distractions of life. Whisper the word, "Stillness." Take your time. When you find that rest in the Lord, enjoy it. Worship Him in it. Be with Him there.

2.   Re-read the passage twice. Allow its words to become familiar to you. Investigate Paul's encouragement to prophesy. What images does it bring to your spirit? What do you see? Become a part of it. What phrases or words especially resonate with you? Meditate especially on those shreds of revelation. Write those pieces down in your journal.

3.   Read the passage twice again. Like waves crashing onto a shore, let the words of Scripture crash onto your spirit. What excites you? What scares you? What exhilarates you about this revelation of the love of God? What are you discerning? What are you feeling? What are you hearing? Again, write it all down in your journal.

4.   Write the theme of this passage in your journal.

5.   Does this passage rekindle any memories or experiences? Does it remind you of any prophetic words you have given or received? Write those down as well.

The Process Of Prophecy

6. What is the Holy Spirit saying to you through this Scripture? Investigate it with Him — picture the two of you walking through it together. Write those words in your journal.

7. Read the passage two final times. Meditate on it. Is there something God wants you to do? Is there something He is calling you to? Write it down.

8. Pray silently. Tell God what this passage is saying to you. Tell Him what you are thinking about. Write down your conversation together. Picture yourself and the Holy Spirit as two old friends in a coffee shop, chatting about what God is doing.

9. Finally, pray and thank God for His relationship with you. Come back to the passage once a week for the next three months. Read it and let more revelation flow into you. If you feel compelled to, craft a prayer based on this passage for yourself, your family, your friends, or your church. Pray that prayer until you feel God has birthed it in you.

Notes

Notes

Notes

Notes

MODULE THREE

THE PURPOSE OF PROPHECY

The Purpose of Prophecy

WHAT YOU WILL LEARN IN THIS SEGMENT:

- Why prophecy is vital in a post modern world.
- The difference between prophecy and teaching.
- Prophecy releases a personal impartation of the purposes of God.
- The importance of being and the grace of doing.
- Prophecy and humility are irrepressible companions.
- Prophecy restores dignity and self respect.
- How to edify, comfort and encourage.
- Releasing correction and warning properly.
- Provide direction and enhance personal vision.
- Complement teaching and confirm the revealed word.
- Release the church into new truth and practice.
- Prophecy provides insight in pastoral situations.
- Produce evangelistic breakthroughs.
- Provide a prayer agenda for individuals and groups.
- Know the difference between the supernatural and the spectacular.
- Understand institutionalized opposition to the prophetic.
- Develop two relationships with God as Abba and Father.
- Childlike trust in the bedrock of mature faith.

The Purpose Of Prophecy

IMAGINE THE LIFE OF MOSES as he led a million Israelites through forty years in the wilderness. Life could not have been much fun for the man. First, he was openly envied by others for his close relationship with God. Second, he was blamed, despised, criticized, and ridiculed any time a problem cropped up along the way to the Promised Land. The people ran the man ragged. Bread from Heaven wasn't enough; they wanted meat. Water from a rock wasn't enough; they wanted more. The law of God itself was resisted.

On top of all of that, Moses was forced to listen to the life issues and difficulties of more than a million people. In each of those cases, he felt compelled to pray and seek out the Lord for His judgment. Such a process would be exhausting for a pastor of a hundred-member church; one can only imagine the strain on Moses.

Fortunately, there were people who loved Moses, and whom the prophet trusted. When his father-in-law, Jethro, watched Moses judge cases from dawn to dusk, he was appalled.

"What is this thing that you are doing for the people? Why do you alone sit, and all the people stand before you from morning until evening?" he asked in Exodus 18:14.

"Because the people come to me to inquire of God," Moses replied in verses 15 and 16. *"When they have a difficulty, they come to me, and I judge between one and another; and I make known the statutes of God and His laws."*

Jethro, an outsider who had just arrived in the Israelite camp, saw a pattern in the constant stream of questions and answers that Moses endured, and proposed a plan. He told his son-in-law to record the problems and answers he had already faced so they could be used as a precedent for others to judge what was going on. With such material in hand, Moses could appoint deputies to deal with those complaints using the prophet's own words and answers. Moses, meanwhile, could preside over new situations, listening and providing the word of the Lord. Thousands of years later, our court systems use the same principle of precedence as Jethro laid out.

Jethro's wisdom probably saved Moses' life, leadership, and sanity. The children of Israel learned to interact with and interpret the written, or revealed, Word of God, and the new word given by Moses through prophetic utterance. This pattern still exists today. The present-day Church has the revealed Word of God in Scripture, which allows us to understand and follow God's ways. We can be grounded in the Bible and able to determine the heart and will of God for ourselves.

When we encounter situations that don't appear to have a clear precedent or answer in Scripture, we may need to access the prophetic ministry. This gift will echo the Bible faithfully, drive us to the feet of Jesus, and never usurp our will or force us into unsound judgments or actions.

> The Kingdom of heaven is present-future, therefore...

I teach my prophetic students to always keep one question at the forefront of their minds when they are asked for a word: "Is this person's need best served by an increased understanding of Scripture, or do they need a *now* word, aligned with Scripture, that will personalize God's Word in a way that increases faith and confidence and releases them from hindrances and bondage?" When we discern that God's answer for their need is obviously contained in Scripture, we should refer them to a teacher who has the gift to exposit that precedent to them.

The Bible clearly distinguishes between prophecy and teaching. It emphasizes that both prophetic and teaching gifts exist and that the two have separate functions with the common goal of growing people into spiritual maturity. *"He Himself gave some to be apostles, some prophets, some evangelists, and some pastors and teachers,"* the Apostle Paul wrote in Ephesians 4:11. Paul went even further in 1 Corinthians 12:27–31:

> *Now you are the body of Christ, and members individually. And God has appointed these in the church: first apostles, second prophets, third teachers, after that miracles, then gifts of healings, helps, administrations, varieties of tongues. Are all apostles? Are all prophets? Are all teachers? Are all workers of miracles? Do all have gifts of healings? Do all speak with tongues? Do all interpret? But earnestly desire the best gifts.*

The Purpose Of Prophecy

Both prophecy and teaching are needed in the Church. One does not have precedence over the other; it is not our preference or prejudice that determines which gift we should use, but rather the demands of the situation we find ourselves in. Prophecy and teaching have different goals, and both are vital if we are to understand God's ways.

> *... it requires a prophetic people to establish its rule.*

The Difference Between Teaching And Prophecy

While teaching allows us to gain a full understanding of God's principles for life; prophecy imparts the purpose of God in our current situation. Teaching reveals to us the mind of God while prophecy deals with His heart. God, like us, both thinks and feels. *"But I am poor and needy; yet the* LORD *thinks upon me,"* says Psalm 40:17. *"Jesus wept,"* records John 11:35. Christ both thinks about us and feels for us.

God loves to express His heart toward us and make His thoughts plain. Those feelings will never countermand Scripture, which is profitable for our teaching, correction, reproof, and exhortation (2 Timothy 3:16). In fact, it was the Holy Spirit-inspired word of the prophets that enabled the heroes of our faith to write Scripture in the first place. One could argue that by believing in the Bible, we automatically believe in prophecy! We cannot separate the two on any level. *"For prophecy never came by the will of man, but holy men of God spoke as they were moved by the Holy Spirit,"* says 2 Peter 1:21.

Many people rightly worry that an over-dependence on experience, at the expense of the solid grounding in the Word that good teaching builds, may lead to error and abuse. On the flip side of that coin, others are rightly concerned that the ministry of the Word without the spirit of revelation, which the prophetic enhances, can lead to a correct, but sterile, formality.

All knowledge must lead to an actual experience if our spiritual life is going to develop. Knowledge that fails to capitalize on experience is not worth anything in the spiritual realm. It ensures that our head is filled with instruction that has not progressed to life changing enlightenment. We are scholars who never graduate because we fail every life test. We know in our head but our heart is untouched. We can quote scripture but we do not encounter the God who breathed it into life.

I know from personal experience that it is possible and beneficial to have both prophets and teachers operating together. After all, that's the way God intended it.

To move in even the simplest prophetic gift requires an understanding of the mind and heart of God and how to release that revelation to others.

Prophetic words have different strengths of impact depending on the situation, circumstances, faith level and understanding of the receiver, and also the ability, experience, understanding, and relationship of the giver to the Holy Spirit.

Prophecy is a gift of the Holy Spirit; it does not belong to people. The Spirit gives gifts at His own discretion. Anyone can be used in the gift of prophecy provided they believe and have accepted Jesus Christ as their Saviour, are filled with the Holy Spirit, and are open to moving in the supernatural.

Knowing that all Spirit-filled Christians can prophesy does not make everyone who does a prophet. Prophetic anointing contains various levels and stages, beginning with the shallow end of basic prophecy, encouragement, edification, and comfort. However, moving through levels of prophetic ministry and into the office of a prophet requires considerable training, experience, and development over many years. On average, it takes about twenty years to fully form a prophet, depending on the training, discipling, and mentoring one has received.

A strong, clean, purposeful relationship with God, wedded to a life of prayer, study, and meditation of Scripture, will always be more productive spiritually than a casual familiarity in those areas.

Humility Is The Key

> *When our ego is small, the Presence of God is enlarged*

One of the most difficult questions for Christians to grapple with is "How do I receive the gift of prophecy?" Unfortunately, even the question is flawed. Prophecy is not for some people more than others. It is not a reward for faithful years of Christian service; it cannot be earned. Prophecy is a gift given freely by the Holy Spirit.

However, the ministry of a prophet is not open to everyone. That is a specific calling and anointing.

We are all required to witness to the unchurched people in our community; that does not make us all evangelists in the five fold tradition.

We are all expected to give advice, help and support to one another as an act of lovingkindness and relationship. That does not make us pastors. We can all impart truth and learning in a sharing environment but we are not specifically teachers.

Our western mindset leads us to believe that *doing* is more important than *being*. We feel as though we always have to be doing something spiritually to earn God's favour: cleaning the church, teaching Sunday school, driving kids to football practice, working late, running errand after errand after errand. But this is not God's desire for us: He only wants to live with, and in, us. He longs for a relationship separate from the work of His Kingdom. He wants to *be* with us.

We each carry a profound and unfathomable call on our life, placed there by God Himself. It is fresh and new and completely beyond our natural ability to accomplish — God has called us to do something we cannot possibly do. We can meditate on that call for the rest of our days, strategize it, and even try and seize it; it doesn't matter. Like reaching for the stars, God's call is beyond us. It's a gift God has given each one of His children. In fact, our inability to accomplish it is exactly why He selected us to carry that call: *"But God has chosen the foolish things of the world to put to shame the wise, and God has chosen the weak things of the world to put to shame the things which are mighty,"* Paul wrote in 1 Corinthians 1:27.

The call must be impossible for us so that we can develop a relationship with the Lord that revolves around Intimacy and Dependency. There is no substitute for a life of joy filled sensitivity to the Person of the Holy Spirit.

Each day we rejoice in the grace of absolute dependence on the Name and the Nature of the Lord. Our walk with Him is filled with a conscious dependence upon who He is for us now in this present situation. Our hope is in Him. Our confidence rises up to meet His intentional nature.

Inevitably, there will be some people to whom God entrusts the gift of prophecy on a regular basis. Those who are moving in an increase of revelatory anointing can be said to be moving into a prophetic ministry rather than just an extensive use of that gift. When that ministry begins to impact whole cultures, nations, and governments, it signifies the change from prophetic ministry to the office of a prophet.

> *Prophecy is a joy to give and to receive*

Prophecy does not make some people better than others — there are no superior or inferior believers. Structural hierarchy has no place in the gifts of the Spirit.

Christians who perform supernatural exploits, or who have been given immense responsibilities within the Kingdom, will have built that influence on a solid base of humility and dependence on God. This level of anointing carries with it a deep sensitivity to, and intimacy with, the Holy Spirit. A lack of humility before God produces an absence of sensitivity to the Holy Spirit; this in turn creates a shortage of compassion for people. The loss of humility is one of the great problems in the realm of prophecy today, and flies in the face of what is taught throughout Scripture. In fact, the book of Proverbs is full of warnings regarding pride:

Humility Is The Key

"Surely He scorns the scornful, but gives grace to the humble." (Proverbs 3:34)

"When pride comes, then comes shame; but with the humble is wisdom." (Proverbs 11:2)

"A man's pride will bring him low, but the humble in spirit will retain honor." (Proverbs 29:23)

When we allow pride to pollute our relationship with God, we lose momentum and trust. Our top mission in life is to love God with everything in us, and love our neighbor the same way we love ourselves. Such dependence on God and respect for others produces the humility necessary for God to live in us.

The Nine Purposes Of Prophecy

Prophecy is a gift and ministry that we should tirelessly encourage and disciple in our churches. Unfortunately, human nature leads us to fear things we do not understand, and many misconceptions about prophecy arise out of a lack of knowledge and understanding about what it is, how it works, and the way in which it should be released in the local church.

Yet prophecy is too powerful a gift to ignore or treat poorly. It can accomplish a number of marvelous purposes:

- Restore people's dignity and self-respect,
- Edify, encourage, and comfort the Church,
- Bring correction or warning,
- Provide direction and enhance vision,
- Open up the teaching of the Word and confirm preaching,
- Release the Church into new doctrine or practices,
- Provide insight into counseling situations,
- Provide evangelistic breakthroughs, and
- Provide an agenda for prayer.

Prophecy Restores People's Dignity And Self-Respect

Many Christians sit in their churches, week after week, with no idea of their own worth and value to the Lord. The enemy, and life in general, conspire to strip people of their God-given identities and concepts of self-worth. For example, many people find it difficult to establish a relationship with God as their Father due to their own poor experience with their family.

> Prophecy declares the beauty that God sees

Hurts, wounds, rejection, and emotional trauma are a part of our lives, both before and after salvation. Fortunately, we serve a God who is committed to our physical, emotional, and mental healing. His goal is to bring us into the fullness of life in the Spirit. He sees us very differently than we see ourselves: *"The precious sons of Zion, valuable as fine gold, how they are regarded as clay pots, the work of the hands of the potter!"* (Lamentations 4:2).

Prophecy is a wonderful part of that healing and renewing process. When the angel of the Lord visited Gideon in Judges 6, he called out the hidden treasure in the Israelite: *"The LORD is with you, you mighty man of valor!"* The Lord looked beyond Gideon's circumstances — and the fact that he was cowering in a winepress for fear of being taken by the enemy — and started renewing his self-image. The human thing to do would have been to slap Gideon down for being a coward. But God had a better plan, and spoke to his potential. The next day, that scared kid pulled down a village stronghold and turned people back to the one true God. When we speak nobility to a person, nobility emerges. If we speak the life of Christ to someone, the life of Christ rises up in them. Prophecy brings us, by direct verbal communication, into contact with God's real perspective on our lives and current situations.

In this context, the goal of prophecy is to open our eyes to God's love and care, enabling us to come to our senses and escape from any snare in which the enemy has tried to entrap us. Prophecy reminds us, in a forthright and loving way, of everything God has provided in Christ Jesus. Prophecy restores our soul, renews our mind, and revives our spirit. Like a cold drink on a hot day, it refreshes us.

Such a prophetic word cuts through the darkness, bringing real light, faith, and confidence. It counters our poor attitudes and negative concepts about ourselves. When Gideon protested God's word, *"Indeed my clan is the weakest in Manasseh, and I am the least in my father's house,"* God just laughed: *"Surely I will be with you, and you shall*

> Goodness is God's theme and personality so it must be ours too

defeat the Midianites as one man." God helped Gideon understand and appreciate his personal value.

Prophecy Edifies, Encourages, And Comforts The Church

In 1 Corinthians 14:3, the Apostle Paul wrote one of the most famous verses on prophecy. *"But he who prophesies speaks edification and exhortation and comfort to men,"* he explained. Often, these are words that explain a part of God's nature in a specific situation. For example, if a prophetic word speaks of the greatness, the majesty, and the supremacy of God, it can stir up the Church to fight, stand its ground, and enter into prevailing prayer and warfare. It has exhorted people to stand firm.

If a word relates to God's compassion, His wholesale forgiveness, and His willingness to extend mercy and cleansing, it will cause people to approach Him and rebuild their lives. It has edified their spirits and released the kind of faith that the Holy Spirit can work with and build on.

Prophecy will not leave the Church feeling confused, degraded, or condemned. It will not make people feel inferior or intimidated. Instead, it will strengthen the ties between God and His people. The word, edification, means "building up," "strengthening," or "improving."

Encouragement is also released by prophecy. At the right time, in the right way, and with the proper word, the Lord can release a magnificent blessing through prophecy. This type of word gives a significant boost to the Church; it will reassure, inspire, and incite people to thanksgiving. It will stimulate faith and create a sense of well-being in the congregation. Put simply, prophecy changes the atmosphere, opening the doors to miracles by injecting faith into people.

Many years ago, I led a conference in a church that mistrusted the supernatural gifts — especially prophecy. The suspicion and unbelief in the room was almost tangible. I knew that unless God moved and did something superb, the weekend would be very difficult.

To prepare, I did the only thing I could do — I rested in the Lord. I resisted the temptation to try and move in the spectacular; instead, I wanted to let the Spirit move in the supernatural. I put all of my energy into being quiet and restful before God, choosing to let my vision be filled up with Him, rather than focusing on my circumstances. When the enemy tries to push anointed ministries into the spectacular, we must resist by humbling ourselves. *"He must increase, but I must decrease,"* was how John the Baptist explained it in John 3:30. We are not here to prove how powerful we are, but merely to serve the Lord.

The Purpose Of Prophecy

SAINT COLUMBA

Lived: 521 to 597

Prophetic Synopsis: Banished from Ireland for his role in starting a war, Columba sailed to the Scottish island of Iona and set up a mission there. The Scots loved him and quickly adopted him as their own. He was a gifted teacher, healer, and prophet. The Holy Spirit would make the saint sound the same to the listener in the front row of his church as he did to someone 1,000 steps away. Once, near Inverness and the fortress of King Brude, he was chanting with monks while Druids tried to distract the crowd with their own songs. Columba came to the walls and sang out Psalm 45:1. His voice was as loud as thunder — the king and the crowd jumped in fear. The Druids ran away.

He was incredibly gifted in prophesying blessing on people. On one occasion, a despised young boy, known in the community for being completely rebellious, snuck up on the saint. As the boy reached out to touch him, Columba grabbed him and pulled him close. Everyone around him said, "Send him away, send him away; why hold on to this wretched and disrespectful boy?" The child was terrified; he shook in Columba's arms.

"Let him be, brothers, just let him be," Columba said. "My son, open your mouth and put out your tongue. Although now this boy seems contemptible to you and quite without worth, yet let no one despise him on that account. For from this hour he not only will not displease you but will find great favor with you, and he will steadily grow from day to day in good conduct and in the virtues of the soul. Wisdom, too, and good sense will increase in him more and more from this day, and in this community of yours he will be a man of high achievement. His tongue also will be gifted with eloquence from God to teach the doctrine of salvation." That boy was Ernene, who became a well-known leader in the Irish church.

Key Comment: "O Lord, grant us that love which can never die, which will enkindle our lamps but not extinguish them, so that they may shine in us and bring light to others."

More: Read *The Life of Columba* by Adamnan

Source: Saint Adamnan, *Life of St Coumba / Adomnán of Iona*; translated by Richard Sharpe (Harmondsworth, Middlesex, England; New York: Penguin Books, 1995).

Prophecy Edifies, Encourages, And Comforts The Church

As the weekend started, I knew I couldn't react to the unbelief and negativity. My job was to be still and very aware of the Lord.

There is a difference between the supernatural and the spectacular. The supernatural is God breaking into our time space world in a way that is astonishing and amazing in its effect on our hearts and lives. Bodies are healed; miracles (producing something out of nothing) occur which leaves us breathless with amazement; the effect of God on our lives on days can be stunning.

That's the point. The *effect* of God is astonishing. The outcome of His work in our lives leaves us with a sense of wonder. However, mostly His entrance and His appearance can be unobtrusive, modest, quiet and restrained.

Isaiah knew Him as "the God who hides Himself" (45:15).

Jesus was present to the disciples but hidden from them on the road to Emmaus (Luke chapter 24). God chose a Bethlehem to reveal Jesus when a Jerusalem would have worked just as well. Elijah discovered that God was not in the wind that could break rocks into pieces. Nor was He in the earthquake on the mighty raging fire, (1 Kings 19). He was in the whisper of sound, like a gentle breeze blowing. A sound so small only a restful, quiet person could hear it. Stillness is so vital in the prophetic gift and ministry.

Without stillness prophetic people can be tempted to make a show. To do something for effect. The difference between the supernatural and the spectacular is in the cause and effect. With God the supernatural is mostly evidenced after He has moved; as in the parting of the Red Sea (Exodus 14:21). There was a strong east wind that worked all night turning the sea into dry land. God mostly works unseen even when He announces Himself!

The spectacular puts on a show up front. Lots of hype, showmanship, rhetoric and bluster. People put on a ringmaster type voice and become the stadium announcer to the audience. The word sounds good but when you write it down later, the content is actually quite minimal. The presentation can be dazzling and the aftermath disappointing.

> *If you can decrease, God will increase in you.*

The one thing that is visible is the prophet! All we have done is encountered someone's individual anointing rather than being engaged by the Living God. Under pressure, prophetic people can try to pull something out of the hat themselves. To make something happen. Fake it till you make it. Cause people to think that God is on the move.

The Lord doesn't work that way. He is normal, humble, gentle and mostly, not loud (He has His moments!). He works simply, quietly, honestly and

The Purpose Of Prophecy

SAINT AIDAN

Lived: 600 *(estimated)* to 651

Prophetic Synopsis: When King Oswald sent for help to evangelize his kingdom in 635 A.D., Aidan answered the call. He traveled across Britain and set up a community on the holy island of Lindisfarne. Aidan loved the Northumbrian people, walking all over northern England, preaching the Gospel and healing the sick. As the Venerable Bede wrote, "He took pains never to neglect anything that he had learned from the writings of the apostles and prophets, and he set himself to carry them out with all his powers."

Aidan was helped by Oswald, who often traveled with the little monk, interpreting for his people. Aidan and Oswald built churches throughout Northumbria. Aidan "cultivated peace and love, purity and humility," wrote Bede.

He was a significantly prophetic man. One Easter, Oswald and Aidan were sitting down to a feast in Oswald's castle. A servant came to Oswald and told him there were several poor people sitting hungry outside the wall. Oswald ordered the food to be taken to the poor, and a silver dish broken into pieces to give them spending money. "Why should these fast while I am feasting?" Oswald said. "God loves all alike, and not less the poor, but rather more." Aidan was so touched by Oswald's act that he grabbed the king's hand and said "May this hand never perish!" Three hundred years later, when Oswald's body was moved from its original burial site, monks found his hand was still perfect.

On another occasion, a man named Utta asked him for a blessing for his boat trip to Denmark. Aidan prophesied that a storm would strike his ship and gave him a bottle of holy oil to keep him safe. Sure enough, when the storm was at its worst, Utta poured the oil into the sea. Even as the sailors screamed "Lost! Lost! Lost! We'll die," the oil hit the sea and the storm stopped.

Key Comment: "The love of Christ — that wins and conquers all."

More: Read *The Ecclesiastical History of the English People* by Bede

---

Source: Bede, *The Ecclesiastical History of the English People; The Greater Chronicle; Bede's Letter to Egbert*, eds Judith McClure and Roger Collins. (Oxford, NY: Oxford University Press, 1994).

directly. Often you only know He has been there by the result, the miracle that has occurred. Heaven is not a three ring circus. God makes a show of the enemy, seldom Himself (Colossians 2:15). The best prophecy that has the most effect and excellent content is delivered quietly and humbly, even in the presence of thousands of people. It occurs because the prophet is only aware of God and the person who is receiving a word; all else disappears. Real prophets are not crowd-conscious but God-responsive. They engage with the intentionality of God both in the words and the manner in which they can be presented that will do the most good.

In the first meeting, as I stood to teach, God gave me a vision and pro-phetic interpretation for one of the young men present. In my spirit, I saw the man's father driving a yellow truck. The Lord showed me what company he worked for and the depot where he was based. I told the boy he could find his father there and that the Lord was doing a work of reconciliation. I told the boy quietly and very matter-of-factly. I wanted to be conscious of his feelings and how the Father would speak to him in a crowd. The church went wild! Apparently, the young man had recently accepted Christ, and the church had been praying that God would allow him to meet his father, whom he had not seen since he was four years old.

Talk about an encouragement for that church! The spontaneous applause showed how hungry they were for the hope of Christ to be revealed to them. The Lord did not want to focus on the church's unbelief, instead choosing to move in the opposite spirit. He did something that made their faith explode. That one prophetic word blew the weekend wide open for the supernatural presence of God to come in and change people. Faith began to rise; indi-viduals began to understand that the Lord was mighty and powerful and involved with them. The young man followed up on the prophetic word and has since reconciled with his father. It has bore incredible fruit.

Because prophecy so powerfully encourages us, it naturally sparks a spirit of thanksgiving and praise. It can reveal to people exactly what is on God's heart now and what we should do next in response to the moving of the Spirit. While I was speaking at a con-ference many years ago, the Lord showed me there was a woman in the auditorium who had been fasting and pray-ing for her unsaved daughter. He told me that this mother was desperately concerned that her rebellious daughter would get into drug-related prob-lems or be taken advantage of sexually.

Prophecy provokes thanksgiving

As I prayed for her, the Lord gave me the prophetic assurance that He was actively involved in this girl's life and that she would come to no harm.

Furthermore, the prophetic word told the mother that God had heard her prayers and was moving to answer them. In response to that, the prophecy continued, the mother was to stop praying and begin giving thanks, praising God for His involvement.

For several months afterwards, the mother gave thanks and praised God. In the first few weeks, very little changed for the positive — in fact, the situation worsened considerably. Still, the mother held on to the prophetic word and continued in praise and gratitude to the Lord.

God did exactly what He said He was going to do. The daughter has been fully restored to the Lord and her family, and the mother's life has been changed too. She now has a spirit of thanksgiving and a grateful heart. She is a woman who knows how to be released in praise and worship, and is a catalyst to lead others to do the same.

God's blessing should propel us into thanksgiving — our excitement over what He is doing must manifest itself in gratitude. Thankfulness is a test we need to pass every day of our lives. Whether life is good or bad, we always have something to give thanks for.

Every church will face tests of character, integrity, and commitment to God and one another. These tests are a vital part of corporate growth and development. If we fail them, we lose vital ground in the realm of the Spirit.

The Church will face many barriers, hindrances, and obstructions, as the enemy tries to move us away from our corporate identity and vision, reduce our expectancy for the supernatural, and eliminate any active faith from our community's lifestyle. Discouragement will constantly nip at our heels. When we enter seasons like this, we must release the prophetic amongst the congregation or send for a prophet to help us.

Encouragement in prophecy releases God's perspective and brings confidence and hope. The western understanding of hope has devalued it — true hope is absolute confidence in God. This type of confidence is at rest in turmoil because it laughs at the actions of the enemy. It produces enough faith that we can stand still and see God — or even march forward in power and expectancy.

Prophecy also releases comfort into lives that have been made bitter by hardness, pain, and difficult circumstances. God does not always shield us from the troubles of life, although He does promise to be with us as we go through those fires. People die for their faith every day. In 2003, some 160,000 people gave their lives for Christ. Loved ones die, children become terminally ill, people's lives are reduced to rubble by unfaithfulness and divorce. Money issues strangle families. Inexplicable tragedy can strike out of the blue.

Prophecy Edifies, Encourages, And Comforts The Church

Into every human tragedy, the Holy Spirit can drop a word of consolation to alleviate pain, reduce stress, invigorate hearts, soothe tension, and provide a wealth of support that will ultimately refresh people and gladden their hearts.

Prophecy Can Bring Correction And Warning

In Scripture, people were often given warnings through prophetic words, and called to repentance and change. In the New Testament the best example of this is found in the letters to seven churches in the book of Revelation chapters 2 and 3. We will look at just two of these churches, Ephesus and Pergamum.

> *Prophets must be Good News, even if that news is repent*

Each church was struggling with a particular issue and the word of prophecy to each was a considerable source of clarity, definition and strength. When looking at these words it is helpful to note a similar pattern in each.

Firstly there is a grace base to corrective prophecy. Secondly there is an understanding of the problem. Thirdly the honoring of what is honest and principled. Fourthly there is a clear word spoken directly to the issue. Finally there is a clear call to repentance and change. Prophecy is always for the common good (1 Corinthians 12:7) therefore people must profit from prophecy. A prophet must be Good News, even is that news is repent!

To the church at Ephesus there was a call to return to intimacy with the Lord. This is a good hardworking church, full of perseverance, who have tested false apostles and who are strong in the ways of God. In the midst of all of this they had slipped away from the first commandment.

Actually this is a common problem amongst churches today where the Great Commission has taken precedence over the First Commandment. In such places, worship is relegated to a minor role and the people are not discipled in a lifestyle of praise, thanksgiving and rejoicing. Thus there is no intimate connection with the Lord in the hearts of the congregation.

Ephesus used to be excellent in these things but had settled back into a working relationship with the Lord and not a friendship relationship that involved expressions of love and intimacy. In this prophecy there is a clear call to repentance, to think again, and to return to the things they did at first in worship.

The church at Pergamum had been brave enough to plant a church in the heart of the occult district in the city, "where Satan's throne is". They were caught up in the unending struggle between light and darkness. One of their number had been martyred as they constantly faced the battle to speak out for the Lord.

In such a contentious place the temptation always is to compromise or become tolerant of other beliefs. Tolerance is the new spirit of the age in our times. The church is being told to compromise its language and beliefs on a wide variety of issues in our culture and society. The church in Pergamum had dropped its guard and was allowing a variety of things to be taught that were harmful to the spiritual growth of its people.

Pergamum is a tough place to start a church and it needs tough people who stand up for the things of God even if their stand leads to death as in the case of Antipas. The call to repentance is a reminder that the call on them as a church is to stand up and fight. This is a corrective word that enables the church to regroup and recover their initial calling.

There is a protocol necessary in the church for prophetic words of this type. We will deal with this much more thoroughly in the second journal of this series which is Prophetic Protocol.

Prophecy Can Provide Direction And Enhance Vision

Direction, purpose, and vision are vital for individuals and groups. Where there is no vision, the people perish. From within a church, a prophetic word can be released that will provide a focus for our goals and plans. Personal and corporate vision can be birthed with a depth of faith. It is vital we understand and have confidence in the Lord's call upon our lives.

> *Confirmation is a vital part of prophecy*

We may need to be cautious where there has been a great deal of internal prophecy bringing direction and envisioning. All words need to be tested, especially those that pertain to the direction of a church. To avoid error or deception, it is a good idea to ask an established, mature prophetic ministry, unattached to the particular church, to give some confirmation from the outside. This person has no ax to grind and no flag to wave, therefore they can be impartial and objective, both in the judging process and in bringing a confirming word.

Words of direction and vision that come into the church from the outside can have a transforming effect on the work. Just as a word blessing the hidden treasure in an individual can bring that gift to the surface, so too can a word ignite a body. I have lost count of the times when God has used me in this manner. All over the world, I have been given the great opportunity to speak prophetically to churches. In many cases I have confirmed ideas, concepts and dreams that have been part of the conversation and prayers of leadership teams as they have deliberated on the next stage of their vision and calling.

On one particularly memorable occasion, I prophesied a conversation between two elders that had taken place while they were riding to the very meeting I was speaking at. They had been surprised to discover that they both had the same idea about creating a new pastoral initiative. During that meeting, I called them both out and laid hands on them for a new pastoral anointing. It was a God-given confirmation.

Prophecy can provide dynamic insight into situations not made clear by Scripture. It provides a distinctive perception of the things of God that may not be gained from the counsel of the Bible. Scripture provides an overall picture of the grand design of God and how to live in the Spirit, but it does not always give us the means or the method to do that effectively. Put simply, the Bible gives strategy while prophecy reveals tactics.

> Prophecy counters negativity

In 2 Chronicles 20, we see a powerful example of the power of prophecy. When some of Judah's greatest enemies aligned against King Jehoshaphat, the people did the one thing they knew to do: they gathered together to seek the Lord for His help. In the face of overwhelming opposition, they prayed.

Jehoshaphat stood before his countrymen and prayed, reminding God of how He had made a covenant with their forefathers. He spoke of the historical accounts of how God had delivered His people again and again. *"For we have no power against this great multitude that is coming against us; nor do we know what to do, but our eyes are upon You,"* Jehoshaphat concluded in verse 12.

Tradition stipulated that they should fast and pray when under attack, but it was the entrance of the prophetic that increased their faith and confidence — *"Then the Spirit of the LORD came upon Jahaziel the son of Zechariah, the son of Benaiah, the son of Jeiel, the son of Mattaniah, a Levite of the sons of Asaph, in the midst of the assembly,"* verse 14 records. Jahaziel prophesied what was to come:

> and he said, *"Listen, all Judah and the inhabitants of Jerusalem and King Jehoshaphat: thus says the Lord to you, 'Do not fear or be dismayed because of this great multitude, for the battle is not yours but God's. 'Tomorrow go down against them. Behold, they will come up by the ascent of Ziz, and you will find them at the end of the valley in front of the wilderness of Jeruel. 'You need not fight in this battle; station yourselves, stand and see the salvation of the Lord on your behalf,*

SAINT PATRICK

Lived: 387 to 461

Prophetic Synopsis: Ireland's patron saint was actually English; as a young boy, he was taken as a slave to Ireland. Years later, he escaped back to his homeland, but God had other plans for him.

One night, Patrick saw a vision of a man, "whose name was Victoricus, coming as it were from Ireland, with countless letters. And he gave me one of them, and I read the opening words of the letter, which were, 'The voice of the Irish'; and as I read the beginning of the letter I thought that at the same moment I heard their voice — they were those beside the Wood of Voclut, which is near the Western Sea — and thus did they cry out as with one mouth: 'We ask thee, boy, come and walk among us once more.'"

Patrick followed the prophetic call of God and returned to the nation that had enslaved him. He performed many miracles, planted several churches, and led thousands to Christ. He even prophesied of an Irish saint who would follow him by returning the Gospel to Britain: "A man-child shall be born of his race, he will be a sage, a prophet, a poet, a beloved lamp, pure, clear, who will utter no falsehood." This prophecy was fulfilled when Saint Columba left Ireland for Scotland.

Key Comment: "Christ be with me, Christ within me, Christ behind me, Christ before me, Christ beside me, Christ to win me; Christ to comfort and restore me; Christ beneath me, Christ above me, Christ in quiet, Christ in danger, Christ in hearts of all that love me, Christ in mouth of friend and stranger."

More: Read Saint Patrick's *Confession* and *Breastplate*

Sources: Charles W. Colby, *Selections From the Sources of English History*, BC *55–AD 1832*. (London: Longmans Green, 1920). Northumbrian Community. "Celtic Night Prayer." (Glasgow: Marshall Pickering, 1996).

Prophecy Can Provide Direction And Enhance Vision

o Judah and Jerusalem.' Do not fear or be dismayed; tomorrow go out to face them, for the Lord is with you." (2 Chronicles 20:15–17)

Prophecy made them tactically aware of God's plan for the situation. It was prophecy that pinpointed the exact whereabouts of the enemy, and showed Judah how to fight and what to expect. The entrance of the prophetic birthed confidence: *"Then the Levites of the children of the Kohathites and of the children of the Korahites stood up to praise the* LORD *God of Israel with voices loud and high"* (2 Chronicles 20:19). We need to live by every word that comes from the mouth of God, ordering our lives by Scripture and being led by the Holy Spirit. To be sons and daughters of God, we must earnestly desire to move in prophecy.

Prophecy is also vital in spiritual warfare. *"This charge I commit to you, son Timothy, according to the prophecies previously made concerning you, that by them you may wage the good warfare,"* Paul wrote in 1 Timothy 1:18. We need to use prophecies to fight the enemy and the circumstances of life.

Just as Jehoshaphat defeated the enemy on the basis of the prophetic word given to him, so we too can harness the power of the prophetic and defeat our spiritual enemies. Judah had been so energized by Jahaziel's word that it broke camp singing. We must never underestimate the power of the prophetic.

Joshua followed a similar pattern of listening and responding to a prophetic word in Joshua 6:1–5:

Now Jericho was tightly shut because of the sons of Israel; no one went out and no one came in. The Lord said to Joshua, "See, I have given Jericho into your hand, with its king and the valiant warriors. "You shall march around the city, all the men of war circling the city once. You shall do so for six days. "Also seven priests shall carry seven trumpets of rams' horns before the ark; then on the seventh day you shall march around the city seven times, and the priests shall blow the trumpets. "It shall be that when they make a long blast with the ram's horn, and when you hear the sound of the trumpet, all the people shall shout with a great shout; and the wall of the city will fall down flat, and the people will go up every man straight ahead."

> Prophecy increases faith

Jericho fell exactly as Joshua had been told it would. The method of Jehoshaphat and Joshua should never have worked; you won't find them in any kind of war manual as a way to win a battle. Great generals don't mimic their strategy. No record exists of other armies being destroyed by singing, nor a fortified city falling to marching feet and shouting voices. But in God's realm, prophecy and warfare go together.

Prophecy Opens The Teaching Of The Word & Confirms Preaching

In 1 Corinthians 13:2, the Apostle Paul wrote, *"And though I have the gift of prophecy, and understand all mysteries and all knowledge."* In Biblical language, a mystery is a secret, hidden thought concealed by God from humanity for a period of time. Several times in my life, the Lord has given me a flash of revelation that has driven me to search Scripture and opened up new areas of truth for me. Until that revelatory insight, those things had been hidden from me. The revelation inspired fresh study into the Scriptures.

It is sad when people get the flash of insight but don't follow it through. This can cause heresy and error rather than birthing deep revelatory truth. They present a portion of truth and a lot of speculation. They inadvertently corrupt the word with their own ideas and concepts which, if left unchecked, can cause real damage. Continuous revelation leads to study and prayer.

As the flow of revelation has increased in my life, I have scaled back my scheduled commitments. I want to have the time necessary to study, meditate and pray as part of my response to the words given to me. I currently spend four months each year in meditation.

The Apostle Paul understood the power of revelation in unwrapping the mysteries of the Kingdom of God. *"By revelation He made known to me the mystery... which in other ages was not made known to the sons of men, as it has now been revealed by the Spirit to His holy apostles and prophets,"* he wrote in Ephesians 3:3–5. Passages like this highlight the need for prophets to promote and provoke active judging and weighing of all prophetic utterances. By opening up the Word, we can wander into the danger of having false doctrine being added to the hazard of false prophecy. We must relentlessly seek God on issues like these.

Prophecy by itself will not save us from ignorance, nor will it solve all of our problems. The Corinthian church had a well-established prophetic presence, but still struggled with sin, immorality, and carnality. As Paul told them in 1 Corinthians 13:9, *"For we know in part and we prophesy in part."* Our prophecy can be incomplete, and we must remember that.

Prophecy can also confirm the preaching of the Word, both before and after teaching. It is common

> There is no breakthrough without follow through

in many churches to see a word given during worship tie in perfectly with the sermon to come.

As good Bereans we love to search the scriptures to see if these things are true. Prophetic input will drive us to the Bible not as Pharisees to disprove something (because they already hold a mindset, they have no intention of changing) but to look for confirmation and connection. Prophecy is a *complement* to scripture, not an addition.

Prophecy Can Release The Church Into New Doctrine Or Practices

The gift of prophecy also has a future aspect to it — a "now, but not yet," paradoxical feel to it. The book of Revelation is a perfect example of this; it is entirely predictive and prophetic, forth telling and foretelling.

When I write that prophecy can release a church into a new doctrine, I want to make it clear that we are not talking about new doctrines or practices never before heard of in the universal Church. Rather, I am speaking of a doctrine that might be completely new to a particular body of people.

Several years ago, the Lord gave me a series of prophetic words for certain churches concerning the type of people God would give them in five years' time. One church in particular was primarily Caucasian and very wealthy; the Lord told me that He was about to send them people who were broken, used, downtrodden, abused, abusers, addicts, alcoholics, involved in the occult, single parents, fatherless, and outcast.

> *Prophecy can open us up to new experiences of God*

To their eternal credit, the church came back several weeks later, asking for help. They fully understood that the arrival of these people would totally change the face of their church. The repercussions of the word were astounding. They knew they had been given time to make changes, and they wanted to be ready.

With a prophetic promise of harvest on the horizon, we knew the enemy would increase its attack on the church. To help them survive the storm, we taught the church about defensive spiritual warfare. This was a concept they had never considered before. They learned how to keep their own homes and lives free from spiritual attack, and how to fight off sickness and financial need. For many of these people, this was new ground; it was a revelation of a new truth and a new practice.

Later on, we taught them offensive warfare in life, prayer, and worship. We became more militant in our outlook. In worship, the church praised Jesus as the warrior King. After that, we taught about having a Joshua mindset; they became people who spoiled for a fight. They became people who

SAINT BRIGID

Lived: 450 to 523

Prophetic Synopsis: Renowned for her generosity and hospitality, this Irish saint was also wonderfully prophetic. In a prophecy eerily similar to one given by her contemporary, Saint Patrick, she foretold the ministry of Saint Columba, even giving the saint's Irish name and mother's identity: "The man-child of longsided Ethne, as a sage he is a-blossoming. Columcille, pure without blemish. It is not oversoon to perceive him."

As a child, Brigid was taken by the Holy Spirit to Bethlehem. It was an experience that changed her life.

When she was young, she would give her father's personal belongings and food to the poor. No matter how many times her father told her not to, she would give away clothing, pottery, and food to anyone who needed it more than she did. Her father became so frustrated that he decided to sell her to a king. He left her at the castle gate while he went in and discussed a price. Meanwhile, out at the gate, Brigid was approached by beggar, asking for money. She gave the poor man her father's sword. Her dad and the king were amazed. The king wouldn't buy her, saying: "She is too good for me — I could never win her obedience."

In an age where women had little authority, God gave Brigid hers. When the time came for Brigid to become a nun, she and a group of women asked Bishop Mel to bless them. Brigid was silent out of humility and respect before the great leader. But as the Bishop prayed, he saw the Spirit of God descend on her. He called her out: "I have no power in this matter," the Bishop said. "God has ordained Brigid."

Key Comment: "May God our Father, our strength and light, bless you beyond even all you would ask. For the weather is always right for the sowing of good seed."

More: Read *Brigid's Cloak* by Bryce Milligan and Helen Cann or *The Celtic Saints* by Nigel Pennick

---

Sources: Bryce Milligan, *Birgid's Cloak: An Ancient Irish Story*. (Grand Rapids, MI: Eerdmans Books for Young Readers, 2002). Nigel Pennick, *The Celtic Saints: An Illustrated and Authoritative Guide to These Extraordinary Men and Women*. (Sterling Pub Co Inc, 1997).

could move into new territories promised by God, expecting a fight and expecting to win.

After the calling comes the training. A similar pattern was unfolded in Acts 10, when Peter led Cornelius and his Gentile household to Christ. When God called Peter to go, he did. His prophetic vision on the rooftop the day before prepared him for a new call. Peter was given the same prophetic vision on three occasions. The interpretation of which called Peter to break with a centuries old tradition and open up a way for Gentile people to know the Lord. In that day and time this was scary stuff, small wonder that Peter was perplexed and had misgivings!

Indeed, it was only when he actually crossed the Gentile threshold of the house of Cornelius that revelation dawned on him. *"In truth I perceive that God shows no partiality,"* Peter said in Acts 10:34–35. *"But in every nation whoever fears Him and works righteousness is accepted by Him."* This lifted the early Church out of its Jewish context and made the salvation of Christ available to the whole world. It released men like Paul, Luke, Barnabas, Silas, John Mark, and Philip to preach the Gospel to all nations. A new doctrine had been released through Peter's prophetic vision and his willingness to follow Christ's commands.

Prophecy Provides Insight Into Counseling Situations

Counseling is a vital ministry in the Church today; it has become a necessary part of working out our salvation before God. However, the Church has done a great disservice to many of these people by preaching a poor quality of Gospel. Too many believers have received the Gospel of "having your needs met in Christ." This has created a generation of people who expect God and, by extension, the Church, to do everything for them.

The real Gospel, the one preached in Acts, was that Jesus was both Lord and Christ. The apostles' challenge to the unsaved was: "Jesus is Lord; what are you going to do about it?" Two thousand years later, we have developed a Church with an invalid culture not a warrior mindset.

Counseling should be conducted as part of the introduction to church life and the foundations of a Spirit-filled walk with God. To be most effective, it needs the cooperation of evangelists, pastors, teachers, and prophets — four ministries working together to bring about a good birth and a strong upbringing in the things of God.

> Prophecy introduces a new mindset for life

The prophetic can get to the heart of a problem in a profound way. *"Even now the ax is laid to the root of the trees,"* Jesus said in Matthew 3:10. *"Therefore every tree which does not bear good fruit is cut down and thrown into the fire."* A prophetic word allows us to focus on Jesus, a paradigm shift which sparks movement and change. Without the supernatural, counseling can focus on problems and processes rather than on Jesus the deliverer.

Prophecy can save a lot of time in counseling sessions. A prophetic word, in season, can save months of work by getting to the basics of an issue. It strips away unhelpful attitudes and layers of deception which people can hide behind. Prophecy, with its attendant associates of words of knowledge and wisdom, can save us from endless hours of dialogue by exposing situations and bringing a quick release. It causes an accelerated breakthrough.

The arrival of the supernatural means we cannot hide behind lies or deception. We can cover nothing up. Understanding this will provoke a level of honesty and godly fear that will break any stranglehold of sin in the lives of believers.

Prophecy Can Provide Evangelistic Breakthroughs

Paul's call in 1 Corinthians 14:24–25 is something to which every church should aspire:

> But if all prophesy, and an unbeliever or an ungifted man enters, he is convicted by all, he is called to account by all; the secrets of his heart are disclosed; and so he will fall on his face and worship God, declaring that God is certainly among you.

Everyone has a dream for their life. The Pharisees were the dream thieves of their day. They stole peoples dream of God giving them instead a sterile atmosphere filled with rules rather than an encounter with a loving God who understood their aspirations.

Many times the Lord has enabled me to see the dream of an individual and to relate it to them in joyful humility. In every case there has been an astonishment and delight (and not a few tears!) as people have understood for the first time, who they are in themselves. To be known by God when you are not fully aware of your own identity is a powerful moment that provokes worship in all manner of people.

> *Prophecy produces a greater awareness of God's nature*

It is amazing to see what can happen when a pre-Christian witnesses dynamic, dramatic, and accurate words of prophecy. They are always strongly affected by such obvious ministry of the Holy Spirit. For many, this is their first real introduction to the Lord and they fall in love with the God of dreams and want to follow Him.

I have seen many atheists and agnostics come to Christ through the gift of prophecy. This should come as no surprise; after all, Jesus Himself outlined the Holy Spirit's role in John 16:8–11:

> And He, when He comes, will convict the world concerning sin and righteousness and judgment; concerning sin, because they do not believe in Me; and concerning righteousness, because I go to the Father and you no longer see Me; and concerning judgment, because the ruler of this world has been judged.

Prophecy, by uncovering past needs and issues, can provide an agenda for repentance, restitution, and revival.

Prophetic evangelism is a growing phenomenon in the Church today. It causes the supernatural power of God to break through into people's lives. A number of churches around the world are going door-to-door in their communities and working by words of knowledge and prophecy. God knows which homes are ready for sowing and ripe for reaping. Gaining God's perspective provides a prayer agenda that will enable us to go to certain houses with something specific to say.

Prophecy Provides An Agenda For Prayer

Prayer, in its purest form, is finding out what God wants to do and then asking Him to do it. *"And whatever things you ask in prayer, believing, you will receive,"* Jesus said in Matthew 21:22. Why, then, do we seemingly receive so few answers to prayer today? Prayer, as it is taught today in most churches, is sporadic in its effect. Most of us have been brought up in a tradition that when something bad happens, prayer must begin immediately. This seems reasonable and even righteous, but on a deeper level, it actually hinders the power of God to work on our behalf. In my experience in churches and friendships, I have seen that when we pray too soon, we usually pray in unbelief. We find ourselves praying out of the shock or trauma of the situation itself, and we pray out of our panic, our worry, our anxiety, and our concern.

We enter God's presence with thanksgiving and His courts with praise. Rejoicing as a lifestyle enables us to live doubt free in our faith. It maintains a closeness of connection to the Father so that faith, peace and joy are operating on a high level continuously.

KING OSWALD

Lived: 605 to 643

Prophetic Synopsis: Oswald, born in Northumbria, the northeastern corner of England, spent seventeen years on the Isle of Iona, learning to be a monk. When his uncle, King Edwin, died, the murderous Cadwallan seized the throne and tormented Oswald's people. So the good prince returned, with his older brother Eanfrid, to rid Northumbria of Cadwallan. But Cadwallan killed Eanfrid almost immediately, leaving Oswald to fend for himself in Northumbria.

Oswald gathered an army of pagan people — men who had never even heard of Jesus Christ. He took his army to a place called Heavenfield to face Cadwallan in one final battle. The night before the battle, Oswald had a dream in which Saint Columba promised him victory. The next morning, Oswald brought together all of his warriors and ordered them to take a knee. He erected a huge wooden cross and bowed his head in prayer, saying, "Let us all kneel and jointly beseech the true and living God Almighty, in His mercy, to defend us from the haughty and fierce enemy, for He knows that we have undertaken a just war for the safety of our nation."

Oswald's army defeated Cadwallan and his much-stronger army. Oswald's warriors looked around and decided that there was no earthly way they could have routed Cadwallan so harshly, except for the miraculous intervention of Oswald's God. His dream and prayer opened the people's hearts and made them hungry for this newfound Saviour. Oswald sent for help from Iona, and received it in the form of Saint Aidan.

Key Comment: "Why should these fast while I am feasting? God loves all alike, and not less the poor, but rather more."

More: Read *The Ecclesiastical History of the English People* by Bede

---

Sources: Bede, *The Eccleciasticaly history of the English People; The Greater Chronicle; Bede's Lettter to Egbert,* eds Judith McClure and Roger Collins. (Oxford; New York: Oxford University Press, 1994).

Prophecy Provides An Agenda For Prayer

A joyful heart finds it easy to trust and to hear the voice of God. We can come before the Lord in worshipful listening in order to hear what His heart is for us in this situation.

Jesus is praying for us. The Holy Spirit is praying for us. We are the third part of a threefold cord in prayer. That means we must pray *with* the answer — not to try to find one.5

By asking God for a revelation of His will for a situation, we change the atmosphere of our prayer. When God tells us the way something will unfold, we can't help but pray full of faith and confidence! This is why most successful prayer initiatives have their roots in the prophetic.

In 1982, God began to show me things He wanted to do in the British church. I saw that the Charity Commission would be given real teeth to expose financial malpractice and comment on value for money in all voluntary agencies, including churches. In the two decades since, we have seen the charitable status of several agencies revoked. I also saw that the government would invest millions of pounds in community endeavors. After doing a major value-for-money study, some long-established charities folded, while new ones were created. The Church had the opportunity to step into that vacuum and create real social change.

Some churches did just that. I think of my hometown of Manchester, England, where a group of churches got together and envisioned a long-term plan for the city. To get the ball rolling, they decided to start saving some money. It took them a few years, but finally they had enough money in the bank to put their plan in motion.

Together, the churches approached Manchester's civic government, police department, social services, and business community with an idea called Eden 2000. With the help of the city's experts, they picked the worst neighborhood in Manchester. This particular area was full of crime. The streets were filthy. It had been compared by the media to a war zone. It was a godless, hopeless place.

But the churches were up to the challenge. Together, they mobilized 20,000 Christians over several weeks. These Christians went into the neighborhood and started working. They painted houses… many hundreds. They cleaned up gardens. They picked up trash. They planted roses. They built playgrounds. They prayed for everyone they met. They started two churches. They worked and worked and worked. In

> *Prophecy releases us to explore the future and to own the present*

---

5   The practice of this type of prayer is found in the journal on "Crafted Prayer," part of the Being with God series (www.brilliantbookhouse.com).

those two weeks, not a single crime was committed in the area. At the end of Eden 2000, people were weeping. "Don't leave us!" they cried. The neighborhood has been a changed place ever since.

In 1982, God also showed me that a network of deliverance and intercessory ministries would bloom across the nation. These works provide a strategy for warfare and inter-church (and inter-city) prayer links. They share information, training and equipping programs, and a common warfare strategy. The overwhelming success of the 24–7 Prayer movement is just one highly-visible component of the fulfillment of this word.

A word about unity was also given to me. I used to think the name "United Kingdom" was a joke. However, God has shown me it is a prophetic name. The Lord is raising up champions in the Celtic nations — men and women who have a tremendous anointing for unity. They will turn the hearts of the nations toward one another.

We will have conferences and conventions aimed at more than just unity — they will actively promote reconciliation, apology, and restoration. Forgiveness and healing will flow as the north-south divide in England dies. Inter-country and inter-city rivalry will perish. Lancashire will stop fighting the War of the Roses with Yorkshire. Cities — even Manchester and Liverpool — will be joined in heart and spirit. Strongholds of history, bigotry, treachery, and betrayal will be torn down. As these things are finally dealt with, we will see economic and spiritual revival break out in these areas.

The Holy Spirit came to Jesus' followers when *"they were all with one accord in one place"* (Acts 2:1). The Spirit finds unity irresistible. Conversely, the demonic inhabits disunity. Unity can start with one person making a stand for love. What we need is active personal, individual, and corporate promoting of unity in every church, home, and city in every nation. The Eden 2000 project in Manchester UK is a prophetic template of what God can accomplish when believers unite.

Finally, God showed me that there was a quickening spirit upon the British Church, particularly on established, institutional Christianity. I have spent thousands of hours working with domestic churches in various denominations, thoroughly enjoying the relationships I have built there. These groups offer a fascinating mix of growth, change, passion for Jesus, and a new radicalism about church planting and community involvement. They exhibit a great hunger for reality and the supernatural presence of God.

The British Church is more influential in the western church world now than it has been in centuries. What we thought might take years to accomplish has taken months, thanks to God's grace.

Prophecy Provides An Agenda For Prayer

Each of these prophetic words provided me with an agenda to pray. I have spent countless hours and days praying into these things. In prophecy, God's will is expressed. Where God's will is made known, we have the basis for an ongoing prayer thrust until His will comes to pass.

Four Common Arguments Against Prophecy

While prophecy seems to have come to the forefront of progressive church life in recent years, the truth is that it has been an integral and vibrant part of Christianity throughout the ages. It is a rich part of the heritage of God's people. The Bible makes it clear that Jesus Christ is our Prophet, Priest, and King. Sadly, much of the Church does very little study of the verses which clearly portray Christ as prophet:

> "And the crowds were saying, "This is the prophet Jesus, from Nazareth in Galilee." (Matthew 21:11)

> "Therefore when the people saw the sign which He had performed, they said, "This is truly the Prophet who is to come into the world." (John 6:14)

> "And He said to them, "What things?" And they said to Him, "The things about Jesus the Nazarene, who was a prophet mighty in deed and word in the sight of God and all the people. (Luke 24:19)

When Christians preach that the prophetic gift is not for today, we preach a two-thirds Gospel. If we only own Him as King and Priest, we strip the Church of all supernatural power. Yet a vast percentage of Christians do just that. Put simply, the faulty doctrine of dispensationalism says that the outpouring of the Holy Spirit, with all of His gifts and graces, was simply given to kick start the Church two thousand years ago. Now that we have the Bible, dispensationalists believe, we have no more need for these extraneous things of the Spirit. The moving of the Spirit belongs to another time, or dispensation, as they term it.

Such faulty theology falls down in one important way: the very Scripture they hold incredibly dear instructs Christians to examine prophecy carefully and hold on to the good part of the word after weighing it. "Do not despise prophecies," Paul wrote in 1 Thessalonians 5:20–21. "Test all things; hold fast what is good." In

To argue against the supernatural life is to...

1 Corinthians 14:1, Paul said prophecy should be coveted: *"Pursue love, and desire spiritual gifts, but especially that you may prophesy."*

Prophecy has been in use throughout Church history, greater in some centuries than in others. Many of the most famous Christian leaders throughout the ages have operated in the gift — even if they haven't called it "prophecy." In this book, we have given you snapshots of some of the great saints and leaders throughout history who have operated in the gift of prophecy. Prophecy usually goes into decline when Church leaders usurp authority and try to control what is said and done in the Body of Christ. But Jesus is the true head of the Church (Ephesians 1:22), and since the days of Adam He has consistently used prophecy to speak into the world.

Despite the historical and Scriptural evidence for prophecy, some Christians simply refuse to believe that God speaks today. Their objections break down into four faulty arguments against prophecy:

1. The Bible replaces spiritual gifts,

2. Preoccupation with gifts prevents effective evangelism,

3. Fruit is more important than gifts, and

4. The gifts of the Spirit are dangerous.

Does The Bible Replace Spiritual Gifts?

Essentially, dispensationalists argue that because we have the whole revelation of God in Scripture, the gifts of the Holy Spirit are no longer necessary. Of course, many of the people who hold this view still pray for a miracle or healing when a loved one is sick! Prophecy is done away with, they argue, because the perfect — the Scripture — has come, using an interpretation of 1 Corinthians 13:8–10 as their foundation: *"Love never fails. But whether there are prophecies, they will fail; whether there are tongues, they will cease; whether there is knowledge, it will vanish away. For we know in part and we prophesy in part. But when that which is perfect has come, then that which is in part will be done away."*

Yet this argument falls down when the same perfect Word of God, less than a chapter later, encourages the Church to *"pursue love, and desire spiritual gifts, but especially that you may prophesy"* (1 Corinthians 14:1).

... promote unbelief in the natural world

Dispensationalism has been rightly discredited in a large part of the Christian Church because it conflicts with a number of things Jesus said concerning the Person and work of the Holy Spirit in John 14–16:

> "Truly, truly, I say to you, he who believes in Me, the works that I do, he will do also; and greater works than these he will do; because I go to the Father." (John 14:12)

> "But the Helper, the Holy Spirit, whom the Father will send in My name, He will teach you all things, and bring to your remembrance all things that I said to you." (John 14:26)

> "If you abide in Me, and My words abide in you, ask whatever you wish, and it will be done for you." (John 15:7)

> "When the Helper comes, whom I will send to you from the Father, that is the Spirit of truth who proceeds from the Father, He will testify about Me." (John 15:26)

> "And He, when He comes, will convict the world concerning sin and righteousness and judgment: concerning sin, because they do not believe in Me; and concerning righteousness, because I go to the Father and you no longer see Me; and concerning judgment, because the ruler of this world has been judged." (John 16:8–11)

> "But when He, the Spirit of truth, comes, He will guide you into all the truth; for He will not speak on His own initiative, but whatever He hears, He will speak; and He will disclose to you what is to come". (John 16:13)

> "All things that the Father has are Mine; therefore I said that He takes of Mine and will disclose it to you. (John 16:15)

The doctrine of dispensationalism completely conflicts with Jesus' own teaching of the purpose of His death, burial, resurrection, and ascension — the four most important moments in the spiritual history of the world. Jesus Himself taught that the Holy Spirit was to have a key place in the ongoing life of a Christian. Dispensationalism clashes with the Gospels like a loud cymbal being fiercely played in an otherwise perfectly-orchestrated

SAINT AUGUSTINE OF HIPPO

Lived: 354 to 430

Prophetic Synopsis: Few have done more to shape Christian theology and thought than St. Augustine. Born to a pagan father and devoutly Christian mother, Augustine struggled throughout his early life to find the one true path. The wilder he lived, the less contentment he found.

His mother, Monica, prayed diligently for her son's salvation. In answer to her prayers, God gave her a stunningly prophetic dream. In it, a Man of Light asked her why she was so sad. "When she replied that her tears were for the soul I had lost, he told her to take heart for, if she looked carefully, she would see that where she was, there also was I," Augustine wrote in his *Confessions.* "And when she looked, she saw me standing beside her on the same rule."

Nine years later, her dream would come true when Augustine met the Light for himself. "What I saw was something quite, quite different from any light we know on earth," Augustine said. "I realized that I was far away from You. It was as though I were in a land where all is different from Your own and I heard Your voice calling from on high, saying, 'I am the food of full-grown men. Grow and you shall feed on Me. But you shall not change Me into your own substance, as you do with the food of your body. Instead you shall be changed into Me.' And, far off, I heard Your voice saying, 'I am the God who is.' I heard Your voice, as we hear voices that speak to our hearts, and at once, I had no cause to doubt."

Key Comment: "Faith is to believe what you do not see; the reward of this faith is to see what you believe."

More: Read Saint Augustine's *Confessions* and *City of God*

Sources: St. Augustine of Hippo, *Confessions,* ed. John Rotelle, trans. R. S. Pine-Coffin (New York: Penguin, 1961). Saint Augustine, *The City of God,* trans. Marcus D. D. Dods. (New York: The Modern Library, 1950).

symphony. It is a confusing, offensive, and disturbing hypothesis that does not align with the Bible.

The true meaning of 1 Corinthians 13:12 simply refers to the end of all things and a full revelation of God to each believer. For now, we see dimly in comparison with that face-to-face, eternal revelation to come. In Heaven, we will fully know — and be fully known. This verse is clearly not talking about this life, but the eternal life to come. In that place, prophecy will not be needed: absolute perfection and communion with God will reign. I can hardly wait for that time!

The idea of dispensationalism is an insult to the person and sacrifice of Jesus. In all of His teaching on the Holy Spirit, He never once mentioned that the gifts were temporary, or that they would run out before His return. In fact, the Holy Spirit, and His gifts and graces, are a permanent fixture in the Church to enable the Bride of Christ to be made ready and presentable for her Bridegroom. The Spirit empowers us to preach the Gospel, with signs and wonders following, to the very ends of the earth. There is so much work to do; we need the Holy Spirit now more than ever. Why would God withhold the Spirit from every generation, except one, when He has given us so much to accomplish?

Dispensationalists believe that around the time the final early Church apostle died, the gifts of the Holy Spirit evaporated. If this is true, why is there no mention of it in early Christian writings? Surely the whole of Christendom would have been brokenhearted that the heavens suddenly turned to brass. How did it happen? When did it happen? Was it immediate? Was it the instant the Apostle John died? If someone had prayed at 11:55 a.m. for a healing, would it have happened? If that same person prayed six minutes later, after the gifts were taken, would they have missed their chance? It just seems so ludicrous to forget healing, wholeness, and fullness — Heaven is now closed! You're on your own, folks. One moment, healing is a sign of God's power and the expression of His heart to the world; the next it's gone.

At Pentecost, the Apostle Peter spoke these words (Acts 2:38–39):

> Peter said to them, "Repent, and each of you be baptized in the name of Jesus Christ for the forgiveness of your sins; and you will receive the gift of the Holy Spirit.

> "For the promise is for you and your children and for all who are far off, as many as the Lord our God will call to Himself."

It's hard to get further off than two thousand years later, but Peter's promise still rings through the ages and includes us.

Peter's prophetic word was given in a moment where the Holy Spirit was being poured out. Tongues and interpretation were commanding the attention of those who did not believe. Healings were about to become everyday occurrences for believers. It was made in the context of the supernatural invading the earth, causing an explosion of understanding and desire for God. The Holy Spirit turned that city upside down and inside out. This revolution had massive repercussions around the world.

> The Kingdom of Heaven is a show and tell realm of power and miracles

Into that context, Peter spoke prophetically to those early, and largely unsaved, people gathered to witness a miracle. He stood and taught them from history, weaving in the truth of Jesus for the present day, and prophesying of the future.

The gifts of the Holy Spirit are indeed for today; to believe otherwise is to believe deception.

Does Preoccupation With The Gifts Prevent Effective Evangelism?

Adherents to this idea teach that one needs to strip themselves of anything that would divert them from the primary objective of preaching the Gospel. It cannot be denied that some churches and small groups have become self-indulgent "bless me" clubs where the gifts are practiced endlessly on other believers. This breeds a type of "spiritual junkie," an addict looking for another hit of prayer. Many people chase that experiential relationship with the Holy Spirit for the purpose of self-gratification and excitement. They bounce from church to church, looking for the next "move of God." Much of this adolescent spiritual behavior is due to the fact that many Christians have a poor understanding of the Kingdom of God.

There are three aspects to establishing the Kingdom of God on earth, in a post modern world. They are Renewal, Revival and Reformation.

First and foremost, we are lovers of God. It is our primary goal to live by the first commandment: "love the Lord your God with *all* your heart, soul, mind and strength". The present day church needs a Renewal of her first love experience. We must value intimacy and have a vision for it as part of individual and corporate life. We must prize worship and take steps to improve and increase our worship on every level. We must disciple people into a continuous joyful encounter with the Living God. We need to teach them how to: praise the Lord; practice continuous thanksgiving; and to embrace the joy of rejoicing as a lifestyle.

Revival is not about the lost getting saved. One cannot revive something that has never been alive. Revival is therefore about the church returning to a place of passion for the world in which we live and the lost in particular. Revival is about the restoration of passion for that which Jesus died to save. Revival occurs when the church joyfully takes up the ministry of reconciliation and becomes ambassadors for Heaven. The Great Commission and the Second Commandment are one and the same.

> *The Gospel is not just in word but power!*

When the church lives fully in the first and second commandments then we are moving fully in Renewal and Revival in the Spirit. The two when combined will force the world to experience a Reformation. The walls of the church are knocked flat and what we have as our habitation experience of His presence is suddenly let loose on an unsuspecting world just as it was on the day of Pentecost.

When this occurs we will hear the world crying out today as they did in the early church… the people who have turned the world upside down are here, too!" (Acts 17:6)

We are here to preach the Gospel of the Kingdom, not just build the Church. The Church comes out of the Kingdom — not vice versa. When we understand that we must lay aside everything to seek the Kingdom, we will see a renewal occur that will truly honor the Lord.

When we appreciate the fact that everything we know and have must be channeled into establishing the Kingdom, we will see Church, leadership, lifestyle, pastoring, teaching, and the gifts of the Spirit in a completely different light. When this happens, revival will be upon us.

Revival is actually about the Church coming back to her original purpose before God.

This will occur when we allow Jesus to inhabit us. For me, revival can be defined as the Church coming back to a place where God can trust us with the things He really wants to give us. When that happens, there will be a reformation. God will knock down the walls of His Church, and what we have in a Sunday meeting or weekend conference will be the same as what we have in the world. Miracles will happen, God will be in full evidence, people will get saved by the hundreds and thousands, and creation's longing for the sons of God to move in power will be answered.

I believe strongly in prophetic evangelism, words of knowledge for the unsaved, gifts of healing across the whole community, and expressing God's heart prophetically in the earth to all people. This is the Gospel I read about in the book of Acts. I have been privileged to see pre-Christians respond to a prophetic word and begin their journey into the Kingdom. The supernatural presence of the Holy Spirit, through His graces and gifts, can impact a hard community in a way that simple preaching cannot. The Apostle Paul himself said that his preaching was not in word only, but by demonstration of the Holy Spirit.

The truth is that spiritual gifts get people's attention, which makes the Word vibrant and irresistible to them. When I worked in a training company many years ago, I would listen carefully to the things God told me to do. Once, I doubled the value of a contract during a pitch because the Lord told me to. When we won the bid — at a huge profit — my employer's eyes were opened to the power of God. It gave me many opportunities to speak into his life.

It doesn't have to be a million-dollar contract to be God. I have visited strangers' houses and prayed for washing machines to work. What am I, a Maytag repairman? Of course not! I'm just someone who wants God to do miraculous things. "Healing" a washing machine — several times — gave me the opportunity to share my faith with a family that I would have otherwise never met.

I have prophesied many times to pre-Christians and seen some spectacular results as they come to God. One woman had not seen her daughter for four years following a family argument. On a whim, she came to a church where I was preaching. She was shocked when I prophesied over her that not only was her daughter safe, but that she would see her in four days and their rift would be healed. No one in that church knew her or her issue — but God did.

> People love to see god at work!

She was astonished when the word came true in the few days following the meeting. "It was like Heaven opened and I realized that God knew me, but I didn't know Him," she told me afterwards. "The knowledge that He was interested and concerned about her family drove her to want to know Him for herself."

Is The Fruit More Important Than The Gifts?

In Galatians 5:22–23, the Apostle Paul listed the fruit of the Holy Spirit: *"love, joy, peace, longsuffering, kindness, goodness, faithfulness, gentleness, self-control."* It is absolutely true that the Church has many people with supernatural gifting and difficult, shoddy characters. It is also correct to say that there are many nice Christians with no overt manifestation of the power of the Holy Spirit in their lives.

We need both good character, as defined by the fruit, and the power of the Spirit. While it is undoubtedly true that the gifts without the fruit are made worthless (1 Corinthians 13:1–2), it is also true that the Gospel cannot be preached effectively without power (Romans 1:16). The word must be confirmed by signs following. People were attracted to Jesus by both His personality and His miracles.

In my schools of prophecy, I have seen many people grow in love because of their training in the gift of prophecy. Their desire for God matures their love for others. They inherit the characteristics of the God whom they want to share with people. I have said countless times that God is the kindest person I have ever known. Every day, He shows me more of His kind nature. He is full of matchless grace, peace, and rest. His love stretches from everlasting to everlasting. His mercy, patience, and long-suffering are legendary. He is slow to anger and swift to bless, abounding in lovingkindness. Every fruit of the Spirit is in full bloom in His nature. These truths cannot be communicated without affecting the giver, as well as the word's receiver.

> The Father is relentlessly kind

The fruit is not more important than the gift. We must not let the enemy push us into a choice that the Holy Spirit has not asked us to make. In matters of morality, the fruit of our characters must always take precedence. In times of development, fruit and gift grow together. Fruit does not grow well in a vacuum. We want the fullness of God — both gift and fruit.

Are The Gifts Of The Spirit Dangerous?

Are the gifts of the Spirit dangerous? I certainly hope so! They should be dangerous to the world, hazardous to the health of the enemy, and a threat to our apathy and indifference. Prophecy is attacking, stimulating, and provoking. It is designed to put a sharp edge on our relationship with God in how we live our lives and handle truth.

The Bible itself says truth is dangerous. *"For the word of God is living and active and sharper than any two-edged sword, and piercing as far as the division of soul and spirit, of both joints and marrow, and able to judge the thoughts and intentions of the heart"*. says Hebrews 4:12. It can cut both ways and needs careful handling. We would never stop using Scripture, even if it cut us to the quick — why then fear the cut of prophecy?

We can no longer afford to ignore things because they are dangerous. Apathy is the most dangerous attitude in the Church, but there are entire

SAINT CUTHBERT

Lived: 635 to 687

Prophetic Synopsis: Cuthbert was fifteen years old when his life changed forever. While out tending sheep on a hill in Northumbria, he had a vision. As he described it: "Methought I saw a dazzling radiance shine suddenly out of the darkness, and in the midst of the streaming light a choir of angels descended to earth and lo! They were bearing away as in a globe of fire a happy soul." He went to Melrose Abbey and told the monks of his experience. It turns out he had the vision at the exact moment Saint Aidan died. His vision became known as the Passing of Saint Aidan.

Eata, whom Aidan discipled, in turn took Cuthbert and discipled him. Eventually, Cuthbert became the leader of Melrose Abbey. He was very popular throughout Northumbria. "Cuthbert was so skillful a speaker and had such a light in his face and such a love for proclaiming his message that none presumed to hide their inmost secrets, but openly confessed all the wrongdoing for they felt it impossible to conceal their guilt from him," wrote the historian Bede.

Soon, Cuthbert became the spiritual leader of all of Northumbria, taking over at the holy island of Lindisfarne. He loved to be alone with God, to pray and read Scripture.

Cuthbert even prophesied his own death to his best friend, Herebert, who would visit him once a year. Herebert and Cuthbert had a unique relationship: Herebert would spend several hours every day praying for God to help Cuthbert in his leadership duties. Then, once a year, Herebert would visit his friend and Cuthbert would encourage him. One year, Cuthbert told Herebert to ask him for anything because Cuthbert was about to die. Herebert asked him for just one thing: that they would die together. Both died on March 20, 687.

Key Comment: "Christ's soldier is the fittest champion to fight the powers of darkness."

More: Read *The Ecclesiastical History of the English People* by Bede

Sources: Bede, *The Eccleciasticaly history of the English People; The Greater Chronicle; Bede's Lettter to Egbert*, eds Judith McClure and Roger Collins. (Oxford; New York: Oxford University Press, 1994)

communities who have not managed to avoid it. Unbelief is like a dangerous cancer to the things of God, but millions of people are affected by it.

No one would ever suggest that we cease preaching or teaching in case we fell into error. Instead, we must work together in defense of truth and the proclamation of the Word of God. In prophecy, we must teach people how to be in the Spirit when they speak. Whether we prophesy, preach or teach, the same principle applies; there is safety in the anointing of God.

Truth: The Best Safeguard

In the Church today, we are seeing a resurgence of the prophetic gift and ministry. Unfortunately, with the true comes the counterfeit. Abuse, misuse, and deception will abound along with the correct use of prophecy. Clearly, we need to know how to handle the gift, ministry, and impact within the work of God.

Throughout Church history, there has been false prophecy and false teaching. If we look objectively at the past two millennia, we find that many more churches have been ruined by false teaching than by false prophecy. For example, teaching on accountability in the 1970s led many leaders into heavy shepherding and accusations of control and domination. Accountability is right and proper, but only if it is God-centered — not man-centered. The truth of proper Biblical accountability has been marred by the practice that was taught and encouraged. Should we now abandon this truth for fear of further misuse or abuse? Or should we seek to introduce proper use of accountable behavior as an honor to God?

Where there has been abuse, we must work even harder to reclaim the truth. The alternative is to have dozens of "no-go" areas in our churches and to lose massive parts of the Gospel.

Many people's lives have been damaged by wrong pastoral advice — far more than the prophetic. Hardly any checks and balances exist for the role of a pastor. It seems pastors can get away with almost anything. There are even some pastors who will not allow themselves to be challenged without an explosion of some sort happening. Yet no one has proposed the need to dismantle the pastoral ministry.

> *The wheat always grows up with the weeds*

One of the major problems in the Church today is the number of people who are inadequately birthed into the Kingdom of God. Salvation is more a process than it is an instantaneous event. Many people's lives are touched by the Holy Spirit and are brought into a measure of real change.

However, if this is not followed up with good teaching, pastoring, and discipling, people's lives will not be fully claimed for the Gospel.

Poor evangelism and preaching have created a back door Christianity, in which people come to Christ on the basis of having their needs met rather than the demand to submit to His Lordship. In spite of this, when people talk about balance and accountability, it is inevitably connected with prophetic ministry. It is true that a prophet on his own is out of balance — but then, a pastor, teacher, or evangelist on his own is also out of balance.

This factor has caused more widespread damage in the Church of Jesus Christ than any loose prophetic cannon. The only answer to misuse in all areas of Church life is not non-use — but proper use. Truth is always our best safeguard against deviation.

Spiritual leaders must not discourage gifting on the basis that it could be wrong or dangerous. We must use every opportunity to exercise our people in rightly hearing the word of truth. Sadly, many leaders are more concerned with avoiding conflict and difficulty than prospering from those words.

It is far easier to create suspicion and fear in people's minds than to tackle the issues involved. Allowing these things grieves the Holy Spirit, however, and our only response must be to apologize, repent, and change our ways.

Since the earliest Bible times, there has been false prophecy. Why should we be surprised by it today? Why don't we accept that the existence of a counterfeit only further proves the existence of the authentic?

Our Response

Our hearts must be filled with a desire for God's truth. This hunger needs to consume everything within us. Integrity is created when we are prepared to break through every barrier, cost, and issue in order to be what is right and proper. We need to *be* the truth, not just *know* it. The truth that prophecy is for today must be appropriated by the whole Church. Part of that ownership is a determination to work through all of the anomalies and dilemmas of releasing the prophetic gift and ministry properly.

The Church is pregnant with the prophetic. Care is needed to bring that prophetic seed to full term. The labor pains are yet to come for the whole ministry; the joy of birthing a new prophetic environment throughout the whole Body of Christ will be worth all of the suffering we must endure.

Jesus said, "My sheep know my voice". The heart of the issue is not just about a spiritual gift. It is concerning our relationship with the Lord. We cannot build a relationship with someone if we cannot hear what they are saying. If a Christian chooses to believe that God no longer speaks to His people, then they had better get as close as possible to God so that they can lip read!

This boils down into a quest for true spiritual maturity. God's goal is to see His children walk as fully mature sons and daughters — believers who can be trusted completely.

The Lord has sent His Spirit into our hearts whereby we cry "Abba, Father" (Galatians 4:6). This is a relational paradox.

A paradox is two opposing ideas contained in the same truth. God is a father and also a judge. He is full of mercy and also justice. He has compassion and also moves in judgment.

We have two types of relationship with the Lord. Firstly we learn to live before Him as a much loved child. We practice a child like faith and innocence. We learn to simply relax and trust in His greatness. When under utmost pressure we know we can lift our arms up and expect His greatness to overwhelm us and lift us up into a higher place. Children are uncomplicated, simple and trusting.

> *Childlike trust is the bedrock of mature faith*

Secondly we learn to say "father" as an adult in the Spirit. To speak out of a place of growing maturity in who the Lord is making us to be. "For as many as are led by the Spirit of God, these are the sons of God" (Romans 8:14). A significant difference exists between being a child of God and being a son of God. We are all children of God, but not all of us, yet, are sons (daughters) of God.

The difference between the two is "learned" experience. As we grow in Christ we experience the other side of the relational paradox. We learn how to move from a different place of relational anointing. We do not outgrow the childlike stage so as to discard it. Rather we move across the range of relational power from Abba to Father. We need both. The childlike faith and trust in the bigness of God is hugely important to maintain as we move out in the Spirit and encounter the wide variety of problems, issues and crises that life will present. It is the bedrock of our relationship with the majesty of God.

The adult son is just as necessary and vital to the increase of the Kingdom. We are mature men and women who can move out in the faith, power and authority that we have allowed the Holy Spirit to develop in our relationship with the Father in Jesus. It is so wonderful to be in Christ Jesus, praying to the Father by the power of the Holy Spirit.

Every time we encounter a new level of anointing and warfare we do so as a much loved child. We explore this new realm with childlike trust and wide eyed wonder. We appropriate it with the grace and simplicity of child like relationship. Then the Holy Spirit teaches us to move out in presence, authority and power into a place of dynamic faith as a mature person in our experience of God. It is most delightful for us to have that range of relational experience to develop in the course of life with all its attendant issues and difficulties.

As a child before the Father we revel in His bigness. We are in awe of His majesty and His capability. He really can do anything! We are amazed at His capacity for us. His willing heart toward us. We revel in His intentionality and promise. We trust him implicitly; He is our Daddy.

As an adult before the Father we revel in His authority, passion, vision and faith. We love to stand in the problem, holding on to the promise, knowing that the provision will come to us. We love His values and principles. We treat them as our own.

As a child we are trusting the Lord. As an adult son, we are learning to be trusted by Him. Our goal is to get to the place where our maturity is a source of great delight to the Father. "This is My beloved Son, in whom I am well pleased," (Matthew 3:17). That moment signified a huge upgrade for Jesus, from carpenter's son, into His supernatural call to be the Messiah. Fully mature sons and daughters receive an anointing that they have never walked in before. They know by experience how to be available to the purposes of God and constantly wait on and attend to Him. They are consistent in their service to Him. Developing spiritual maturity is the call of every Christian... and every prophetic voice.

Notes

Notes

The Purpose of Prophecy

Reflections, Exercises, and Assignments

The following exercises are designed with this particular chapter in mind. Please work through them carefully before going on to the next chapter. Take time to reflect on your life journey as well as your prophetic development. Learn to work well with the Holy Spirit and people that God has put around you so that you will grow in grace, humility, and wisdom in the ways of God.

Graham Cooke.

What Constitutes Maturity

We live in a show and tell world. People want to see something not just hear something. We have a magnificent opportunity to develop a supernatural presence in the Holy Spirit.

In this context we need prophecy that is capable of an expression from heaven whilst being rooted in the parameters of scripture. It is so important that this vital gift is not left merely in the hands of the idle, the unprepared and those without a sense of purpose.

Maturity is earned in this context by the following:

- Develop a relationship between your love of scripture and your use of the gift. All prophecy in the Bible is planned, developed, prepared, rehearsed and clearly thought through. What must change in your style of delivery, content and preparation of prophecy in order to conform to a biblical base and preparation?

- Prophecy provides much needed insights, perspectives and wisdom in order to enable the receiver to achieve powerful breakthroughs. Prophecy has impact. It arises out of a solid prayer agenda. Too much spontaneity in prophecy will eventually lead us into a place of mediocrity. How would you upgrade your relationship with the Holy Spirit so that your prophesying can move to a higher level of intentionality?

- Humility is a prerequisite when we are seeking to move in the supernatural realm. We need grace to become a different person who has seen something more of God. We need grace to move to a higher level of purpose and intentionality. What must change in your approach to people and the church so that you can become much more purposeful with your gifting? What new area of prophetic impact is the Lord giving you permission to step into for your friends, neighbors and members of your church?

What Constitutes Immaturity?

One of my mentors, Graham Perrins, once described some prophecy as "an empty thought passing through an empty head". Admittedly this was in the period 1979–1984, but it does still hold true in many places today.

What we love we think about. What we wish to excel in, we practice. We rehearse, prepare, study and train so that we can achieve excellence. Jesus is worth all our energy and zeal. Prophecy represents Him and therefore needs to be as exemplary as teaching, as superb as the best preaching, as outstanding as a quality prayer. Our communication must be excellent.

Immaturity cuts corners. It relies more on the spontaneous than the well prepared. It cloaks its lack of content with hype, showmanship and sensationalism. The loudness of the delivery is open not passion released but paucity disguised.

- Immature prophecy is unprepared, unrehearsed. It is off the cuff, low level, mostly spontaneous and lacking in power and impetus.

- The Holy Spirit is a genius. He is purposeful, highly articulate, deeply intentional and totally focused. *"I know the plans I have for you, declares the Lord. Plans for your welfare not your calamity, to give you a future and a hope," (Jeremiah 29:11).* If we are still moving in prophecy the same way we started after several years we are not growing or developing. We are moving backward.

- All things grow. It is time for an upgrade. What was acceptable a few years ago is a sign of immaturity now!

- Describe how the intentionality of God makes you feel about yourself.

- Explain the difference in context, presentation and impact between a specific prophecy and a general one.

- Define the current level of your prophetic gift and specify what you must do to upgrade it to a higher level.

AN ASSIGNMENT

Think of a person around your life at this time who may be going through a troubling period of life.

Read Psalm 126.

When God moves in our life it is like the stuff of dreams. The Gospel is so good it is almost too good to be true. The Lord can turn every life circumstance on its head. Our testimony is always about His greatness. He only does great things.

To walk with Him is to smile, to laugh, to shout with the sheer joy of being alive and in Him. When we forget Who He is for us then we are taken captive by our circumstances. We become pioneers of anxiety, worry, fear and doubt. We lose our peace as faith disintegrates. In times like this we must sow in to the greatness of God. Take the tiny mustard seed of faith and plant it into the Name of Jesus.

We have to sow in order to reap a harvest. The spirit filled life is one of constant sowing. God is faithful and generous. He takes the little that we have and multiplies it so that a few fish sandwiches feeds a multitude of people. We are never beaten as long as we can sow one more thing into His greatness. We always sow into our own future. God is so amazing in this regard. He loves us to reap. He loves to guarantee our future in Himself. When we sow, we partner with Him in the present, for our future.

Read the Psalm and study it. Ask the Lord for His own perspective, so that you can think what He is thinking.

- What is your friend going through at this time that is difficult for them?
- What do they need to see turned around in their own life?
- The rule of life in the Spirit is simple for moments like this. It is: "Whatever you need the most, be the first to give it away," *i.e.*, if you are ill, go and pray for someone who is sick. Sow to the Spirit. If you are in debt, give some money to the poor in your community. Sow to the Spirit. If you are under attack, give a blessing to someone else. Sow and reap.
- How would you encourage your friend to believe in the greatness of God at this time?

- What words from the Father's heart would inspire them to stir themselves and sow to the Spirit?

- Everyone has seed. It is part of our relationship with God. The power does not lie in the amount of seed that we possess but in the incredible fertile nature of the soil in which we place it. That soil is God's goodness.

- How could you speak this prophecy out in such a way that it would stimulate your friend to action?

Think of your own life. Do you need to sow to the Spirit now, for your future? Take some advice. Never stop sowing. In hard times, sow more. Sow every day. Sow in every conceivable way. It is how to invest in your own future.

Now, write out a prophecy. Craft a word of life for your friend that will inspire, encourage and stimulate them to reach out to the Lord with the little seed that they have.

Think about how you should deliver the word. The power of the spoken word creates an impact that breakthrough every hostile barrier. Sometimes our heart gets surrounded by doubt, fear and hopelessness. Prophecy has the anointing and the power to break down that wall. (See Jeremiah 1:9 & 10!) Prophecy has power to build people in the Spirit and to plant new hope and faith in their life. The secret of that power lies in the way that you say the word. Always allow your heart to be touched and inspired by the word you have received for another.

- How would the Lord say it? Ask the Holy Spirit to empower you with the same intentionality.

- Choose the right moment and the right place. Don't make a big production of it and do not be too casual either. Choose a time when there are no distractions, if you can. Possibly take someone with you, so that you can join faith and pray for them.

- Deliver the word properly with due consideration and respect but also with power. Record it on tape if you are able. Give them the written version at least. Often is it important to give them both.

- Think about yourself. Do you need to sow to the Lord?

FRUIT OF THE SPIRIT

"The fruit of the Spirit is love, joy, peace, patience, kindness, goodness, faithfulness, gentleness, self-control; against such things there is no law." Galatians 5:22, 23

- What is your biggest challenge in becoming Christlike at this point in time? Identify and explain.
- Which fruit of the Spirit will most help you in overcoming this obstacle?
- What particular fruit of the Spirit is the Father most wanting you to develop in this next twelve months?
- How will the development of this aspect of God's nature most help you to: *a)* Draw near to God in a place of intimacy? *b)* Be enabled to build better relationships? *c)* Become a better person in your attitude and approach to life? *d)* Be empowered to overcome the schemes of the devil? *e)* Develop a stronger prophetic gifting?
- Ask the Lord to give you a word of prophecy about one of the fruits of the Spirit. What would you say to encourage someone in this regard? How would you speak out a word of prophecy challenging someone to step up into one of the attributes of the Spirit? How could you match the content with the delivery and give a clear prophetic blessing?

NB. For your advice. When you identify a fruit of the Spirit that the Father wants to develop in you in the next time season, then it is vital to understand the following life principle…

… All your tests in the following season area allowed by the Lord to establish this particular fruit in your life. As you cooperate with the Holy Spirit and choose the fruit He has indicated then every situation you encounter will only establish that attribute in your life by experience. It is not easy but it can be done!

CASE STUDY:
MATCHING PROPHETIC DELIVERY WITH CONTENT

The delivery of a prophetic word must match its content. One cannot grab someone by the throat and prophesy love and peace; likewise, a prophecy about warrior strength cannot be properly prophesied in an airy whisper. The context must match the content.

Below are a few prophetic words I have given to individuals enrolled in my prophetic schools (I have changed the names for privacy reasons). In this exercise, read the prophetic word and answer the questions following it.

Prophetic Word

Laura, I see a big bowl of water, and a brick being dropped into the middle of it. It's caused a big splash, and displaced the water. God wants to drop a huge dollop of love in the middle of your fear, so that the fear will actually be shot out of your life. This is who God is. Perfect love casts out fear. Nobody is safe from that blessing.

Answer the following questions:

1.   What is the crux (focus) of this word?

2.   What is the emotion and plan God has for Laura?

3.   What would be the best way to deliver this word? What tone of voice would be best to use? What body language and position should be used?

4.   After delivering the word, what would you pray over her?

When I find someone who is fearful, I get excited, because I know what God wants to do in the coming months. Instead of majoring on the problem of fear, I prophesy of the love of God, because we have the Scriptural and experiential precedent of how God deals with fear. When God brings His love, it displaces fear. One casts the other out. The next few months are always incredible as God lavishes His love on the person. He is in the business of bringing His love in stronger and stronger ways.

LECTIO DIVINA

Lectio Divina (Latin for *divine reading*) is an ancient way of reading the Bible — allowing a quiet and contemplative way of coming to God's Word. *Lectio Divina* opens the pulse of the Scripture, helping readers dig far deeper into the Word than normally happens in a quick glance-over.

In this exercise, we will look at a portion of Scripture and use a modified *Lectio Divina* technique to engage it. This technique can be used on any piece of Scripture; I highly recommend using it for key Bible passages that the Lord has highlighted for you, and for anything you think might be an inheritance word for your life (see the *Crafted Prayer interactive journal* for more on inheritance words).

Read the Scripture:

For even as the body is one and yet has many members, and all the members of the body, though they are many, are one body, so also is Christ. For by one Spirit we were all baptized into one body, whether Jews or Greeks, whether slaves or free, and we were all made to drink of one Spirit. For the body is not one member, but many.

If the foot says, "Because I am not a hand, I am not a part of the body," it is not for this reason any the less a part of the body. And if the ear says, "Because I am not an eye, I am not a part of the body," it is not for this reason any the less a part of the body. If the whole body were an eye, where would the hearing be? If the whole were hearing, where would the sense of smell be? But now God has placed the members, each one of them, in the body, just as He desired. If they were all one member, where would the body be?

But now there are many members, but one body. And the eye cannot say to the hand, "I have no need of you"; or again the head to the feet, "I have no need of you." On the contrary, it is much truer that the members of the body which seem to be weaker are necessary; and those members of the body which we deem less honorable, on these we bestow more abundant honor, and our less presentable members become much more presentable, whereas our more presentable members have no need of it. But God has so composed the body, giving more abundant honor to that member which lacked, so that there may be no division in the body, but that the members may have the same care for one another. And if one member suffers, all the members suffer with it; if one member is honored, all the members rejoice with it.

Now you are Christ's body, and individually members of it. And God has appointed in the church, first apostles, second prophets, third teachers, then miracles, then gifts of healings, helps, administrations, various kinds of tongues. All are not apostles, are they? All are not prophets, are they? All are not teachers, are they? All are not workers of miracles, are they? All do not have gifts of healings, do they? All do not speak with tongues, do they? All do not interpret, do they? But earnestly desire the greater gifts. And I show you a still more excellent way. (1 Corinthians 12:12–31)

1.   Find a place of stillness before God. Embrace His peace. Chase the nattering thoughts out of your mind. Calm your body. Breathe slowly. Inhale. Exhale. Inhale. Exhale. Clear yourself of the distractions of life. Whisper the word, "Stillness." Take your time. When you find that rest in the Lord, enjoy it. Worship Him in it. Be with Him there.

2.   Re-read the passage twice. Allow its words to become familiar to you. Investigate Paul's word picture of the body. What images does that bring to your spirit? What do you see? Become a part of it. What phrases or words especially resonate with you? Meditate especially on those shreds of revelation. Write those pieces down in your journal.

3.   Read the passage twice again. Like waves crashing onto a shore, let the words of Scripture crash onto your spirit. What excites you? What scares you? What exhilarates you about this revelation of the nature of God? What are you discerning? What are you feeling? What are you hearing? Again, write it all down in your journal.

Reflections, Exercises, and Assignments

4.   Write the theme of this passage in your journal.

5.   Does this passage rekindle any memories or experiences? Does it remind you of any prophetic words you have given or received? Write those down as well.

6.   What is the Holy Spirit saying to you through this Scripture? Investigate it with Him — picture the two of you walking through it together. Write those words in your journal.

7.   Read the passage two final times. Meditate on it. Is there something God wants you to do? Is there something He is calling you to? Write it down.

8.   Pray silently. Tell God what this passage is saying to you. Tell Him what you are thinking about. Write down your conversation together. Picture yourself and the Holy Spirit as two old friends in a coffee shop, chatting about what God is doing.

9.   Finally, pray and thank God for His relationship with you. Come back to the passage once a week for the next three months. Read it and let more revelation flow into you. If you feel compelled to, craft a prayer based on this passage for yourself, your family, your friends, or your church. Pray that prayer until you feel God has birthed it in you.

Notes

Notes

Notes

Notes

MODULE FOUR

MOVING FROM PRAYER
TO PROPHECY

Moving From Prayer to Prophecy

I first received this whole workshop in a dream more than 25 years ago. In the dream I saw myself doing this workshop in a conference. When I awoke I wrote out the workshop verbatim and have not changed it from that day to the present.

Tens of thousands of people have stepped into the prophetic gift with absolute ease using this particular model.

This exercise can be done on your own; with another person or as part of a group exercise where people split into pairs. (If it's a group exercise try and get with someone you hardly know). You will need: pen, paper and bible.

Workshop

S PECIFIC INSTRUCTION:

1.   Bring yourself/the group to peace and rest. Quietly acknowledge God's Presence and relax.

2.   Take one step at a time and complete as close to the time allotted as possible.

Step One: Find a partner!

- Think about the person you are with.
- Ask the Lord questions about them re: How He sees them.
- Get God's heartbeat for them — How much He loves them — What He wants to be for them.

Imagine you have a bow and arrow and that the arrow represents the prayer God is going to give you. Where would you aim this arrow? Into what part of their life would you aim a prayer of blessing and encouragement, *e.g.*, Home, finances, health, job, ministry, marriage, relationship with God, etc.

- Write down the target area (probably the first one you think of is it).
- In the light of your target area being identified does your prayer need to change and become more specific? Write accordingly.

Allow 4–8 minutes.

Step Two:

- Write out a prayer of Blessing, Release and Encouragement.
- Allow any pictures, visions, scriptures to come to mind.
- It is helpful to imagine yourself praying for them. Let a prayer rise up in your heart and write down the main points then amplify it.
- Write between 4–6 sentences in your prayer.

Allow 5–10 minutes.

Step Three:

Recap: Now we have a prayer of blessing and encouragement for a particular area of life.

- Imagine a computer screen… with your prayer on the screen!
- Change the wording from a prayer to a simple prophetic statement by altering some key words and phrases.

Example: Turning a Prayer Into a Simple Prophetic Statement

Prayer

Father, I pray that you will bless David and take your relationship with him to a whole new dimension of the Spirit. I pray that you will become his heart's desire.

I ask that he know you and that your love for him will set his heart on fire with a new passion for intimacy and worship. I ask that you will give him a spirit of wisdom and revelation to know you and your ways to a new depth of understanding and experience.

Prophetic Statement

> *David, you are coming into a season of blessing that will take your relationship with God to a whole new powerful dimension of the Spirit.*
>
> *You are going to see, know, understand and experience God in intimacy and worship in a way that will set your heart on fire with a burning passion.*
>
> *There is a spirit of wisdom and revelation that God is pouring out into your heart in this next season, that will impact you greatly and will lead you into a deeper place of the Spirit.*
>
> *This deeper place of the Spirit will become a strategic well of devotion and praise that will touch the hearts of many people with whom you come into contact.*
>
> *The anointing upon you will empower people to break free of unbelief and poor vision of God to embrace the Lord in a powerful way.*
>
> *You will have an anointing to awaken people to a new depth of first love experience in the Lord.*

NB. It is inevitable that in turning the prayer into a simple prophetic statement that the word will be expanded to some degree.

- Write out your simple prophetic statement of encouragement and blessing. Add whatever you feel is necessary!

Allow 10–15 minutes.

Step Four: Choose who will begin!

The one speaking: Pray for your partner.
- Give the word slowly and clearly.
- Don't rush it! Be humble and considerate.
- Don't mumble. Don't apologize.
- Trust the Lord in what He has given you.

The recipient: Open your heart to receive encouragement.
- Smile! Nod your head, be attentive.
- Enjoy the experience. The worst thing that can happen is that you get a blessing in the wrong area of your life! (If that happens, ask the Holy Spirit for the right target area yourself and apply the encouragement!)
- Change over so that both people have equal opportunity to speak and receive.
- Pray for one another to seal in the prophecy.
- Exchange papers!!

Allow 10–15 minutes.

If you finish before the allotted time share what the word meant to you and encourage your partner.

Step Five: Review of the exercise.

- Who enjoyed it?
- Who was a little scared?
- Who received a blessing?
- Who felt that God spoke to them?
- Who felt God speaking through them?
- What did that feel like?

The premise for this workshop is: if you can pray, you can prophesy!

The same faith faculty that reaches out to the Lord for a prayer is identical to the ones we use when moving in prophecy, *i.e.*, care, love, concern, the heart of God, desire to be a blessing, a will to encourage another, a belief in God's goodness, etc.

- Halfway through this workshop it ceased to be a workshop only and became body ministry.
- God has spoken to you at this time and the word you have is yours to keep and use.
- Meditate on it and expect the blessing.
- You are now an encourager so keep going! Do this exercise at least twice a week either with another person or on your own and write a card to mail to someone else.

What have you learned?

1. To sit quietly in God's Presence.

2. To receive His heartbeat for another person.

3. To hear the Lord in prayer.

4. To receive a sense of direction (arrow) ... this is a word of knowledge.

5. How to be sensitive to the Holy Spirit.

6. To write a crafted prayer of blessing and encouragement.

7. How to craft a prophetic word that will edify, encourage or comfort.

8. How to give a simple prophecy with sensitivity and faith.

9. How to record prophecy by writing. (The more your practice and become attuned to God's heart you may want to consider upgrading the recording aspect to buying a handheld recorder and tapes.)

10. How to convey God's love and desire.

11. How to touch a person's life in a personal way from the Lord!

12. How to seal the word in prayer.

Practice makes perfect. If you will continue this exercise over a period of months, your capacity to hear God and receive prophecy will grow in a very powerful way.

Blessings!

—Graham

Notes

Notes

Notes

$\mathcal{N}otes$

Notes

FINAL
APPLICATIONS

Final Applications

THIS SERIES OF ASSIGNMENTS INCLUDE:

- A Meditation Explanation and Exercise.

- A Relational Value and its application regarding Non-Negotiable Love.

- A Life Principle for Prophetic Ministry and its application regarding The Nature of God.

- What Kind of Partnership with Leaders?

- A checklist for dialogue, discussion and relationship building.

- What Help and Support from Leaders?

- Development issues to safeguard the prophetic gift in the church.

- A Prophetic Word to be read, studied and acted upon.

- A Recommended Reading List.

A MEDITATION AND EXPLANATION EXERCISE

TO MEDITATE MEANS TO THINK deeply about something or someone. It means to explore with mind and heart, allowing what you think to touch your innermost being.

Meditation is creative thought which leads us to the higher realm of revelation and wisdom. It takes us beyond the place of reason to where joy is seated and faith is activated.

Meditation allows us to search inside and outside the box of our current paradigm. What you see and hear there touches you profoundly. It adds a ring around the core truth of Christ which his God within, the certainty of freedom.

Fruitful meditation is therefore not a casual seeking for revelatory insight. Initial creative thoughts are merely the X that marks the spot. There is treasure in meditation, a guarantee of wealth in the pursuit of God.

Many are satisfied with collecting random truth on the surface of their consciousness. It is good wholesome stuff but it does not satisfy and it cannot challenge the complexities of life in a warfare context.

Deep truth has to be mined over days and weeks. It takes joy and patience to take truth down to its deepest level. Beyond meeting our current needs. Beyond the depth of understanding the power it releases to us against our adversary. Down to the depth where God lives in the highest places of heaven. For all meditation must ultimately come before the throne of His majesty, sovereignty and supremacy. He fills all things with Himself.

Our current situation requires wisdom, but even more it years for Presence. Meditation allows us to experience both, through the word coming alive in our spirit. Meditation leads us to God and the permission of His heart. Learn to be in the question peacefully with God. Let the Holy Spirit teach you how to abide. Turn inwardly and rest, wait patiently... He will come. When your heart gets restless turn to worship. When the interior atmosphere settles return to listening.

Write down initial thoughts but do not pursue them just yet. Do not be distracted by what you hear initially. Set it aside, come back to it later.

When fist entering a lifestyle of meditation, take care to ease into it slowly. An hour at first, then longer until half a day and so on.

Always have a focus, do not try to wait in a vacuum. In this next exercise is a particular statement, followed by a series of questions. This is both to give you practice in meditation and to bring you into revelation of God through the focus statement.

Use the questions as the Spirit leads. This exercise is not prescriptive but merely a guide to enable your contemplation. No doubt you will discover better questions as the Holy Spirit tutors you. Enjoy!

Meditation Exercise

> *"... stand in your problem, holding onto the promise, looking for the provision."*

- Engage your heart with the picture this statement provokes.
- What does this mean for you?
- What problems currently require God's blessing?
- What particular promise is the Holy Spirit drawing to your attention? Ask for scriptural support.
- Study the promise(s). Look for key words and phrases. Write down specifically what the Lord is guaranteeing to you in your current circumstances.
- How will you stand and position yourself before the Father?
- What level of confidence does the Father wish to bestow upon you?
- What fear, unbelief and inadequacy must you give up in favour of the promise?
- View the promise and the provision together until they fill your vision and hope/faith begin to rise.
- Now, through the lens of the promise, look at the problem. What has changed in your: *a)* heart? *b)* viewpoint? *c)* mindset?
- Compose a prayer before the Lord, a request for His grace, kindness and power to enable you to receive.
- Write a psalm of thanksgiving to the Lord for what He has done in and for you in this current situation.
- Write out in full a confession and a declaration that you can speak into your circumstances by the power of the Holy Spirit.
- As you challenge your circumstances with your newfound revelation a boldness and confidence will enter your speech. How did you feel?
- Continue declaring, believing and challenging daily until God speaks further or the problem disappears.

- What has changed in you?
- What have you learned?
- What have you become in Christ?
- Finally, enter all these things in your journal. Keep a record of your walk with God in this way not only to encourage you in later times but also as a legacy to your family and friends.

A Relational Value

- Do not merely treat this value as an exercise but as an opportunity to develop Christlike intent for yourself.
- Develop this value into a prophetic word in order to demonstrate the importance of your ministry arising out of your relationship with the Lord.
- Read the scriptures out loud several times.
- Think through the introductory paragraph and the main points.
- Work through the Action Points 1–8.
- Improve the Value Statement and make it your own.

NB. This exercise can be done by individuals or groups of 2–4 working together using dialogue. This guide is understated deliberately to allow for wide ranging thinking or discussion.

A group should be able to take the concept further in dialogue.

Follow up the action points with each other and get personal feedback from everyone regarding their progress.

Non-Negotiable Love

Scriptures
John 15:9
Romans 12:10
Colossians 3:12–17
1 Corinthians 13:1–7
1 Peter 4:8

There is nothing we can do to make God love us more, and there is nothing we can do that would make Him love us less! His love is based on who He is within Himself, not on our performance.

He is consistent and faithful in how He loves us. His love is never on the negotiating table when we are in dispute and disrepute with Him. How can we be anything less for each other?

His love enables us to be true to one another when we have difficulties. Keeping His way of loving in the forefront of our minds in times of complexity helps us to be true to God in the way that we hold on to one another.

- Love means being patient and expressing kindness.
- Love does not remember slights, hold grudges or recall bad history.
- Love is unselfish and thoughtful.
- Loving people bear all things well and believe the best of others.
- Truly forgiving and forgetting is the hallmark of God's love in us.
- Love is not provoked and foregoes vengeance.
- Love never fails.
- Be devoted to one another in brotherly love.
- Love is an action not just a word.
- Real love allows people to change.

Action

1.　Think of someone recently where you have not fully been the loving person the Holy Spirit was expecting you to be in the situation... and be reconciled.

2.　Take time to thoughtfully upgrade your love with the people around you.

3.　Using the above scriptures and comments develop a word of prophecy on the theme of God's love.

4.　Who is the intended target for this word?

5.　How would you deliver it in a way that fulfilled the objective?

6.   Record the word in writing or on tape.

7.   Deliver it to the person concerned.

8.   Write an evaluation of the process and result.

Value Statement

Non-negotiable love is being the best expression of Christ to another human being. Putting love first and last in every situation keeps us in the abiding Presence of God.

Non-negotiable love can heal and seal every problem that may occur in any relationship.

A Life Principle for Prophetic Ministry
We must pursue our calling within a working structure of intentional relationships. This process will inevitably on days revolve around being purified, moving in loving confrontation and the discipleship necessary to enable each one of us to grow up into all things in Christ. Cultivating values and principles in how we use our gifting will enable us to be pro-active in our own development into a place of freedom and maturity.

We are all responsible for our own behavior. We are answerable to the Lord and to one another in the improvement and expansion of our gift and calling.

This Life Principle if followed will enable us to understand and experience the personality and character of the Lord Jesus as it relates to moving in the gift of prophecy.

The Nature of God

Scriptures
Exodus 34:6–9
Matthew 5:43–48
John 13:34, 35
Philippians 2:1–13
2 Thessalonians 3:5
1 John 4:7–21

All of life is an exploration into the secret place of God's heart for humanity. The Father is extremely intentional towards not only His own people but to all mankind.

Prophetic people proclaim Who God is for people. In order for those words to be authentic they must be backed up by our experience of His essential nature in our own lives.

"The testimony of Jesus is the spirit of prophecy" (Revelations 19:10). We prophesy from the same place of revelatory insight as our current experience of God. We all have a testimony of what God is like to us on a consistent basis. Our mouth speaks of what our heart knows to be true.

God is good. He is loving, kind, generous and compassionate. He does not lie, so what He says about Himself is the whole truth and fit for prophecy. He is everlastingly unchanging and consistent. He is good news. Prophecy is the proclamation of the steadfast nature of God.

Therefore the way that we move in the gift of prophecy must be consistent with His Name and Nature.

What we think about God is the most important issue in the world to us. (Matthew 16:15).

- A true perspective on God's nature is essential in our prophesying.
- It is important then that we upgrade our image of God within our own hearts.

Action Points

Answer as many questions as you need to!

- What is your current picture of God? Write it down in 4–6 sentences or phrases.
- How long have you had this image? Is it time for an upgrade?
- Is your image biblical? Can you put scripture(s) alongside it? Do so!
- What do you need to change?
- What do you need God to be in you in this current season?
- Sit quietly, relax and ask the Holy Spirit to give you a vision of God for this next season. Keep persevering until the whole picture emerges *and* your faith begins to rise and worship flows.

- What scripture can support this image?
- What is the Spirit saying to you through this picture and the word?
- How can you become this image of God to the people around you? What must change in you?
- Now keep this picture alive through praise and worship!

Principle: I must discover the nature of God for myself, and develop that revelation into an actual relationship experience.

I must only prophesy out of that place of internal relationship and truth.

What Kind Of Partnership With Leaders?

1. Leaders are looking for appropriate levels of accountability and a developing sense of responsibility.

2. A teachable spirit when loving feedback is given regarding methodology and presentation of prophecy.

3. Leaders want the personal life and relationships of people moving in gifting to have appropriate levels of Christlike behavior.

4. Leaders are looking for a servant spirit in which to invest and develop a greater sense of responsibility for the body as a whole.

5. A partnership should begin with prophecies that release encouraging, edifying and comforting words only then progresses as capability increases.

6. Develop meetings where prophecy can be targeted at specific people, problems and situations. Follow up with prayer.

7. Give personal input to develop a greater perception of God.

8. Where necessary provide specific opportunity to upgrade personality to a more positive outlook.

9. Be generous but tough when people are not getting the message.

10. Provide a team context in which to learn and develop gifting. Provide a team leader who is part of the wider leadership team.

What Help And Support From Leaders?

1. Prophetic people need encouragement and effective constructive feedback on their gifting, methodology and content of their words.

2. Guidelines need to be issued that allow people the freedom to upgrade and improve their gifting.

3. People need to be free to make mistakes while learning humility, honesty and accountability.

4. Develop workshops to provide opportunities for practice, practice and more practice. Offer dialogues and discussions on case histories, right habits, and improved content and presentation.

5. There should be training in the church on the disciplines of hearing and waiting on God through meditation, listening prayer and contemplation.

6. There should be devotional training that teaches people how to relate, respond and be intimate in worship to God.

7. Upgrade the level of prophecy in the church through a deliberate partnership and loving relationship.

8. Provide practical loving support when people get it wrong, not just to close down their gift. People do not learn successfully in a vacuum. To restrain people without development is actually punishment.

9. Prophetic people need a place in which to use and develop their gifting, ideally a small group setting in order to encourage their movement and minimize any mistakes.

10. Prophetic people need a focus that has been agreed upon with the leadership regarding their own development. It should be in the form of an action plan that at least agrees with the parameters for this next season.

A Prophecy

WE ARE IN A SEASON of Divine Acceleration. There is a Quickening Spirit abroad in the earth. The Lord is redeeming time because the days we are living in are becoming progressively more wicked. Time is the currency that our lives are running on, not money. God redeems time by speeding up the process by which we are transformed. I say to you that there is a quickening spirit upon your life should you choose to accept it.

What you thought would take years, will take months. What you thought would take months, will take weeks. What you thought would take weeks, will take days. What you thought would take days, will take hours and moments. The favor of the Lord is upon you to accelerate your development in this next twelve months. In this Divine Acceleration the gap between prophecy spoken and prophecy fulfilled will get narrower and narrower. Eventually the gap will be so small we will see the release of the "Let there be" word from Genesis One. Creative words of prophecy that will bring immediate release and empowerment particularly to situations where the church is contending with the enemy for breakthrough.

The Lord will give you five years growth in the next twelve months. BUT!!! You have to learn to run! You must say yes, much faster and mean it. You must stick with the process. Acceleration is a paradox. It is not always easy and it is hugely enjoyable.

I believe the Lord would say to you that, "This is how I want you to see the next twelve months; it is indeed a crash course in the Glory of your God. He would say to you, did I not say to you that if you would believe you would see the Glory of God.

This next twelve months, as you progress, as you speed up in the Spirit, I will give you an anointing. I will renew you in the Spirit of your mind. I will open your heart. Your eyes of your heart will be enlightened and you will see the hand of God everywhere in your life. You will look and there will be days, says the Lord, when you will look at your life through My eyes and you will see what I see.

Your heart will be overwhelmed with joy, with laughter. There will be a faith that rises up. There are many quick victories that I intend to give you.

The Lord says, do not look at the next twelve months in the way you've looked at the last ten years. I'm giving you new eyes, I'm giving you a new heart and I am giving you a new mind. You will perceive totally differently.

A Prophecy

You will believe more freely and you will think the way I think. Because this is what I am doing, I am elevating your thinking to my level. You will think on a level that I think. You will behold in the spirit what I am beholding. You will understand what I'm holding out to you and you will take the provision of your God and spread it around in your own life.

You will come into a place of successive, easy and quick victories. There will be some situations says the Lord when I will hold up victory for awhile so that your revenge can be complete.

There will be times says the Lord when I will allow the enemy to contend with you so that I may establish you in something deep and powerful and profound. The Father says when you come into a situation that is resisting you, I want you to smile. Because the hand of your God, I intend through the resistance to give you a double portion. It is not about what the enemy is doing. It is about what I am allowing. I will allow him to come against you so that I may give you a double portion and that I may increase the anointing upon you in those days.

Your life will be a balance of easy victories and times when the enemy will contend, but it is on those days of contention I have a divine increase for you. The Father says, look for increase in a time when the Power seems to have slowed down. Look for the increase and stand and worship. You will know Me, for I will reveal myself to you and I will come to you. I will establish in you the very things that I want you to have and you will behold the power of your God. You will start to think with a level of wisdom and intelligence you have never seen before, you will start to see in the realm of the spirit in a way you've never seen before.

Out of your mouth will come words of faith, says the Lord. You will completely lose the ability to worry or be anxious because I am making war on anxiety. I am making war on panic. I am making war on fear. You will not be subject to those things but you will know your God. You will be strong in your God and you will do exploits this next twelve months. You will do exploits in your own life.

When those things are established in you, I will lead you. I will bring you across the path of people who are victims in the area you have just won through. You will assist them, you will help them and you will be a breakthrough anointing to them. As they breakthrough, your anointing will go to a deeper level, still, that as you give out so the anointing in you will increase and abide and will abound. In this way, says the Lord, in the next twelve months you will make years and years of growth.

Final Applications

You will become the man and woman you were always suppose to be and you will come into a place where nothing will overwhelm you. You will come into a place where you will cease to be a foot soldier in the body of Christ. You will take on the stature of a warrior. You will take on the stature, like onto one of David's mighty men. I will cause a greatness to rise up within you. I will make you a power in the land. Even as you come to the end of this twelve months of training, say the Lord, I will begin to show you and declare to you what your personal inheritance is, so that you may be a stake holder in the territory of the spirit that I choose to bestow upon you. You will come into your ministry. You will come into your anointing. You will come into a place of abundance. You will certainly and most definitely and assuredly come into the place of your favor. You will know what the hand of God is upon you. You will know what your assignment is, you will know who you are, you will know your identity and you will know your inheritance. You will begin to stand in and trade upon the favor that is present over your life. Then, says the Lord, when that quickening spirit has done that work, then I will open a window in heaven and I'll pour things out upon you because this next twelve months is just the beginning. It's just boot camp. It's to get you up to speed with who I am and then the real adventure begins.

This next twelve months you will see the Glory of God in your own life, in your own circumstances. I will cause you to rise up and occupy a place of overcoming. You shall overcome yourself, that you will no longer be your own worst enemy. When you have conquered yourself, then I will send you out on a great adventure. Nothing will overwhelm you because I will teach you that every obstacle is indeed an opportunity and every opposition can be laid low. That which will rise up in you in this next twelve months will be nothing less than the sovereignty and the declared majesty of your God. It is My intention, says the Father, that you would know Me, that you would be strong and that you would do exploits. You would be filled to overflowing with the goodness of God, that you would know the majesty of God, that you would have the joy of the Lord. The power of God will overshadow you and erupt within you. You will no longer be the person that you once were but I will turn you into a different man and a different woman. Then, says the Lord, then, we will really get on with the business of the living Father.

This next twelve months, it's for you to discover who I am for you. It's for you to come to a place of trust, a place of peace, a place of rest and a place of faith. It is for you to discover who I am for you and as your Father. I intend to enjoy myself this year because during this year you will actually

A Prophecy

stop whining. You will begin worshipping and that will be good for My ears. I intend to enjoy Myself beloved. In this next twelve months, I want to bring you into a place where your life is a joy and a delight to yourself. Where you will enjoy your life and you will be delighted with your life and you will be ecstatic about who you are becoming. I will banish low self esteem. I will do violence to self hatred. I will bring you into a place where you are happy and relaxed about who you are because when I look at you, I'm happy, I'm relaxed. You are not much of a challenge to Me, says the Lord. I know you are amazing but you are not much of a challenge to Me. I can beat you with My little finger. You are not much of a challenge. I will do something so compelling so wonderful that I will make you a challenger against the enemy for the rest of your life."

Recommended Reading

Title	Author	Publisher
Hearing God	Dallas Willard	InterVarsity Press
The Gift of Prophecy	Jack Deere	Vine Books
Surprised by the Voice of God	Jack Deere	Zondervan
Growing in the Prophetic	Mike Bickle	Kingsway
The Seer	James Goll	Destiny Image
Prophetic Etiquette	Michael Sullivant	Creation House
The Prophets' Notebook	Barry Kissel	Kingsway
User Friendly Prophecy	Larry Randolph	Destiny Image
Prophecy in Practice	Jim Paul	Monarch Books
Can You Hear Me?: Tuning in to the God Who Speaks	Brad Jersak	Trafford Press
When Heaven Invades Earth	Bill Johnson	Treasure House
Knowledge of the Holy	A. W. Tozer	O. M. Publishing
The Pleasures of Loving God	Mike Bickle	Creation House
Manifest Presence	Jack Hayford	Chosen
Living the Spirit-Formed Life	Jack Hayford	Regal
The Agape Road	Bob Mumford	Lifechangers
The Sensitivity of the Spirit	R. T. Kendall	Hodder & Stroughton
Living in the Freedom of the Spirit	Tom Marshall	Sovereign World
Secrets of the Secret Place	Bob Sorge	Oasis House
The Heart of Worship	Matt Redman	Regal
Experiencing the Depths of Jesus Christ	Jeanne Guyon	Seedsowers
The Unsurrendered Soul	Liberty Savard	Bridge-Logos

About the Prophetic Equipping Series

Graham began teaching prophetic schools in 1986. Eight years later he wrote *Developing Your Prophetic Gifting*, a book which has won universal acclaim. Translated into numerous languages, reprinted many times over and published by several companies, it has been a best seller and widely regarded as a classic. Graham has continued to develop new material each year in the Schools of Prophecy. Now after almost twenty years of teaching continuously upgrading material, the School of Prophecy has developed into one of the finest teaching programs on the prophetic gift, ministry and office of a Prophet. This new material effectively makes *Developing Your Prophetic Gifting* redundant.

The Prophetic Equipping Series encompasses six volumes that combine classic teaching with the journal format so popular in the *Being with God Series*. It also embraces a workshop and training manual, with emphasis on producing one of the finest teaching aids on the prophetic gift and ministry. These manuals are appropriate for individual, small group or church-wide use. All Christians can prophesy and would benefit from Graham's wisdom and experience in ministry. The assignments, exercises, workshops, lectio divina and other material are designed to further the understanding of the prophetic gift, ministry and office. If used properly, the process will develop accountability for prophetic people, healthy pasturing of the prophetic, and give relevant questions for leadership and prophetic people to ask one another. The series includes:

Volume 1 – *Approaching the Heart of Prophecy*
Volume 2 – *Prophecy & Responsibility*
Volume 3 – *Prophetic Wisdom*
Volume 4 – *The Prophetic Impact*
Volume 5 – *Prophetic Partnerships*
Volume 6 – *Prophecy and the Ways of God*

To find more information on Graham's training schools and events, please visit www.GrahamCooke.com

About the Author

Graham Cooke is part of The Mission's core leadership team, working with senior team leader, David Crone, in Vacaville, California. Graham's role includes training, consulting, mentoring and being part of a think tank that examines the journey from present to future.

He is married to Theresa, who has a passion for worship and dance. She loves to be involved in intercession, warfare, and setting people free. She cares about injustice and abuse, and has compassion on people who are sick, suffering and disenfranchised.

They have six children and two grandchildren. Ben and Seth both reside and work in the UK. Ben is developing as a writer, is very funny, and probably knows every movie ever made. Seth is a musician, a deep thinker with a caring outlook and an amazing capacity for mischief.

Sophie and her husband Mark live in Vacaville and attend The Mission. Sophie & Mark are the Operations Managers of Brilliant Book House, the publishing company of Graham Cooke. Sophie has played a significant part in Graham's ministry for a number of years, and has helped develop resources, new books and journals, as well as organize events. Mark and Sophie are a warm-hearted, friendly, deeply humorous couple with lots of friends. Mark and Sophie have three daughters. Evelyn (August 2006) is a delight; a happy little soul who likes music, loves to dance and enjoys books. Annabelle (December 2008) is lovely, happy, content and very tiny. Penelope Violet joined us in February 2011 and is adored by her sisters — and all the rest of us!

Their other daughters are Alexis, who is loving, kind and gentle, and very intuitive and steadfast toward her friends; and Alyssa, a very focused and determined young woman who is fun-loving with a witty sense of humor.

Also, Graham and Theresa have two beautiful young women, Julianne and Megan, both in Australia, who are a part of their extended family.

Graham is a popular conference speaker and is well known for his training programs on the prophetic, spiritual warfare, intimacy and devotional life, leadership, spirituality and the church in transition. He functions as a consultant and freethinker to businesses, churches, and organizations, enabling them to develop strategically. He has a passion to establish the Kingdom and build prototype churches that can fully reach a post-modern society.

A strong part of Graham's ministry is in producing finances and resources to the poor and disenfranchised in developing countries. He supports many projects specifically for widows, orphans and people in the penal system. He hates abuse of women and works actively against human trafficking and the sex slave trade, including women caught up in prostitution and pornography.

If you would like to invite Graham to minister or speak at an event, please complete the online Ministry Invitation Form at www.GrahamCooke.com.

If you wish to become a financial partner for the sake of missions and compassionate acts across the nations, please contact his office at office@ myemerginglight.com, and his administrative assistant will be happy to assist you.

You may contact Graham by writing to:

Graham Cooke
865 Cotting Ln, Ste C
Vacaville, California
95688, USA

www.GrahamCooke.com
www.BrilliantBookHouse.com

going on in the spirit when God seems to be distant and when He is drawing close, understanding God's nature and many others. *Brilliant* boasts an extensive collection of Graham's work. We distribute his CDs, MP3s, DVDs, books and Interactive Journals and offer a direct link between Graham and our customers through our newsletters, YouTube channel and podcasts.

Become a fan of Graham Cooke on Facebook!

Search for "Graham Cooke" on Facebook and be the first to receive updates on new projects, events and resources.

"*At Brilliant Book House, we believe you have a unique call on your life that can only be found in God. He has something for you that is far beyond your wildest dreams. As you step out into that purpose, we want to stand with you, offering you encouragement, training and hope for your journey. We want to equip you for what God wants to do in you, and through you. That is our promise to you.*"

–*Graham Cooke*

Brilliant Book House is a California-based publishing company founded and directed by Graham Cooke and is dedicated to producing high-quality Christian resources and teaching materials. Our vision is to equip all of our readers to lead brilliant lives, confidently led by the Holy Spirit into the destiny God has for them.

Brilliant has a passion for the Kingdom of Heaven, a powerful desire to see the Body of Christ comes into full dynamic stature in the earth, and a hunger for everyone in Jesus to discover their rightful places in the purposes of God.

The world needs to see God in a *brilliant* way.

Visit us online today:

www.BrilliantBookHouse.com